PORSCHE 911 1964–69 AUTOBOOK

Workshop Manual for
Porsche 911 1964–67
Porsche 911L 1967–68
Porsche 911S 1966–69
Porsche 911T 1967–69
Porsche 911T Luxe 1968–69
Porsche 911E 1968–69

by

Kenneth Ball G I Mech E

and the

Autopress team of Technical Writers

AUTOPRESS LTD   GOLDEN LANE   BRIGHTON   BN1 2QJ   ENGLAND

The AUTOBOOK series of Workshop Manuals covers the majority of British and Continental motor cars.

For a full list see the back of this manual.

CONTENTS

ISBN 0 85147 166 8

First Edition 1971
Reprinted 1972

© Autopress Ltd 1971

Printed in Brighton England for Autopress Ltd by G Beard & Son Ltd

ACKNOWLEDGEMENT

My thanks are due to Porsche Cars (Great Britain) Ltd. and in particular to Mr. W. H. Aldington for their unstinted co-operation and also for supplying data and illustrations.

I am also grateful to a considerable number of owners who have discussed their cars at length and many of whose suggestions have been included in this manual.

Kenneth Ball G I Mech E
Associate Member Guild of Motoring Writers
Ditchling Sussex England.

ACKNOWLEDGEMENTS

INTRODUCTION

This do-it-yourself Workshop Manual has been specially written for the owner who wishes to maintain his car in first class condition and to carry out his own servicing and repairs. Considerable savings on garage charges can be made, and one can drive in safety and confidence knowing the work has been done properly.

Comprehensive step-by-step instructions and illustrations are given on all dismantling, overhauling and assembling operations. Certain assemblies require the use of expensive special tools, the purchase of which would be unjustified. In these cases information is included but the reader is recommended to hand the unit to the agent for attention.

Throughout the Manual hints and tips are included which will be found invaluable, and there is an easy to follow fault diagnosis at the end of each chapter.

Whilst every care has been taken to ensure correctness of information it is obviously not possible to guarantee complete freedom from errors or to accept liability arising from such errors or omissions.

Instructions may refer to the righthand or lefthand sides of the vehicle or the components. These are the same as the righthand or lefthand of an observer standing behind the car and looking forward.

CHAPTER 1

THE ENGINE

1:1 Description

In September 1964, excited Porsche enthusiasts welcomed the introduction of a completely new engine design. This was a superb piece of engineering—a six-cylinder unit destined for the 1965 cars. It had the designation '2000', with a capacity of 1991 cc and a power output of 130 bhp at 6100 rev/min. After two years in this form, 1967 saw the production of an additional hotted-up version known as the '2000S' which was rated at 160 bhp at 6600 rev/min. A third, and milder, version was introduced in 1968, to be known as the '2000T' and rated at 110 bhp at 5800 rev/min. Car model designations used the same letters for identification, being known as 911, 911S and 911T, but an additional model called 911L indicates one with exhaust emission control and optional Sportomatic transmission, the engine being in the '2000' class. 911E and 911T Lux models have fuel-injection systems and self-levelling suspension.

The cross-sectioned views of the engine in **FIGS 1:1** and **1:2** show most of the outstanding features of this brilliant design and help to explain the reasons for the high power output. Six cylinders are arranged in two horizontally-opposed banks of three, each cylinder carrying its own aluminium head. The cylinders are of cast iron on the '2000T' but are of composite construction on the other models, the aluminium fins and barrels having a thin cast-iron bore to give excellent heat dissipation and a good wearing surface.

The cylinders are mounted on an aluminium crankcase which is split vertically. The crankshaft 4 runs in eight plain bearings, one between each throw, one to take thrust at the flywheel end and a sleeve type in the timing cover (see **FIG 1:2**). The connecting rods have split big-end bearing shells and bushed small-ends. Aluminium alloy pistons carry fully-floating gudgeon pins, two compression rings and one for oil control (see 15 in **FIG 1:1**).

Each aluminium head carries an inlet and an exhaust valve, these being set at a wide angle to each other. Valve guides are detachable and there are valve seat and sparking plug inserts. Rocker gear housings span each set of three heads, carrying the rockers 29 and camshafts 30, the latter running in three plain bearings. **FIG 1:2** shows how the camshafts are driven by two duplex chains 14 from an intermediate shaft 13, this shaft being gear-driven from the crankshaft. Each chain is tensioned by a spring-loaded sprocket.

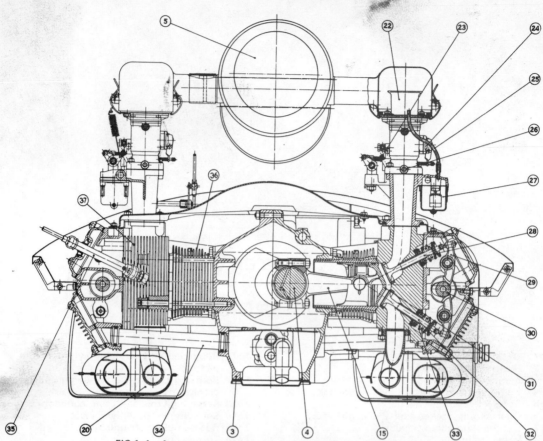

FIG 1 : 1   A transverse cross-section through the type 2000 engine

Key to Fig 1 : 1   3 Crankcase   4 Crankshaft   5 Air cleaner   15 Connecting rod   20 Heat exchanger   22 Air intake horn   23 Idle adjusting screw   24 Accelerator pump   25 Float chamber vent   26 Throttle shaft   27 Float housing   28 Inlet valve   29 Rocker arm   30 Camshaft   31 Piston   32 Exhaust valve   33 Valve spring   34 Oil drain tube   35 Suppressor   36 Cylinder   37 Head

The intermediate shaft also drives twin oil pumps 18 and 19, pressure pump 19 supplying oil to the engine. The larger scavenging pump 18 picks up draining oil from the sump and returns it to a separate oil tank. Before oil from the pressure pump reaches the engine bearings it passes through an oil cooler. When the oil is cold a valve opens to allow oil to arrive at the bearings without passing through the cooler.

The air-cooling system is similar to that employed on Volkswagen cars, a belt-driven blower 7 producing large volumes of air which is ducted over the cylinders and heads by shaped covers. After passing through heat exchangers associated with the exhaust system, the hot air is available to warm the car interior through pipes and valves.

The flywheel 2 normally carries an orthodox diaphragm-spring clutch, but is replaced by a fluid torque converter when Sportomatic transmission is fitted. The flywheel housing is bolted to the transmission casing to provide integral construction of the power unit and drive. Such technical details as compression ratios, firing order and general fits and tolerances will be found in Technical Data at the end of this manual.

1 : 2 Routine maintenance

Before the summer and winter seasons or every 6000 miles, drain the engine oil while it is hot. The plug is part 16 in **FIG 1 : 2**, and it is also shown in **FIG 1 : 3**. Next remove the coverplate 4, followed by the gaskets and gauze strainer 1, 2 and 3. Clean strainer with brush and fuel, not fluffy rag. Remove all traces of old gaskets.

Fit gasket to strainer and replace strainer so that the opening exactly surrounds the inlet pipe inside the crankcase. Refit the second gasket and cover, tightening the nuts on spring washers. **Do not overtighten or the cover may be distorted.** Clean metallic particles from drain plug and refit, then fill up with oil to the upper mark on the dipstick. Use heavy duty oil SAE.30 in summer and SAE.20 in winter. Quantity required is 9 litres (15.8 Imp. or 19 US pints). For normal oil changes the quantity is the same for cars with Sportomatic transmission.

Oil filter:

The throwaway filter is mounted adjacent to the oil filler as shown in **FIG 1 : 4**. It cannot be cleaned and must be renewed every 6000 miles. Unscrew anticlockwise. Fit a new filter after verifying that the rubber seal and seating face are clean and undamaged.

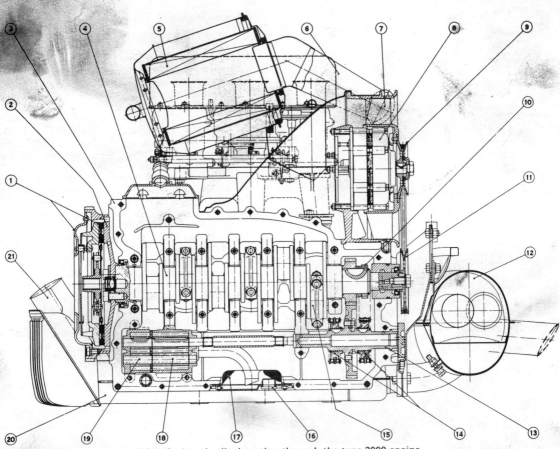

FIG 1 : 2   Longitudinal section through the type 2000 engine

Key to Fig 1 : 2   1 Clutch   2 Flywheel   3 Crankcase   4 Crankshaft   5 Air cleaner   6 Air intake   7 Cooling blower
8 Alternator   9 V-belt   10 Distributor drive gear   11 Crankshaft pulley   12 Exhaust silencer   13 Intermediate shaft
14 Camshaft drive sprocket   15 Connecting rod   16 Oil drain plug   17 Oil strainer   18 Oil scavenging pump   19 Oil pressure
pump   20 Heat exchanger   21 Heating air outlet

Valve clearance:

Check this every 3000 miles. Correct clearance for both inlet and exhaust valves on all engines is .10 mm or .004 inch (cold). Check in firing order 1-6-2-4-3-5, the cylinder numbering being shown in **FIG 1 : 5**. Each cylinder must have its piston at TDC on the firing stroke with both valves closed. At this point it will be found that marks on the crankshaft belt pulley align with the crankcase joint as shown in the top view of **FIG 1 : 6**. Note that there are three marks 120 deg. apart.

Remove cylinder head covers. Turn belt pulley until both valves of No. 1 cylinder are closed and TDC mark (Z1) on the pulley lines up with the crankcase mark. Check clearance with feeler gauge. Adjust as in lower view of **FIG 1 : 6**, slackening the nut on the rocker adjuster and turning the adjuster with a screwdriver. Hold screw while tightening nut and check clearance again.

Continue checking by turning belt pulley clockwise to next mark at 120 deg. or one third of a turn. This should find No. 6 cylinder at TDC with both valves closed. Repeat procedure until all valves have been checked.

In every case, make quite sure that the feeler is being inserted immediately above the valve stem tip.

Rocker arm shafts:

Check tightness every 6000 miles. Refer to **Section 1 : 6**.

Compression:

Check cylinder compressions every 6000 miles.

Blower belt:

Check tension every 6000 miles and adjust if necessary, referring to **Chapter 4.**

1 : 3 Engine removal and refitting

Porsche recommend the removal of the engine and transmission as a single unit. For most operations on the engine it is easier to work on it when it is out of the car, and as the crankcase must be split to attend to the crankshaft, removal is then essential. Proceed as follows:

1 Raise rear of car on firmly-based stands to a height which will permit removal of the engine downwards and to the rear.

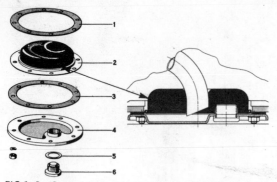

FIG 1:3 Components of the oil strainer. Section on right shows how strainer surrounds oil pick-up pipe

Key to Fig 1:3 1 Gasket 2 Oil strainer 3 Gasket
4. Oil strainer coverplate 5 Sealing ring 6 Magnetic drain plug

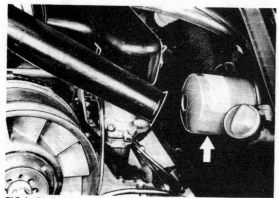

FIG 1:4 Arrow points to renewable oil filter, which is mounted on the oil tank

2 Remove air cleaner and oil tank vent hose. Disconnect battery, then cables from ignition coil, alternator, fuel pump, oil pressure transmitter (see **FIG 1:7**), reversing light switch and starter motor. Remove earth strap. Detach alternator cables from body fasteners.

3 Detach throttle linkage from bell crank and remove hose from oil filler (see **FIG 1:7**). Drain engine oil. Detach hoses from oil tank. See **Section 6:3** for extra details when Sportomatic transmission is fitted.

4 Detach axle shafts (see **Chapter 7**). Detach hot air ducts from front ends of heat exchangers. Detach clutch cable from release lever.

5 Detach fuel hose from connector at float chambers. Remove cover from floor tunnel in passenger compartment. Pull rubber boot forward (see **FIG 1:8**). Cut safety wire and remove square-headed bolt, detaching shift rod clutch from shift control lever.

6 Just take weight of engine on trolley jack. Release engine rear support and transmission support from body mountings (see **FIG 1:9**). Lower jack, keeping engine steady, and pull out rearwards. Detach engine from transmission, taking great care not to let the transmission input shaft hang in the hub of the clutch plate.

Refitting engine:

Adopt the reverse sequence, observing the following precautions:

1 Check transmission input shaft for runout (see **Chapter 6**). Check condition of clutch release bearing. If clutch plate was removed, make sure it is centrally disposed in flywheel and cover (see **Chapter 5**).

2 Put 2 to 3 cc (.06 to .09 fluid oz) of graphite grease in the pilot bush for the input shaft (see 4 in **FIG 1:27**). Put a smear of graphite grease on the shaft splines and the bearing surface, in the starter shaft bush, and on the teeth of starter pinion and flywheel.

3 Clean mating faces of engine and transmission flanges. Keeping engine square with transmission, feed shaft through clutch plate hub, turning crankshaft by means of pulley with transmission engaged until splines are aligned. Push engine into place, being careful to put no strain on the shaft or clutch plate hub.

4 Start bottom screws in flanges first, then push transmission home against engine and tighten all bolts with equal torque.

5 After installation, check clutch free play. Do not reconnect battery until all cables are in place.

1:4 Removing and refitting cylinder heads

One bank of three heads with camshaft housing may be removed as a unit, or individual heads may be removed, with the engine out of the car.

Removing heads and camshaft housing as a unit:

1 Remove carburetters (see **Chapter 2**). Remove distributor cap with plug leads. Detach all cooling air ducts and covers. The alternator need not be removed.

2 Remove rear engine support and silencer. Remove heat exchanger (see **FIG 1:10**). Detach hose between crankcase and chain housing cover. Remove chain cover. Remove chain tensioner (see **Section 1:7**). Remove camshaft sprocket nuts and pull dowel from one of vernier timing holes in sprocket using tool P.212 (see **FIG 1:21**). Lift spring retainer with a screwdriver and pull chain guide ramp from housing.

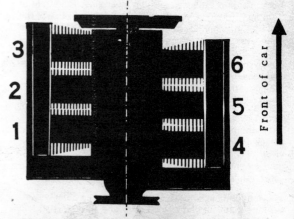

FIG 1:5 For checking purposes, use the cylinder numbering indicated. Firing order is 1, 6, 2, 4, 3, 5

Do not turn camshaft or crankshaft or pistons may hit valves.

3 Withdraw sprocket and flange. Remove key from camshaft. Remove three flange bolts and push out seal through slots in front of housing (see **FIG 1 : 11**). Detach chain housing from crankcase. Loosen cylinder head nuts with Allen key and lift off head and camshaft housing.

4 When refitting, remove the rockers to avoid distortion of the camshaft bearings (see **Section 1 : 6**).

Removing individual cylinder head :

Follow the preceding operations, but remove the rocker shafts and camshaft (see **Section 1 : 6**). Remove camshaft housing nuts and spring washers and the three socket-head nuts. Remove particular head required.

Refitting heads :

Perforations in cylinder head gaskets face cylinder. When camshaft housing is refitted, use sealing compound (Teroson Atmosit) on head faces. Fit housing and oil return pipes but do not tighten fixings. Tighten head fixings to 3.0 to 3.3 mkg (21½ to 24 lb ft). Tighten camshaft housing nuts evenly, inserting camshaft and checking free running. Use a torque of 2.2 to 2.5 mkg (16 to 18 lb ft).

Heads for engines up to No. 900.727 :

When renewing pistons or heads on these engines, use plasticine or a similar compound to check clearance between valves and pockets in piston crown. **Do not turn crankshaft until rocker gear has been fitted and timed correctly.** After turning several revolutions,

FIG 1 : 7 Removing engine. Detach throttle linkage from bellcrank (left arrow). Remove oil breather hose (central arrow). Detach cable from oil pressure transmitter (right arrow)

FIG 1 : 8 Gearshift rod joint under tunnel cover in passenger compartment

FIG 1 : 6 Adjusting valve clearances. Distributor rotor pointing to notch on body and pulley mark Z1 in line with crankcase joint with both valves closed, gives TDC on No. 1 cylinder (top view). Using feeler gauge to set valve clearance (bottom view)

FIG 1 : 9 Righthand and lefthand engine support mountings at rear (top view). Transmission support from below (lower view)

FIG 1:10 Removing heat exchanger flange nuts with spanner P.217

FIG 1:11 Sealing ring 3 and thrust washer 4 determine the end float of camshaft

Key to Fig 1:11 1 Paper gasket 2 O-ring 3 Sealing ring 4 Thrust washer 5 Spacer 6 Camshaft sprocket flange

FIG 1:12 Checking joint face of head for flatness, using a straightedge and feeler gauges

remove head and check clearance. If less than .80 mm (.032 inch) the particular valve seat must be ground back until correct clearance is obtained.

1:5 Servicing cylinder heads

Heads with unserviceable guides, seats or plug inserts may be works reconditioned.

Removing valves:

Remove springs with suitable compressor. Note any washers under spring seats. Remove burrs from cotter grooves in valve stems and push out valves, storing them in correct order. After 6 May, 1965 the valve stem seal need not be removed when lifting off the spring seat.

Checking head:

Check tightness and condition of valve seats and plug inserts. Check both faces of head (see **FIG 1:12**). Distortion must not exceed .15 mm (.006 inch). **The faces must not be machined.**

Check valve guide bores and measure valve stems. Clearance between inlet stem and guide must be .030 to .057 mm (.001 to .002 inch), and exhaust .050 to .077 mm (.002 to .003 inch). Defective guides cannot be renewed with normal workshop equipment. If facilities are available, heat head to 200°C (392°F) and drive out guide with a shouldered drift. Factory guides are oversize and must be machined until there is an interference of .031 to .06 mm (.001 to .0024 inch) between guide and head. Heat head again, put guide in freezer and then fit guide from camshaft side, using tallow as a lubricant. Correct position is shown in **FIG 1:13**. Ream bore to a diameter of 9.015 to 9.00 mm (.355 to .354 inch).

Renewing valve seat inserts also needs considerable skills and precision tools, so that the owner is recommended to entrust the work to a Porsche agent. The old seat is ground away until it becomes loose in the head and is then knocked out without damaging the recess. This recess is then accurately measured for bore and a new seat turned on the outside until it will have an interference fit of .14 to .18 mm (.0055 to .007 inch) for an inlet seat and .16 to .20 mm (.006 to .008 inch) for an exhaust seat. The seats are driven in with a suitably shouldered drift after the heads have been heated to 200°C or 392°F. Let head cool slowly. Reheat to the same temperature and maintain for 2 hours. Allow to cool slowly. Renewal of valve guides and head seats calls for accurate grinding of the new seat to ensure that it is the correct width and is concentric with the guide. Width of inlet seat (see A in **FIG 1:13**) must be 1.25 ± .10 mm (.050 ± .004 inch) and exhaust seat 1.55 ± .10 mm (.060 ± .004 inch). Correct angle is 45 deg.

Checking valves, grinding-in:

Clean valves and check against dimensions in Technical Data. Renew valves with burned seats, worn stems, stem ends and cotter grooves. **Do not try to straighten bent stems.** If grinding with paste will not remove pitting have valve seatings ground on a machine to an angle of 45 deg.

Grind-in with a suction tool and water-soluble paste. Put a light spring under the valve head. With a smear of paste on the valve face, grind-in with a semi-rotary action, letting the valve rise now and then to turn it to a fresh position. Continue until valve and head seats are a smooth matt grey. Wash off all traces of compound and dry thoroughly. Hold valve in place and pour fuel into port. Leakage past valve will be evident.

Checking springs:

Correct lengths and loadings are in Technical Data. Variation on used springs may be 5 per cent. Clean first and check for cracks. If one spring of a pair is defective, renew both. Installed length is shown at A in **FIG 1:14.** For most engines it is $36 \pm .30$ mm ($1.42 \pm .01$ inch) but later 2000 engines after No. 911.001 have an installed length of $35 \pm .3$ mm ($1.378 \pm .012$ inch). On 2000S engines for 911S cars, the installed length for inlet valves is $35.5 + .50$ mm ($1.4 + .02$ inch) and for exhaust valves $35.0 \pm .30$ mm ($1.378 \pm .012$ inch). For 2000T engines the length for both valves is $41.0 - .50$ mm ($1.614 - .02$ inch).

Reassembling head:

Before refitting the valves, check them as shown on the right in **FIG 1:14.** Dimension X must be 45.85 to 47.05 mm (1.805 to 1.852 inch) for both valves with a wear limit of 47.55 mm (1.871 inch). If the valves are the correct length and dimension X is not within the limits, renew the head or have new seat inserts fitted.

It is important to refer to the last instruction in **Section 1:4** when dealing with engines up to No. 900.727, so that there is no risk of contact between valves and pistons.

Put a smear of oil on the stem and fit the valve in its correct position. Fit adjusting shims, spring seat, and a new stem seal. Fit springs and collar, putting the close-coiled end of the outer spring against the head. Compress springs and fit collets.

1:6 Overhauling rocker gear and camshafts

To remove the camshaft housing proceed as instructed under 'Removing head and camshaft housing as a unit' in **Section 1:4,** but do not detach chain housing. Remove rockers as instructed later in this Section. After the seal is removed, push the camshaft to the rear and then detach the housing without disturbing the cylinder heads. Remember that three of the housing fixings have socket heads. Lift off the spring washers before removing the housing.

The housings are interchangeable but the coverplate must be pressed into place according to the housing position. Clean off all gasket material from sealing faces and check security of head studs.

The camshafts:

These are handed and the correct positions are shown in **FIG 1:15.** Clean shafts and check for wear or damage. Inject oil or use compressed air to check that oilways are clear. Refer to **FIG 1:11** and check condition of O-ring 2 and thrust washer 4. Sealing ring 3 is a guide and must be renewed if play is excessive.

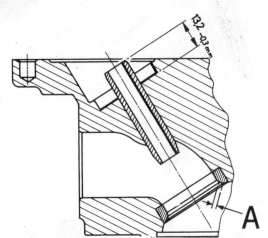

FIG 1:13 Correct position of valve guide with respect to valve spring seat in head. Width of valve seat is indicated at **A**

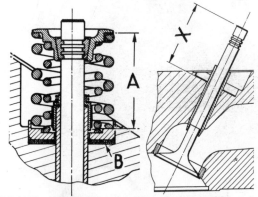

FIG 1:14 Installed length of outer valve spring at **A**, adjustment shims at **B** (lefthand view). Check **X** for length of valve stem projecting above spring seat (righthand view)

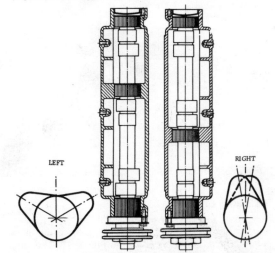

FIG 1:15 Lefthand and righthand camshafts and housings, showing differing cam positions

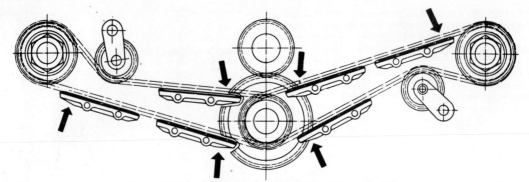

FIG 1:16   Positions of timing chain guide ramps

FIG 1:17   Lifting spring on chain guide ramp out of groove in mounting stud

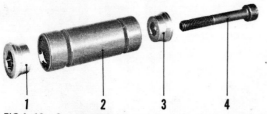

FIG 1:18   Components of rocker shaft. Cones expand ends to secure shaft in housing

Key to Fig 1:18   1 Nut cone   **2** Rocker shaft   **3** Bush cone   **4** Allen screw

Camshaft drive:

With the chain tensioner and camshaft sprocket removed it will be possible to attend to the chain guide ramps. The positions are shown in **FIG 1:16**. The inner ones are removed as shown in **FIG 1:17** after detaching the chain housing. These ramps are attached by stud bolts, and removal is effected by lifting the spring retainers from the groove in the stud and then unscrewing. Check condition of ramps, springs and stud bolts.

When replacing, check that spring locates correctly in groove. Fit new gaskets between crankcase and chain housing. Refer to **Section 1:7** for details of overhauling the chain tensioner. Alignment of sprockets is covered in **Section 1:15**.

Refitting camshaft housing:

Apply a thin coat of sealing compound such as Teroson Atmosit to the cylinder head surfaces. Place housing and oil return pipes on heads, fit a few nuts and washers and tighten finger tight. Fit remaining nuts and tighten diagonally across the head. While doing this, have the camshaft in place and check that it turns freely. If it binds, try altering the sequence of nut tightening.

Refitting camshaft:

With shafts correctly located as shown in **FIG 1:15**, attach gasket 1 with grease (see **FIG 1:11**). Fit sealing ring 3 and O-ring 2 and tighten the three screws. Fit thrust washer 4 and spacer(s) 5. Fit key to shaft and press on sprocket flange 6. The rockers must be detached during all these operations.

Camshaft sprockets are interchangeable but are offset differently when fitted. The one for cylinders 1 to 3 must have the deeper recess visible and the one for cylinders 4 to 6 must have the shallow recess visible. Cylinder numbering is shown in **FIG 1:5**.

Removing and refitting rockers:

Mark rockers for correct reassembly. When removing rocker with valves in position, turn camshaft until rocker is free of pressure before trying to remove rocker shaft.

FIG 1:18 shows the method of securing the rocker shaft 2 by means of expander cones in each end. Tightening screw 4 causes the cones to expand the ends of the shaft inside the camshaft housing, locking it in place and making an oil-tight seal.

Undo screw with an Allen key and push out the shaft. Check shaft and rocker for wear. Oil parts during reassembly.

Refit marked rockers in original positions. Allen screws of end rocker shafts must have their heads facing cylinders 2 and 5 respectively (see **FIG 1:5**).

The shafts must be centrally located so that the grooves are recessed into the camshaft housing bores the same amount each side. This should be 1.5 mm (.06 inch). Use feeler gauges as follows:

Insert feeler between rocker and housing and locate shaft so that feeler drops into groove. Push on shaft at end farthest from groove until feeler is trapped. Withdraw feeler. Push shaft approximately 1.5 mm (.06 inch) further in and tighten Allen screw to 180 cm/kg (13 lb ft).

Adjust the valve clearances as instructed in **Section 1:2**. If the timing gear has been dismantled, adjust the valve timing as described in **Section 1:8**.

1:7 Overhauling chain tensioner—removal and refitting

Removal:

With engine removed from car, disconnect both oil supply hoses from crankcase to chain housing cover. Remove cover and turn engine to TDC on firing stroke of No. 1 cylinder (see top view of **FIG 1:6**). On lefthand side of engine, jam tensioner sprocket against chain with a block between spindle and crankcase. On righthand side tie sprocket arm to a cover stud above it, using wire. Remove tensioner, noting that plunger is under spring pressure (see **FIG 1:19**).

Overhauling:

Refer to **FIG 1:19**. Righthand view shows that spring-loaded piston action is damped hydraulically. Dismantle tensioner by holding piston down and prising out circlip 1 (see lefthand view). Release piston slowly and extract the ball valve parts. Valve seat 3 is a press fit in piston. Clean parts and check fit of piston in bore. Check action of valve. Reject corroded parts, particularly the spring. Reassemble in reverse order.

Hold tensioner vertically in vice and fill oil cup with engine oil. Depress ball with bent wire as shown on right in illustration. Press piston up and down, keep cup filled with oil and continue until no more air bubbles emerge.

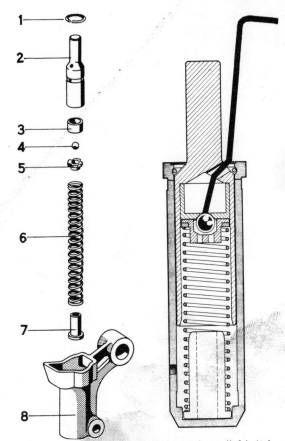

FIG 1:19 Components of chain tensioner (left). Using wire probe to depress valve to bleed tensioner (right)

Key to Fig 1:19 1 Circlip   2 Piston   3 Ball valve seat
4 Ball   5 Ball valve cage   6 Spring   7 Spring guide
8 Tensioner housing

FIG 1:20 Checking valve timing. Outer arrows point to camshaft markings, central arrow to pulley mark Z1 aligned with crankcase joint

Hold piston at bottom of stroke with steel strip bent inwards at each end, to facilitate refitting. This must fit over piston and under tensioner body.

A tensioner with doubtful action must be tested. Use SAE.30 engine oil at approximately 20°C or 68°F. Arrange for a weight of 5.5 kg (12 lb) to rest squarely and centrally on the piston end. During 5 to 10 minutes the piston must not yield by more than 10 mm (.40 inch).

Refitting:

Do this in the reverse order of dismantling, removing the steel strip to release the piston when the tensioner is in place. Remove device used to keep sprocket pressed firmly against chain.

1 : 8 Valve timing

It is essential to check the valve timing if an engine has been completely dismantled or if the camshafts and drive gear have been overhauled. **It is most important that all operations of turning the crankshaft and camshafts with the drive disconnected are undertaken with great care.** Unless the pistons and valves are correctly timed there is a possibility that they will make contact when the top of each stroke is reached. If the slightest resistance to turning is noticed, stop at once, back off a little and reset the relative positions of camshafts and crankshaft.

Adjustment:

Preliminary timing is set as follows:
1 Refer to **FIG 1 : 20** and turn crankshaft so that pulley mark Z1 lines up with crankcase joint.
2 Camshafts are marked on the end with a punch. Turn these marks until they are vertically above camshaft centres (see outer arrows in illustration), taking the precautions mentioned at the start of this Section.
3 One hole in each camshaft sprocket will line up with one in the sprocket flange. Insert the dowel (see **FIG 1 : 21**). Fit spring washer and tighten nut to 10 mkg (72 lb ft).

Accurate timing is obtained as follows:
1 Set inlet valve clearance of No. 1 cylinder to .10 mm (.004 inch). See **FIG 1 : 5** for cylinder numbering.
2 Set up a dial gauge as shown top left in **FIG 1 : 22**. The plunger must rest on the valve spring collar and in line with the valve stem. Arrange for the plunger to extend a further 10 mm (.40 inch) as the valve opens. Zero the gauge.
3 Use a screwdriver to press the tensioner sprocket firmly against the chain, as shown, and block the tensioner in that position. Turn crankshaft through a complete turn so that No. 1 cylinder is now at TDC on the inlet stroke and the inlet valve should have started to open. Read the dial gauge. This will be the amount of inlet valve lift at TDC and figures for the various models are as follows:

If the amount of lift shown by the gauge differs from these figures, adjust as follows:
1 Remove camshaft sprocket nut and spring washer. Withdraw dowel. Ensure that pulley mark aligns with crankcase joint.
2 Turn the camshaft with special tool P.202 as shown. Do this until the dial gauge shows the desirable adjustment value just specified.
3 Find the holes in sprocket and flange which line up and insert dowel. Fit washer and nut and tighten to correct torque.
4 Turn crankshaft two complete turns and check gauge reading. Readjust if necessary.

Repeat the procedure on cylinder No. 4 to set the timing of the other camshaft, making sure the tensioner sprocket is firmly pressed into the chain. When adjustment is completed, remove blocks used to maintain position of tensioners. Note in **FIG 1 : 22** that a screwdriver is being used to press the tensioner into the chain to take up all backlash.

1 : 9 Servicing lubricating system

The layout of the system is shown in **FIG 1 : 23**. There are two pumps 2 and 3. Pressure pump 3 draws oil from tank 9 and pumps it to thermostat 5. If the oil is cold it is prevented from passing through cooler 8 and is forced through passages to the various engine bearings. When the oil warms up, the thermostat opens and allows the oil to pass through the cooler 8 before it goes to the bearings. Draining oil collects in the crankcase and is drawn out by scavenge pump 2. It is then pumped to tank 9, passing through a fullflow filter 12 on its way.

Excessive pressure in the system will open relief valve 7 which allows some oil to escape into the crankcase. If this valve becomes blocked or otherwise inoperative a safety valve 4 will open under excessive pressure to ensure that there is no possibility of the hoses, the cooler or the filter being damaged.

Maintenance of the filter and the crankcase strainer has been covered in **Section 1 : 2**.

Servicing pressure relief and safety valves:

The location of the valves is shown by the arrows in **FIG 1 : 24**. The relief valve is on the left. Both are removed by unscrewing the plugs and withdrawing the springs and pistons.

Examine the pistons and remove score marks with care. Renew pistons if worn or beyond renovation. Check springs as follows:

The springs are identical, the fitted length varying to give the required lifting pressures. Free length is 70 mm (2.75 inch). Pressure at length of 52 mm (2.04 inch) should be 23 lb and at a length of 46 mm (1.81 inch) it should be 31 lb.

2000 engines (up to No. 909.927)	4.2 to 4.6 mm (.165 to .181 inch)
Desirable adjustment value	4.3 mm (.169 inch)
2000 engine (Nos. 911.001 to 912.050 and 3180.001 to 3380.001) ..	3.0 to 3.3 mm (.118 to .130 inch)
Desirable adjustment value	3.15 mm (.124 inch)
2000S engine (from Nos. 960.001 and 4080.001)	5.0 to 5.4 mm (.197 to .213 inch)
Desirable adjustment value	5.2 mm (.205 inch)
2000T engine (from No. 2080.001)	2.3 to 2.7 mm (.091 to .106 inch)
Desirable adjustment value	2.5 mm (.098 inch)
2000L engine (from No. 3380.001)	6.8 ± .10 mm (.268 ± .004 inch)

FIG 1:21 Withdrawing dowel which aligns vernier hole in camshaft sprocket with that in flange

FIG 1:22 Valve timing check. Dial gauge records inlet valve lift while camshaft is turned with tool No. P202

For engines up to No. 901.282 it is necessary to fit a special aluminium sealing ring to the plug for the pressure relief valve. This will give the required length of 57.5 mm (2.26 inch) as shown at A in view 1 of **FIG 1:25**. Measure with a depth gauge.

Later engines had modifications which made distance B in view 2 as 59.5 mm (2.34 inch). The sealing ring then became the same as that fitted to the safety valve plug.

When refitting the piston spring, make sure it does not scratch the bore.

Removing and refitting oil filter and oil cooler:

Instructions concerning the oil filter are to be found in **Section 1:2**. To remove the oil cooler with the engine in or out of the car, proceed as follows:

1 Remove upper coverplate, front coverplate and right-hand coverplate. Refer to **FIG 1:26** and remove upper nuts (top view).
2 Hold hexagon of inlet pipe to prevent it turning and release union from cooler.

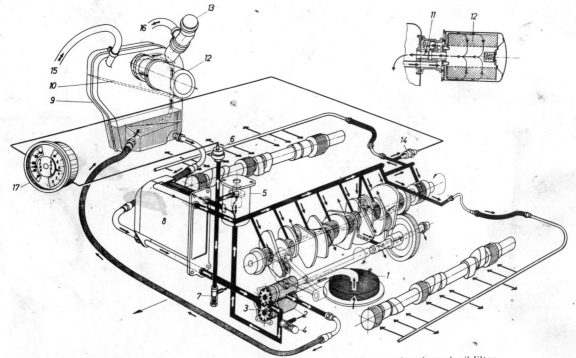

FIG 1:23 Layout of lubricating system. Inset (top right) is a section through oil filter

Key to Fig 1:23   1 Strainer in crankcase   2 Scavenge pump   3 Pressure pump   4 Safety valve   5 Thermostat   6 Oil gauge transmitter   7 Pressure relief valve   8 Oil cooler   9 Oil tank   10 Anti-foaming plate   11 Bypass valve   12 Fullflow oil filter   13 Filler   14 Temperature gauge transmitter   15 Crankcase breather connection   16 Tank breather connection   17 Oil pressure and temperature gauges

FIG 1 : 24 Plug for oil pressure relief valve (left), plug for safety valve (right)

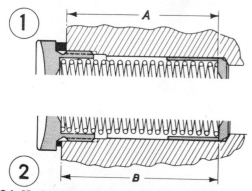

FIG 1 : 25 Length **A** should be 57.5 mm (2.26 inch) on engines up to No. 901282. The plug is fitted with a thick aluminium sealing washer (view 1). Later engines have thinner washer and dimension **B** is 59.5 mm (2.34 inch), as shown in view 2

3 Remove lower nuts (bottom view). Lift cooler away, noting seals to crankcase. Always renew these.

When refitting cooler, make sure the seals are correctly seated and connect the inlet pipe, using the precautions taken to remove it.

Thermostat and oil pressure transmitter:

These are indicated by the arrows in the top view of **FIG 1 : 26**. To remove the thermostat, disconnect cable to transmitter (top arrow), disconnect hose from breather outlet and unscrew transmitter. Remove thermostat (two nuts).

Refit in the reverse order, fitting new O-rings. Offset holes in thermostat flange prevent incorrect assembly.

Oil pump removal and refitting:

The location of the pump can be seen on the left in **FIG 1 : 30**. Note how it is driven by the intermediate shaft (see 13, 18 and 19 in **FIG 1 : 2**).

The pump is removed after the crankcase halves have been parted. Arrows indicate the securing nuts. Remove pump with intermediate and connecting shafts. Withdraw pump from connecting shaft.

The pump cannot be repaired and must be renewed if faulty. Check action after cleaning and blowing out with compressed air. Run at moderate speed. Check sealing surfaces and renew seals.

Refit pump in the reverse order, inserting it complete with shafts and chains. Make sure the seals are correctly fitted and are not displaced. Secure with nuts and tab-washers.

1 : 10 The flywheel and clutch

Removing:

Part the engine and gearbox, then loosen the bolts securing the clutch. Do this a turn at a time, working diagonally to avoid distortion of the clutch cover. Lift away clutch cover and driven plate. With the flywheel secured against turning, use a long-handled wrench to remove the socket-head screws and lever the flywheel squarely off the crankshaft (see **FIG 1 : 27**). Note drive shaft bush 4 and spacer 5.

Reconditioning flywheel:

Check condition of starter teeth, clutch plate surface and centre boss where it mates with crankshaft. Renew flywheel if seriously defective, but have it machined if damage is slight. Gear teeth may be cut back slightly and clutch plate surface may be resurfaced by Porsche agents, who will know the necessary dimensions. From engine No. P901.639 the flywheel was reduced in width and the gear teeth were of finer pitch, the width of the rim being 39 mm (1.54 inch). Flywheels must be rejected if the

FIG 1 : 26 Removing oil cooler. Top view also shows pressure transmitter (top arrow) and thermostat (lower arrow)

clutch driving face is less than 11 mm (.433 inch) from the face of the centre boss.

Check condition and fit of input shaft bush. It may be renewed by pressing out from the front and fitting a new one from the back.

Refitting:

Flywheels and crankshafts may be renewed separately without upsetting the balance. Holes for securing screws are staggered so that flywheel fits in one place only.

Mounting faces of crankshaft, flywheel and spacing washer must be free from oil. Lightly oil threads of screws and tighten them evenly and progressively to a torque of 15 mkg (108 lb ft). Put about 2 cc of graphite or molybdenum-disulphide grease in the input shaft bush. Centralize the clutch plate and refit the clutch cover as instructed in **Chapter 5.**

1:11 Removing and servicing cylinders and pistons

Before removing the cylinders, mark them 1 to 6 as indicated in **FIG 1:5.** After removing the cylinder head, either in sets or individually, as described in **Section 1:4,** detach the air deflector plates and lift off the cylinders.

Removing pistons:

Mark each piston with the cylinder number and indicate how it faces with respect to the flywheel or front of the engine. Push rag into the crankcase apertures to prevent gudgeon pin circlips falling in as they are prised out with a thin screwdriver, using the slots provided. Pistons must be heated before gudgeon pins are pushed out. Electric heaters are available but hot water may be used to get each piston up to a temperature of 80°C or 176°F, taking care that water does not enter the crankcase. Remove pin and lift piston off connecting rod. Remove rings with special pliers.

Cylinder specifications (up to and including 1967 models):

911T engines have cast iron cylinders, all other models having 'Biral' cylinders with iron bores and aluminium cooling fins as shown in **FIG 1:28.** Note how the tolerance groups are designated A and B. If the triangle encloses the figure 5 the height of the barrel from joint face to joint face is 82.2 to 82.225 mm (3.236 to 3.237 inch). If the figure is a 6 the height is 82.225 to 82.250 mm (3.237 to 3.238 inch). **All cylinders in a bank of three must be of the same height.** Specifications are as follows:

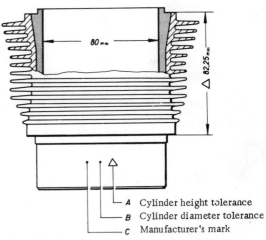

FIG 1:27   How flywheel is secured. Bush 4 supports rear end of gearbox input shaft

Key to Fig 1:27   1 Flywheel   2 Socket-head screws
3 Crankshaft   4 Bush and seal   5 Spacing washer

A   Cylinder height tolerance
B   Cylinder diameter tolerance
C   Manufacturer's mark

FIG 1:28   Location of cylinder marking for height, and bore diameter

Designation B									Bore size
—1	..	..	..	..	..	..	..	..	79.99 to 80.00 mm (3.1492 to 3.1496 inch)
0	..	..	..	..	..	..	..	..	80.00 to 80.01 mm (3.1496 to 3.150 inch)
+1	..	..	..	..	..	..	..	..	80.01 to 80.02 mm (3.150 to 3.1504 inch)
Oversize:									
—1.KD.1	..	..	..	..	..	..	..	..	80.49 to 80.50 mm (3.1689 to 3.1692 inch)
0.KD.1	..	..	..	..	..	..	..	..	80.50 to 80.51 mm (3.1692 to 3.1696 inch)
+1.KD.1	..	..	..	..	..	..	..	..	80.51 to 80.52 mm (3.1696 to 3.170 inch)

Use this table when assessing bore condition in association with the table of piston sizes which follows. Measure bore 30 mm (1.18 inch) up from the bottom. Cylinders may be rebored by any reputable workshop.

Piston specifications (up to and including 1967 models):

Clearance between piston and cylinder should be .055 to .075 mm (.0022 to .0029 inch). Wear limit is .10 mm (.0039 inch). Establish clearance by measuring with internal and external micrometers. Measure pistons at right angles to gudgeon pin about 2 mm below the bottom ring groove. Specifications are as follows:

Piston crown marking	Piston diameter
—1	79.925 to 79.935 mm (3.1466 to 3.1470 inch)
0	79.935 to 79.945 mm (3.1470 to 3.1474 inch)
+1	79.945 to 79.955 mm (3.1474 to 3.1478 inch)
Oversize:	
—1.KD.1	80.425 to 80.435 mm (3.1663 to 3.1667 inch)
0.KD.1	80.435 to 80.445 mm (3.1667 to 3.1671 inch)
+1.KD.1	80.445 to 80.455 mm (3,1671 to 3.1675 inch)

Pair this table off with the cylinder bore table to check wear. Standard pistons are marked —1, 0 and +1. **These are obtainable only as a set with matching cylinder.** Oversize pistons are available individually.

Cylinder specifications (1968 models onwards):

Designation B	Bore size
0	80.00 to 80.01 mm (3.1496 to 3.150 inch)
1	80.01 to 80.02 mm (3.150 to 3.1504 inch)
2	80.02 to 80.03 mm (3.1504 to 3.1508 inch)
Oversize:	
0.KD.1	80.50 to 80.51 mm (3.1692 to 3.1696 inch)
1.KD.1	80.51 to 80.52 mm (3.1696 to 3.170 inch)
2.KD.1	80.52 to 80.53 mm (3.170 to 3.1704 inch)

Use this table in conjunction with the following tables for the three types of piston shown in **FIG 1 : 29**. Note, however, that type C comes in two makes, Mahle and Schmidt, with differing dimensions.

Piston specification for 911L engine (1968 models onwards):

Crown mark	Diameter of piston B at D1 (tolerance ± .005 mm or ± .0002 inch)
0	79.960 mm (3.148 inch)
1	79.970 mm (3.1484 inch)
2	79.980 mm (3.1488 inch)
Oversize:	
0.KD.1	80.460 mm (3.1677 inch)
1.KD.1	80.470 mm (3.1681 inch)
2.KD.1	80.480 mm (3.1685 inch)

Piston specification for 911T engine (1968 models onwards—Mahle):

Crown mark	Diameter of piston C at D1 (tolerance ± .005 mm or ± .0002 inch)
0	79.970 mm (3.1484 inch)
1	79.980 mm (3.1488 inch)
2	79.990 mm (3.1492 inch)
Oversize:	
0.KD.1	80.470 mm (3.1681 inch)
1.KD.1	80.480 mm (3.1685 inch)
2.KD.1	80.490 mm (3.1689 inch)

Piston specification for 911T engine (1968 model onwards—Schmidt):

Crown mark	Diameter of piston C at D1 (tolerance + .006 — .007 mm or + .0002 inch —.0003 inch)
0	79.960 mm (3.148 inch)
1	79.970 mm (3.1484 inch)
2	79.980 mm (3.1488 inch)
Oversize:	
0.KD.1	80.460 mm (3.1677 inch)
1.KD.1	80.470 mm (3.1681 inch)
2.KD.1	80.480 mm (3.1685 inch)

FIG 1:29 Piston types **A**, **B** and **C**. These are fitted to cars 911S, 911L and 911T respectively. For clearance checks, measure at D1

Piston specification for 911S engine (1968 models onwards):

Crown mark	Diameter of piston A at D1 (tolerance ± .005 mm or ± .0002 inch)
0	79.95 mm (3.1476 inch)
1	79.96 mm (3.148 inch)
2	79.97 mm (3.1484 inch)
Oversize:	
0.KD.1	80.45 mm (3.1673 inch)
1.KD.1	80.46 mm (3.1677 inch)
2.KD.1	80.47 mm (3.1681 inch)

Piston clearance (1968 models onwards):

Measure piston at point indicated by D1 in **FIG 1:29**. Measure cylinder bore 30 mm (1.18 inch) up from bottom. Clearance of piston in bore should lie between limits of .035 to .055 mm (.0014 to .0022 inch) for 911L and 911T (Schmidt) pistons. It should be .025 to .045 mm (.001 to .0018 inch) for 911T (Mahle) pistons, and .045 to .065 mm (.0018 to .0026 inch) for 911S pistons.

Gudgeon pins:

These must be a force fit in piston. Any pin which can be inserted easily into a cold piston must be replaced by one of larger diameter. Pins are colour-coded black or white and this marking will also be found on the inside of the piston boss. Piston bore and pin diameter are as follows:

White .. 22 mm (.866 inch), tolerance 0 to —.003 mm (—.0001 inch)

Black .. 22 mm (.866 inch), tolerance —.003 to —.006 mm (—.0001 to —.0002 inch)

When fitting gudgeon pins it is best to fit new circlips. Insert one circlip so that its opening faces to the piston crown or the skirt. Heat piston to 80°C or 176°F and push oiled gudgeon pin into place in one movement. **Do not stop on the way.** Make sure circlips are properly seated.

For correct clearance of gudgeon pin in small-end bush of connecting rod refer to **Section 1:13**.

Piston rings:

Ring gap should be .30 to .45 mm (.012 to .018 inch) with a wear limit of 1.0 mm (.04 inch). Use a piston to push ring about 20 mm up the cylinder bore from the bottom. Measure gap with feeler gauges. Too small a gap may be rectified by judicious filing. Check side clearance of rings in groove with feelers. Correct clearance is given in Technical Data.

Fit rings with marking 'TOP' uppermost and set gaps 120 deg. apart. Use piston ring pliers to avoid breakage.

Decarbonizing pistons:

Clean carbon off piston crown with soft tool, taking care not to scratch surface. Clean carbon out of ring grooves, taking care not to remove metal from the sides of the ring grooves. Check for markings which might indicate a bent connecting rod. These often show as scoring and heavy marking on one side of the piston below the gudgeon pin, with similar marking above the pin on the opposite side.

Refitting pistons and cylinders:

Refit the gudgeon pins as instructed in a preceding section. Lightly oil the pistons, rings and cylinder bores. Stagger the ring gaps evenly. Use a compressor on the rings. Making sure that the mating faces are clean, fit a new gasket to the base of each cylinder and slide the cylinders into place. Check that holding-down studs do not contact cylinder fins. Refit air deflector plates (see **FIG 1:35**).

1:12 Splitting crankcase, removing and refitting crankshaft

With cylinders and pistons removed and crankcase stripped of external parts, remove the chain guide ramps as described in **Section 1:6** under the heading 'Camshaft drive'. **FIG 1:17** shows the operation. Proceed as follows:

1 Remove oil strainer from base of crankcase. Remove flywheel (see **Section 1:10**).

FIG 1:30 Oil pumps and intermediate drive shaft. Arrow points to pump fixings

FIG 1:31 Special spring steel strips hold connecting rods and timing chain upright to facilitate assembly of crankshaft halves

FIG 1:32 Connecting rod dismantled, showing bearing shells

2 Remove oil pressure relief and safety valves (see **Section 1:9**). Remove V-belt pulley. Remove cover at rear end of intermediate shaft (see **Section 1:14**).

3 Detach breather outlet nozzles and adjacent thermostat and oil pressure transmitter (see **FIG 1:26**).

4 Remove all nuts securing crankcase halves. This includes two cap nuts which are located inside the oil cooler mounting flange. Unscrew all through bolts. Remove nut inside the lefthand chain housing aperture.

5 Separate crankcase halves and lift out crankshaft. Remove nuts arrowed in **FIG 1:30** and lift away oil pump and intermediate shaft. Mark bearing shells if to be refitted.

Cleaning and inspection:

Clean off all jointing material. Flush out oil passages with solvent and compressed air. Check crankcase for cracks and damage. Check joint faces for flatness and freedom from burrs.

Examine groove round through-bolt hole in lefthand casing at No. 7 main bearing, counting from the front end. This must be clean and free from jointing compound.

Bolt crankcase halves together and check main bearing bores with internal micrometer. Standard bores for bearings 1 to 8 is 62.0 to 62.019 mm (2.4409 to 2.4417 inch). Bores may be machined at the factory and oversize bearing shells fitted. The bore then becomes 62.269 to 62.250 mm (2.4515 to 2.4508 inch). While the case is bolted together, check the bores for the intermediate shaft. Bearing 1 should be 29.8 to 29.821 mm (1.173 to 1.174 inch) and bearing 2 should be 24.0 to 24.021 mm (.945 to .9457 inch).

Reassembling crankcase:

Service the crankshaft as explained in **Section 1:13** and the intermediate shaft as in **Section 1:14**. Proceed as follows:

1 Refit oil pump and intermediate shaft (see **Section 1:9**). Fit main bearing shells 2 to 7 in both casings, locating the tags in the notches provided. Fit flanged shells for bearing 1. Check that oil holes coincide.

2 Oil bearings and fit crankshaft. At front end, coat outer diameter of seal with jointing compound and fit.

3 Use flat spring strips to hold connecting rods and timing chain in position as shown in **FIG 1:31**. Fit new sealing rings to oil pump and adjacent oil passage. Fit No. 8 bearing, using a new seal and O-ring (see **FIG 1:34**).

4 Smear jointing compound thinly on joint faces, keeping it away from bearings and annular groove round No. 7 bolt hole. Before fitting the lefthand case, check all parts, see that none becomes displaced and lower the casing half into place. Make sure dowel locates bearing No. 8.

5 Fit through-bolts, fitting a double-chamfered washer under each head with smooth face to crankcase. Push on an O-ring and assemble bolt to crankcase. Fit another O-ring followed by a double-chamfered washer and cap nut.

6 The same washers, rings and nuts are used on the studs for No. 1 bearing. These are located on the lefthand side inside the oil cooler flange. Use a washer and nut on the stud for No. 7 bearing, to be found in the chain housing on the lefthand case. Tighten through-bolts and studs evenly to 3.5 mkg (25 lb ft).

7 Fit spring washers to all retaining studs. Tighten all nuts evenly and diagonally to 2.2 to 2.5 mkg (16 to 18 lb ft).

Renewing O-ring for bearing No. 8:

Refer to the lefthand view in **FIG 1:34**. To renew the O-ring without dismantling the engine remove the pulley and push a small screwdriver carefully under the lip of the seal and lever out the ring. Take care not to mark the sealing surface of the crankshaft.

Coat a new O-ring with oil and refit it, using tool No. P.216. This is a steel cup which presses the ring into place by the action of a nut on a bolt which is screwed into the crankshaft.

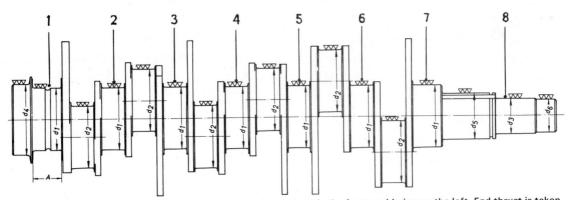

FIG 1 : 33 Main bearing journals on crankshaft are numbered 1 to 8, the front end being on the left. End thrust is taken at bearing 1 as indicated at **A**

Renewing oil seal at front end:

This is possible without splitting the crankcase, after the flywheel has been removed. Displace the seal from its recess with a chisel and then prise it out with a screwdriver. Take care not to damage the sealing surface of the crankshaft. Lightly radius outer corner of recess, removing all swarf.

Take a new seal and lightly coat the outer surface with jointing compound. Press ring into place with tool P.215 so that it finishes flush with the crankcase. Oil the sealing lip and refit the flywheel.

1 : 13 Servicing crankshaft and connecting rods

Removal of the crankshaft has been covered in the preceding Section.

Remove connecting rods:

This is simply a matter of removing the big-end bolts, but make sure that the caps and rods are correctly marked for reassembly. **The bolts must be renewed at each overhaul.**

Check rod weights. They must not vary by more than 5 gr. (.176 oz). This is the weight of a complete rod without bearing shells, and is the one quoted when ordering spares. The rod components are shown in **FIG 1 : 32.**

Check gudgeon pin in small-end bush. It should be a light push fit. Clearance between gudgeon pin and small-end bush should be not more than .020 to .039 mm (.0008 to .0015 inch). Data on oversize pins is given in the preceding Section.

Small-end bushes are renewable, the interference fit being such that the bush must be .014 to .055 mm (.0005 to .002 inch) larger in diameter than the bore in the eye of the connecting rod. The bore of the bush after reaming should be 22.033 to 22.020 mm (.8674 to .867 inch). The pin should then be a light push fit.

Bearing shells:

If scored or breaking up, these must be renewed. If a bearing has 'run', all oilways in the engine must be flushed through at high pressure to remove bearing particles. **Never attempt to rectify bearing clearances by filing or scraping the shells.**

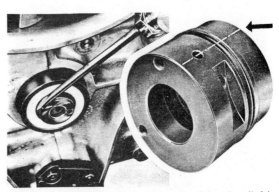

FIG 1 : 34 Removing O-ring from No. 8 bearing (left). Marking position of dowel hole on face of bearing housing to ensure correct location (right)

FIG 1 : 35 Cooling air shrouds fitted below cylinders (top view). Shrouds secured with clamps (lower view)

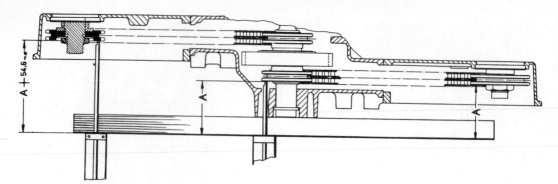

FIG 1 : 36   Checking camshaft drive sprockets for correct alignment, using a straightedge and depth gauge

Dismantling crankshaft:

Remove circlip and use a puller to draw off the distributor drive gear, spacer and timing gear as one assembly. Remove spring washer. Prise out Woodruff key.

Clean crankshaft and oilways and examine shaft for wear or cracks. Support shaft on V-blocks at bearings 1 and 7 and check for eccentricity. Bearing eccentricity at bearings 4 and 8 should not exceed .002 mm (.0008 inch). Bearing numbers are given in **FIG 1 : 33**. Standard diameters of main (d1) and connecting rod pins (d2) are 56.990 to 56.971 (2.244 to 2.243 inch). Of No. 8 bearing (d3) it is 30.993 to 30.980 (1.2202 to 1.2197 inch). Excessive wear may be cured by regrinding mains or crankpins to one of three undersizes, —.25, —.50 and —.75 mm and fitting the appropriate bearing shells. As the shaft needs heat treatment after grinding it is advisable to entrust it to a Porsche agent.

Main bearing and crankpin clearances:

Clearance of main bearings 1 to 7 must lie between .030 and .088 mm (.001 and .0034 inch). Clearance for big-end bearings is the same. Clearance for main bearing No. 8 should be .048 to .104 mm (.002 to .004 inch). End float is .110 to .195 mm (.004 to .0076 inch).

Check by measurement of bore of shells when assembled and by diameters of main and big-end journals. Alternatively, use 'Plastigage' between the assembled bearings and check the width of the squashed material against the gauge supplied, to determine the clearance. Remember that main bearing shells may become loose in the crankcase bores and this may be cured by machining, and then fitting shells which are oversize on outside diameter (see **Section 1 :12**).

Reassembling crankshaft:

Having carefully removed any scoring where the gears are pressed onto the shaft without actually impairing the fit, slide on the spring washer and insert the key. Heat the gear to 150°C or 302°F in an oil bath or on a hotplate and push it onto the shaft with its shoulder facing forward. Fit the spacer and distributor drive gear after heating the gear to 100°C or 212°F. Check that gears are tight when cool and fit circlip.

Inject oil through the crankshaft passages and fit the connecting rods. Make sure the shells are correctly located in the rod and cap, oil the bearing and assemble cap to rod so that the identification numbers coincide. Fit new bolts and tighten to a torque of 5 mkg (36.2 lb ft). If bearing seems tight, tap big-end lugs with a copper hammer to settle cap and rod together. When lubricated the rods should fall freely under their own weight.

1 :14 Servicing the intermediate shaft

This is shaft 13 in **FIG 1 : 2** and its function is to drive the two camshafts through sprockets 14. The front end of the shaft is coupled to oil pumps 18 and 19. A crankshaft gear immediately behind No. 7 main bearing drives the intermediate shaft.

Great care is needed when servicing the shaft to ensure satisfactory meshing of the gears. Firstly, the shaft and gear must be renewed as an assembly because the gear is machined in situ to make sure it is concentric with the shaft. Secondly, there was a change in design during production and gears and crankcases must be paired together, due to an alteration in shaft centres.

First-type intermediate shaft assembly

Nominal distance between crankshaft and intermediate shaft is 104 mm. Deviation from this dimension is stamped on the rear face of the lefthand crankcase-half adjacent to the alternator mounting. The gears have the deviation from pitch radius of the teeth stamped on the sides. Deviation values are in 1/100 mm. Gears must be mated so that the installed tolerances are nil, with a maximum clearance of 1/100 mm.

Second-type intermediate shaft assembly:

An identifying number, either 0 or 1, will be found on the rear face of the lefthand crankcase-half adjacent to the alternator mounting. The gears are stamped in the same way.

When the crankcase number is 0, fit a pair of gears stamped 0. The gear backlash will then be .029 to .049 mm (.001 to .002 inch). It is permissible to fit a No. 1 crankshaft gear with a No. 0 intermediate gear, the backlash then being .016 to .042 mm (.0006 to .0016 inch). It is also permissible to fit a No. 0 crankshaft gear with a No. 1 intermediate gear, the backlash being .017 to .043 mm (.0007 to .0017 inch).

If the crankcase number is 1, fit a pair of gears stamped 1. Backlash will be .012 to .041 mm (.0005 to .0016 inch). It is permissible to fit a No. 0 crankshaft gear with a

No. 1 intermediate gear to give a backlash of .025 to .049 mm (.001 to .0019 inch). Also permissible is a No. 1 crankshaft gear and a No. 0 intermediate gear, the backlash being the same.

Servicing shaft:

Bearing clearance in crankcase must be .020 to .054 mm (.0008 to .002 inch). Wear limit is .10 mm (.004 inch). Shafts which have seen much service should have the internal bore cleaned of residue. Access is by removal of the aluminium plug at the rear end. This is drilled and tapped and a bolt used to withdraw it, a piece of tubing 1 inch long and slightly larger in bore than the diameter of the plug, being used as a spacer. Clean the bore of the shaft and press in a new plug, taking care not to damage the oilway.

Fitting shaft to crankcase:

Being satisfied with the condition of the gear teeth and the bearing surfaces of the shaft, place the shaft in the crankcase, complete with pump but without timing chains. Check for freedom of movement. Altering position of connecting shaft splines may cure binding. When satisfied remove shaft without altering position of connecting shaft, fit the chains and continue with crankcase assembling as instructed in **Section 1:12.**

End float of intermediate shaft:

Later engines have no provision for adjustment of end float because the rear bearing has renewable inserts with thrust flanges. When fitting the inserts, take care to locate the tabs in the crankcase notches.

On earlier engines, end float is controlled by a thrust plate secured to the rear face of the crankcase. One paper gasket must always be fitted, and adjustment made with shims, before the chain housings are fitted.

Through the chain aperture, lever the sprocket forward to take up all play in the shaft and install the plate with gasket and a thread of 'Plastigage' between the contact faces. Lever the shaft to the rear, remove the plate and measure the 'Plastigage'. Alter shims until the correct end float of .08 to .12 mm (.003 to .0047 inch) is obtained.

The Porsche method of checking uses a dial gauge fitted to a plate which takes the place of the thrust plate so that the plunger can bear on the end of the intermediate shaft to record end float directly.

When reassembling a stripped engine, do not install the thrust plate until the timing sprockets have been checked for alignment as instructed in the following Section.

1:15 Reassembling a stripped engine

1 Fit the intermediate shaft and oil pump as instructed in **Sections 1:14** and **1:9.** Fit a new oil seal and O-ring to the housing for bearing No. 8 and mark the position of the dowel pin hole on the housing face as indicated by the arrow on the right in **FIG 1:34.** Fit to the crankshaft.

2 Fit main bearing liners, making sure oil holes coincide in righthand crankcase half. Coat all bearing surfaces with oil or molybdenum disulphide compound. Fit assembled crankshaft into righthand crankcase half

FIG 1:37 Pipe connections to torque converter oil pump on cars fitted with Sportomatic transmission. Pump is driven by front end of lefthand camshaft

FIG 1:38 Cover removed from torque converter oil supply pump to show rotors (Sportomatic transmission)

(see **Section 1:12**), making sure that the dowel for No. 8 bearing housing is in the correct hole.

3 Fit lefthand crankcase half. Fit flywheel (see **Section 1:10**). Check that crankshaft turns freely, but ensure that the timing chains cannot jam.

4 Fit pistons (see **Section 1:11**). The deeper recess in piston crown is for the inlet valve, so that it must face upwards. Fit the cylinders, holding each in place with two opposite nuts and spacers. Fit head gaskets with perforated face to cylinder. Assemble valves in heads.

5 If cylinder heads and camshaft housings are assembled together, fit these on the cylinders, at the same time inserting the oil return tubes into the recesses in crankcase and in camshaft housings. The tubes must be initially prepared by fitting them with new O-rings which are oiled to facilitate entry.

6 Fit the washers and nuts and tighten them evenly and diagonally to a torque of 3 to 3.3 mkg (21½ to 24 lb ft). Make sure the camshafts do not bind as the nuts are tightened (see **Section 1:4**).

7 If cylinder head and camshaft housings are to be refitted separately, follow the instructions in **Section**

1:6 and take the same precautions to ensure that the camshafts do not bind. The rocker arms and shafts must not be installed. In all operations where the crankshaft and camshaft are not correctly timed together, take particular care not to continue turning either of them if the valves can be felt to contact the piston crowns or serious damage could result. Alter the relative positions and try again with extra caution.

8 Refit the camshafts and rockers as described in **Section 1:6**. Fit chain guide ramps in crankcase, making sure the springs locate properly in the stud grooves. Fit the chain housings, then the sealing flanges round the sprocket ends of the camshafts. These operations are covered in **Section 1:6** where instructions will also be found for refitting the camshaft sprockets.

9 The next task is to align the sprockets correctly. The diagram in **FIG 1:36** shows a straightedge in use for this purpose. The coverplate over the rear end of the intermediate shaft must be removed to reveal a small hole just below. Push the intermediate shaft and camshafts forward as far as possible and use a depth gauge to measure from the straightedge to the face of the drive sprocket, as shown by the central A in **FIG 1:36.** Keeping the straightedge firmly pressed against the crankcase face, check the distance shown by the righthand A. Any difference must not exceed .25 mm (.01 inch). Check the second camshaft as indicated by the lefthand A, but note that 54.8 mm (2.157 inch) must be added to compensate for the offset.

10 If checking reveals any misalignment of the sprockets, correct this by adding or removing spacers (see **FIG 1:11**). Fit the chains and ramps, followed by the tensioners (see **Section 1:7**). Adjust the valve timing according to **Section 1:8**.

11 It is preferable not to invert the engine once the tensioners are fitted because of the oil scoop in each tensioner. For this reason it is often more convenient to fit the heat exchangers before installing the tensioners. Now install the distributor body, fitting a new O-ring to the neck. With cylinder No. 1 at TDC, set the distributor as described in **Chapter 3**.

12 Install chain housing covers, but first check condition of seals for oil supply to the camshafts. Each seal is pressed into its cover and a defective one must be prised out and a new one pressed into place. Refit the oil supply pipes from crankcase to chain covers.

13 The diamond flange on the lefthand chain cover carries the mechanical fuel pumps (when fitted). At least two gaskets and an intermediate plastic flange must be fitted between the lowest point of the eccentric nut and the mounting surface of the pump. Distance from the mounting face must be measured with a depth gauge. It must be 51.4 mm (2.024 inch).

14 Refit the remaining parts in the reverse order of dismantling. Centre the clutch driven plate before fitting the pressure plate (see **Chapter 5**). The rear engine support leaf spring must be horizontal when fitted. Place a straightedge along the carburetter connecting plate so that it projects over the support. Measure from the top edge of the support spring to the straightedge on both sides of the engine and adjust until the measurements are the same.

1:16 Torque converter oil pump

If the car is fitted with Sportomatic transmission, there is a camshaft-driven oil pump to supply the torque converter. It is mounted in line with the lefthand camshaft as shown in **FIG 1:37**.

Testing pump:

Oil flow should be 3 litres ($5\frac{1}{4}$ pints or 3.2 US quarts) per minute at a maximum pressure of 29 lb/sq in. Check action of pump by disconnecting the oil return pipe from the torque converter at the oil tank while the engine is running. Oil should flow from the pipe if the pump is working.

If an engine is run while it is out of the car, connect the pump to a supply of oil in a container to keep the system full of oil. **Never run the pump dry.**

Removing pump:

Remove rear wheel on lefthand side. Remove lefthand heat exchanger. Detach pipelines (see arrows in **FIG 1:37**). Remove pump.

Dismantling and reassembling pump:

Remove cover (see **FIG 1:38**). Drive dowel pin out of shaft and remove rotors. Remove relief valve cover (two nuts) and lift out spring and plunger.

Clean parts and inspect for wear or damage. Renew rotors as a pair. Fit inner rotor and shaft. Press dowel pin into shaft until it is midway. See that cover dowel protrudes 4 mm (.16 inch) above joint face. Fit outer rotor with bevelled edge leading. Oil parts liberally. Fit cover on a new gasket and tighten down with temporary bolts. The rotors should turn freely. Remove bolts and then fit relief valve, putting the O-ring in the cover.

Refitting pump:

Before doing this, check the driving pins in the end of the camshaft. They are roll-pins and must be fitted in such a way that the pump driving pin cannot rest on the roll-pin slots. The pins must project 8 mm (.315 inch) from the camshaft end.

Install the pump on a new gasket, setting the driving shaft pin between the camshaft roll-pins. Fit heat exchanger using new gaskets, tightening the bolts and nuts uniformly.

1:17 Testing after overhaul

Before starting the engine, check the contact breaker points and the ignition timing (see **Chapter 3**). Check fan belt tension (see **Section 1:2**). Fill up with correct Heavy Duty oil to upper mark on dipstick (approximately 9 litres, $15\frac{3}{4}$ pints or $9\frac{1}{2}$ US quarts).

Use the starter for a few revolutions without switching on the ignition. Start the engine and check the oil pressure at once. It must rise immediately and failure to do so will starve the bearings of oil. The red ignition warning light should go out when a fast idling speed is reached.

Let the engine warm up at 2000 to 3000 rev/min until it reaches a temperature of 60°C approximately. Check all joints and oil pipe connections for leakage and inspect the oil filter and oil cooler. Adjust carburetter (see **Chapter 2**). Check oil level in tank at idling speed. The oil pressure at a temperature of 80°C at 5000 rev/min should be 78 to 200 lb/sq in. Set ignition with a stroboscopic lamp.

After running for some time, check that the rocker shafts are tight, tighten the cylinder head nuts, check the valve clearance and check the fan belt tension.

1 :18 Fault diagnosis

(a) Engine will not start

1 Defective ignition coil, carbon brush in distributor cap not contacting rotor arm
2 Faulty distributor capacitor (condenser)
3 Dirty, pitted or incorrectly set contact breaker points
4 Ignition wires loose, insulation faulty
5 Water on sparking plug leads
6 Battery discharged, corrosion of terminals
7 Faulty or jammed starter
8 Sparking plug leads wrongly connected
9 Vapour lock in fuel pipes
10 Defective fuel pump(s)
11 Overchoking or underchoking of carburetters
12 Blocked fuel pump filters or carburetter jets
13 Leaking valves
14 Sticking valves
15 Valve timing incorrect
16 Ignition timing incorrect
17 Engine flooded with fuel

(b) Engine stalls after starting

1 Check 1, 2, 3, 4, 5, 10, 11, 12, 13 and 14 in (a)
2 Sparking plugs defective or gaps incorrect
3 Retarded ignition
4 Mixture too weak
5 Water in fuel system
6 Fuel tank vent blocked
7 Incorrect valve clearances

(c) Engine idles badly

1 Check 2 and 7 in (b)
2 Air leaks at manifold joints
3 Carburetter idling adjustment wrong, jets blocked
4 Over-rich mixture
5 Worn piston rings
6 Worn valve stems or guides
7 Weak exhaust valve springs

(d) Engine misfires

1 Check 1, 2, 3, 4, 5, 8, 10, 12, 13, 14, 15 and 16 in (a), 2, 3, 4 and 7 in (b)
2 Weak or broken valve springs

(e) Engine overheats

1 Weak mixture, ignition over-advanced
2 Fan belt slipping
3 Defective oil thermostat
4 Oil cooler blocked or choked with dirt
5 Loss of cooling air through badly fitted covers

(f) Low compression

1 Check 13 and 14 in (a), 6 and 7 in (c) and 2 in (d)
2 Worn piston ring grooves
3 Scored or worn cylinder bores

(g) Engine lacks power

1 Check 3, 10, 12, 13, 14, 15 and 16 in (a), 2, 3, 4 and 7 in (b), 6 and 7 in (c) and 2 in (d). Also check (e) and (f)
2 Leaking joints and gaskets
3 Fouled sparking plugs
4 Automatic ignition advance not working
5 Exhaust system blocked

(h) Burnt valves or seats

1 Check 13 and 14 in (a), 7 in (b) and 2 in (d). Check (e)
2 Excessive carbon in head

(j) Sticking valves

1 Check 2 in (d)
2 Bent or scored valve stems, defective guides
3 Defective stem seals
4 Incorrect valve clearance

(k) Excessive cylinder wear

1 Check 11 in (a) and check (e)
2 Dirty or insufficient oil. Wrong grade
3 Piston rings wrongly gapped, gummed or broken
4 Bent connecting rods
5 Dirt under cylinder mounting flanges

(l) Excessive oil consumption

1 Check 6 and 7 in (c), check (k) and 3 in (j)
2 Ring gaps too wide
3 Oil control rings ineffective
4 Scored cylinders
5 Oil level too high
6 External oil leaks
7 Incorrect grade of oil

(m) Crankshaft or connecting rod bearing failure

1 Check 2 and 4 in (k)
2 Blocked oilways
3 Bent or worn crankshaft
4 Bearing shells wrongly fitted
5 Worn oil pump, defective lubricating system
6 Loose bearings or connecting rod caps

(n) High fuel consumption

1 Car in poor mechanical condition
2 Bad driving habits, excessive acceleration in low gears
3 Incorrect ignition or carburetter adjustments
4 Flooding float chamber, fuel leakage
5 Incorrect jet sizes
6 Carburetter accelerating pump wrongly adjusted

(o) Engine vibration

1 Mounting failures
2 Loose alternator mounting
3 Fan out of balance
4 Clutch and flywheel unbalanced
5 Misfiring due to mixture, ignition or mechanical faults

CHAPTER 2

THE FUEL SYSTEM

2:1 Description of system

Engines up to No. 907.000 have six Solex carburetters, type 40.PI (see **FIG 2:1**). After that number the installation changes to a triple-throat Weber carburetter on each bank of three cylinders (see **FIG 2:13**). Starting with the 1969 models, 911E and 911S cars have a fuel injection system which is fully described in **Section 2:12**.

The Solex system differs from orthodox layouts because the supply of fuel needs an electric pump and two mechanical pumps. The electric pump (see **FIG 2:3**) passes fuel from the tank to a separate float chamber below each bank of three carburetters. Each mechanical pump (see **FIG 2:5**) takes fuel from its own particular float chamber and pumps it to a spill-tube fuel well in the body of each one of a set of three carburetters. This well is on the right in **FIG 2:7**, the fuel level in the spill-tube controlling the fuel level in the jet system to the left of it. Surplus fuel overflows from the tube and returns to the float chamber. This method provides a constant level of fuel to the jets, whatever the driving conditions.

The mechanical pumps are mounted on the lefthand chain housing cover, being operated by a cam nut on the camshaft and a plunger reciprocating in the mounting flange. **FIG 2:5** shows that the pumps are of the normal diaphragm type with inlet and outlet valves.

The electric pump for the Solex system is shown in **FIG 2:3**. A pumping piston is reciprocated by a solenoid and spring, current control being made by a magnetic contact breaker.

Each triple-throat Weber carburetter assembly has two float chambers and an accelerating pump. **FIG 2:3** includes a section through one of the carburetters and shows how fuel is drawn from the float chamber.

The mechanical pumps are not needed for the Weber installation and fuel is pumped by the Hardi electric pump shown in **FIG 2:6**. This has a pumping diaphragm which is reciprocated by an electric magnet and a throw-over contact breaker, inlet and outlet valves controlling the flow.

2:2 Routine maintenance

Cleaning mechanical pump filters:

Refer to **FIG 2:2**, unscrew the cover bolt and withdraw the cover, gasket and filter gauze. Remove dirt from filter with a brush and fuel. **Do not use a fluffy rag.** Clean out the filter recess in the body. Refit filter, gasket and cover, making sure that the gasket is in good condition and properly seated. Run the engine and check for leaks.

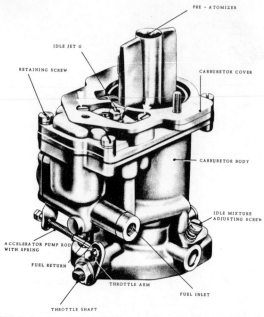

FIG 2:1   One of the six Solex carburetters, type 40.PI, as fitted to engines up to No. 907.000

Labels on Fig 2:1:
PRE - ATOMIZER
IDLE JET G
RETAINING SCREW
CARBURETOR COVER
CARBURETOR BODY
IDLE MIXTURE ADJUSTING SCREW
ACCELERATOR PUMP ROD WITH SPRING
FUEL RETURN
THROTTLE ARM
FUEL INLET
THROTTLE SHAFT

FIG 2:2   Removing one of the filters on twin mechanical fuel pumps

Cleaning Bendix electric pump filter:

Refer to **FIG 2:3** and remove the bottom cover 7 by turning it to release the bayonet catches. Remove filter 5, clean it with a brush and fuel and then with compressed air. Clean the bottom cover and magnet and check that gasket 6 is in good condition. Reassemble parts, turning cover clockwise to its stop. Run the engine and check for leaks.

Cleaning Hardi electric pump filter:

Refer to **FIG 2:6** and remove lower plug to release filter 10. Clean filter with a brush and fuel. **Do not use a fluffy rag.** Check condition of gasket for plug and reassemble. Run engine and check for leaks.

Cleaning air filter:

The filter body contains a large paper element which becomes clogged according to road conditions, so that servicing periods cannot be fixed. It is better to service too frequently, if in doubt. Refer to **FIG 2:4**, release the spring

clips indicated and remove the filter cover. Extract the element. If it is seriously loaded with dust it is best to renew it. **Do not attempt to clean the element with a solvent and do not oil it.** The best method of cleaning is to tap it lightly, at the same time blowing dry compressed air through it from the outside.

Clean the inside of the casing with an oily rag. Do not use cotton waste or anything of a fluffy nature. Check the condition of the gasket. When reassembling, fit the cover so that the mark on it points to the upper lefthand clip.

Cleaning Weber carburetter fuel filters:

There are two banjo bolts securing the fuel feed pipe to each bank of three carburetters (see **FIG 2:17**). Remove the bolts for access to the tubular filters. Clean filter gauze with a brush and fuel. Renew gaskets if faulty.

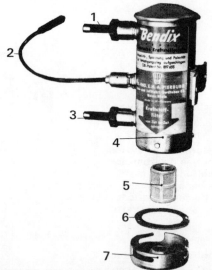

FIG 2:3   The Bendix electric fuel pump showing the bottom cover removed for access to the filter

Key to Fig 2:3   1 Fuel outlet   2 Electrical connection
3 Fuel inlet   4 Pump housing   5 Filter   6 Gasket
7 Cover with magnet

FIG 2:4   Arrows point to spring clips which secure the air filter cover

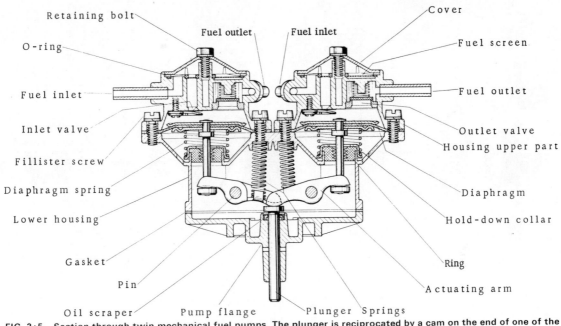

Retaining bolt

O-ring

Fuel inlet

Fuel outlet

Fuel inlet

Cover

Fuel screen

Fuel inlet

Inlet valve

Fillister screw

Diaphragm spring

Lower housing

Gasket

Pin

Oil scraper

Pump flange

Plunger Springs

Fuel outlet

Outlet valve

Housing upper part

Diaphragm

Hold-down collar

Ring

Actuating arm

FIG 2:5 Section through twin mechanical fuel pumps. The plunger is reciprocated by a cam on the end of one of the camshafts

Setting hand throttle lever:

From 1968 models onwards, a hand throttle lever is incorporated in the handbrake mounting on 911L, 911S and 911T-Sportomatic cars. This is the small lever with the round knob. This knob is a push fit.

To adjust the friction of the lever pivot, remove the handbrake boot and turn the pivot nut. Correct setting, using a spring balance at right angles to the hole in the lever on the underside is that the lever should not begin to move until a pull of 6 kg (13 lb) is recorded.

There is a hole in the tunnel just below the knob of the lever and this will reveal a clamping collar on the throttle control rod. Correct adjustment is such that the engine should be running at 4000 rev/min with the lever fully opened. Adjust by resetting the position of the clamp.

2:3 Checking fuel system

If faulty operation is suspected, check as follows:
1 Check that there is fuel in the tank. Make sure the vent hole in the filler cap is clear.
2 Detach fuel hose from carburetter, operate starter (or switch on ignition) and see if fuel spurts from hose. If fuel is pumped, check pump pressure and cleanliness of all jets and fuel passages. Also check floats and float needle valves.
3 If fuel is not pumped, check pump filters, pump valves, tightness of diaphragm flange screws and electrical connections. Check contacts of throw-over breaker in Hardi pump. Check fuel feed pipes from tank and use compressed air to clear possible obstructions. Do not pass compressed air through pumps.

2:4 Servicing mechanical fuel pumps

Details of the pumps can be seen in **FIG 2:5**. As the plunger is forced inwards by a cam nut on the camshaft

it pulls down the diaphragms by pressing on the rockers or actuating arms. The resulting suction above each diaphragm induces fuel to enter the pumping chambers through the inlet valves. On the return stroke, spring pressure below each diaphragm forces fuel out of the outlet valves and so to the carburetters, the inlet valves being closed. The function of the pumps is to draw fuel from the Solex float chambers and deliver it to each of the six carburetters.

Removing and refitting pumps:

This is a simple matter of pulling off the fuel hoses and removing the bolts from the pump flange. When refitting the pumps, use a new flange gasket, reconnect the hoses and check for leaks by running the engine.

Overhauling pumps:

1 Remove covers and filters (screens). From each pump flange remove six fillister-head screws and lift off upper bodies.
2 Remove screws and detach pump flange with plunger. The actuating arm pins are held in place by lock rings. Remove one ring and drive out the pin for each pump, which will release the arms and springs.
3 Lift off the diaphragms complete with actuating rods, springs and seals.
4 Working inside the upper bodies, remove the inlet valves by unscrewing one screw from each retainer. The outlet valves cannot be removed.

Clean all the parts in fuel and check for wear and corrosion. Suck and blow on the outlet valves to check their operation. Check condition of diaphragm, diaphragm springs and seal. **Do not stretch the spring in an attempt to modify pump performance.** Check for wear of the actuating arms and pivot pins. Check fit of plunger in flange. Renew worn parts.

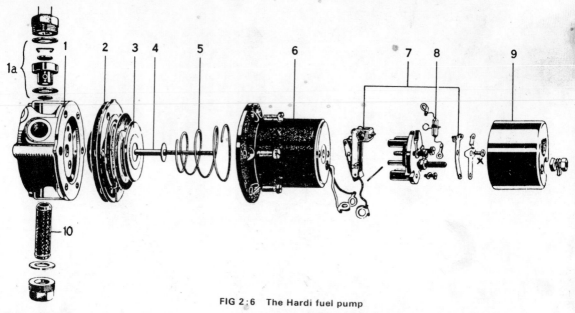

FIG 2:6   The Hardi fuel pump

Key to Fig 2:6   1 Valve housing   1a Valve components   2 Diaphragm   3 Armature   4 Pressure rod   5 Spring   6 Magnet housing   7 Rockers and contact points   8 Condenser   9 Cap   **X** Contact adjusting screw

Check seats of inlet valves, assemble valves and suck and blow to test them for correct action.

Reassemble pumps in the reverse order. When joining the pump halves, make sure that the diaphragm is not creased and then tighten the screws diagonally, a turn at a time. Renew the cover gasket if faulty or leaking. Fit a new gasket to the pump flange. Lubricate the plunger and check that its seal is working.

Checking pump flow:

Pumps are tested one at a time, the pump not under test being connected to both banks of carburetters by a T-piece. The object of the test is to determine the rate of flow under a certain amount of outlet pressure. This pressure is arranged by connecting a vertical length of tubing to the outlet of the pump being tested. The top of the tube must turn over into a suitable container, and the total vertical lift of fuel must be 650 mm (25.6 inch).

With the engine running at 3000 rev/min, the pump must deliver not less than 800 cc (27 fl oz) of fuel in one minute. Check both pumps by changing over the T-piece and the vertical tube.

2:5 Servicing electric fuel pumps

The Bendix pump:

This is the one illustrated in **FIG 2:3**. A central brass tube houses an inlet valve at the bottom, a spring and a sliding piston of steel containing a fuel transfer valve. At rest, the piston is at the top of its stroke and its presence affects the field of a trigger magnet on the outside of the brass tube. The trigger magnet tilts and closes electrical contacts. Lower down there is a solenoid coil round the outside of the tube. When the ignition is switched on, the closed contacts allow current to flow through the coil which produces a powerful magnetic field. This pulls the piston down against the spring and fuel flows through the transfer valve into the bore above the piston. Withdrawal of the piston from the trigger magnet field causes it to tilt in the opposite direction and open the contacts. The solenoid becomes de-energized and the piston is forced upwards by the spring, pushing fuel out through the outlet connection. At the same time, suction below the piston induces fuel to flow into the bore below the piston past the inlet valve. This operation continues all the time fuel is needed.

Much of the pump assembly is sealed and the electrical components work in helium gas to prevent contact erosion. Overhauling is restricted to removal of the

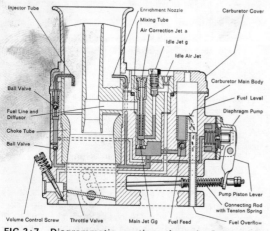

FIG 2:7   Diagrammatic section through Solex carburetter, type 40.PI. Note how the fuel level is controlled by the height of the spill-tube above the fuel feed

bottom cover and filter for cleaning. It is, however, possible to remove the valve carrier from the central brass tube (3 screws). It will then be possible to check the pump parts, the valves and the spring. The first check in the case of faulty operation is on the electrical connection to the pump to ensure that it is sound. Failure of the sealed part of the pump calls for the attention of an electrical service station dealing in this type of Bendix pump.

The Hardi pump:

This is illustrated in **FIG 2:6**. The main parts are a valve housing 1 and a magnet housing 6. These are secured together with a diaphragm 2 in between. A pressure rod which is attached to the diaphragm passes through the magnet housing and is connected to a throw-over mechanism incorporating a contact breaker 7. The valve housing carries inlet and outlet valves and connections.

Assuming that the contact points are closed and the ignition is switched on, the magnet is energized and it attracts a polepiece or armature 3 which is secured to the diaphragm. Consequent suction in the chamber of the valve housing induces fuel to flow in through the inlet valve. The movement of the diaphragm and pressure rod eventually causes the contact breaker mechanism to throw-over and the contacts separate. The breakdown in magnetism allows spring 5 to push the diaphragm towards the valve housing, the inlet valve closes, the outlet valve opens and fuel is pumped to the carburetters. The action is repeated so long as fuel is required.

Removing and refitting Hardi pump:

Disconnect fuel pipe banjos. Detach cable from terminal on pump cover. Remove mounting bolts and detach earth lead. Check mounting grommets.

When refitting pump, make sure that the electrical connections are clean and tight, and check that the banjo gaskets are sound. Switch on and check for leaks. Rapid action without pumping fuel may be due to air leaks on the suction side. Sluggish action may be due to a blocked filter or trouble with the valves. Another cause of faulty operation may be dirty contacts. These are cleaned by drawing a strip of paper between them while pressing them together.

Overhauling Hardi pump:

1 Remove outlet connection from valve housing and extract valve assembly 1a.
2 Separate housings (six screws). Unscrew diaphragm 2 by turning anticlockwise. Collect spring, and also impact washer on pressure rod.
3 Remove breaker adjusting screw X, condenser 8 and breaker platform. Make a careful note of the electrical connections.
4 If necessary, release the throw-over mechanism by pushing out the pivot pin.

Clean and examine the parts. Check valve assembly 1a by sucking and blowing. Check the diaphragm for cracks. Parts 2, 3 and 4 are an assembly and must be renewed as such. Check breaker points 7 and renew pivot pin if worn. This pin is hardened and a genuine spare must be used.

Reassemble in the reverse order, putting a tiny drop of oil on the breaker pivots. **Oil must not reach the contact points.**

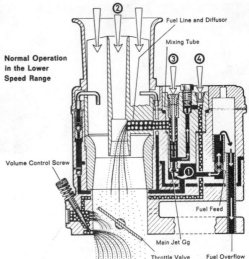

Normal Operation in the Lower Speed Range

FIG 2:8 Throttle partly opened on the Solex carburetter, type 40.PI. All jets are producing air and fuel emulsion

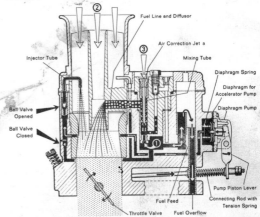

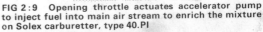

FIG 2:9 Opening throttle actuates accelerator pump to inject fuel into main air stream to enrich the mixture on Solex carburetter, type 40.PI

FIG 2:10 Solex installation, type 40.PI. Lefthand arrow points to float chamber. Central arrow indicates throttle stop. Righthand arrow points to link connecting bellcrank shaft to throttle shaft

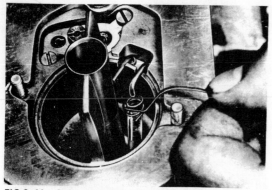

FIG 2:11 Solex carburetter, type 40.PI. Checking fuel delivered by accelerator pump to injection nozzle

FIG 2:12 Solex carburetter, type 40.PI. Four screws secure cover for pump diaphragm. Arrow on left points to retaining pin for pre-atomizer. Lower arrow on right points to adjustment for pump operating rod

Fit the diaphragm and spring, screwing the pressure rod into the contact breaker trunnion. Press on the diaphragm so that the points are open and adjust the contact gap to 1.2 mm (.05 inch) by turning the adjusting screw. The diaphragm spring must have its large end against the magnet housing. **Do not try to alter pump performance by stretching the spring.**

Continue to screw in the diaphragm rod until the contacts will no longer open when the diaphragm is pressed in towards the magnet housing. Now turn the diaphragm anticlockwise until a point is reached where the contact points will just begin to open when the diaphragm is pressed in. From this point, unscrew the diaphragm a further 300 deg. or five holes in the edge of the diaphragm. Fit the body halves together and tighten the screws diagonally and evenly. The electrical connections must be clean and tight. After switching on, check for leaks.

2:6 The Solex carburetter

FIG 2:1 is an external view of the carburetter and FIGS 2:7, 2:8 and 2:9 show some of the principles of operation. In FIG 2:7, the central part of the section shows how the jets are mounted in a carrier which is readily removable. The darker shaded passages indicate the fuel level, and this is maintained by the height of the spill-tube in the well on the right. Surplus fuel which overflows will return to the float chamber by the tube illustrated.

FIG 2:8 shows how the carburetter operates in the lower speed range. At idling speed there will be no flow from the fuel line and diffuser, and the throttle valve will be almost closed, so that emulsion will flow from the orifice below the volume control screw but not from the passages just above.

In power metering, as shown, fuel flows, in part, from the main jet into the chamber containing the mixing tube and air correction jet 3. The emulsion formed by fuel and air issues from the fuel line and diffuser to mix with the incoming air in the right proportions for correct combustion.

Where rapid throttle opening during acceleration calls for an enriched supply of mixture, the diaphragm pump comes into operation as shown in FIG 2:9. The pump connecting rod is attached to the throttle control and operates the pump lever. Fuel is forced through the passages shown until it lifts the upper ball valve on the left, to squirt from the injector tube into the stream of incoming air 2. The pump recuperates as the diaphragm flexes to the right and draws in fuel through the lower ball valve, the upper valve closing. When full power is needed at large throttle openings, additional fuel is provided by the enrichment nozzle shown in FIG 2:7.

2:7 Servicing Solex carburetter

Idling adjustment:

Run the engine until the oil temperature is approximately 60°C and remove the air filter. Check ignition timing and contact breaker gap. Check that ball joints in carburetter linkage are properly seated. Disconnect links from operating shafts (see righthand arrow in FIG 2:10). Accurate setting is best achieved with a synchronizing device which fits on the air intake, but careful work with a length of rubber or plastic hose will give reasonable results. One end of the tube is held to the ear and the other placed on the lip of the air intake in the same position every time. The hiss which is heard must be of the same intensity for all carburetters. With either device, set the engine to run at 1200 to 1400 rev/min and synchronize the throttle valves to give equal results. Adjust the idling mixture screws (see FIG 2:1) so that the engine runs smoothly. Readjust the throttle stops (central arrow in FIG 2:10) to set the idling speed to 900 ± 100 rev/min. Use the synchronizing tester or listening hose to check that each throttle opening is correct and then readjust the idling mixture screws.

When satisfied that all carburetters are correctly synchronized, reconnect the operating links, adjusting the length so that the ball joints fit without preload. Refit the air filter and try a minor adjustment of the idling mixture screws. Check the throttle return damper. The plunger travel should be approximately 4 to 5 mm (.16 to .20 inch).

Throttle valve adjustment:

Unsatisfactory idling may sometimes be due to damaged idling screws or to lack of unison in throttle closing. Remove the idling adjustment screws and check that the points are smooth and not bent. Equal closing of the throttle valves is obtained by turning the knurled nut in the centre of each throttle lever link.

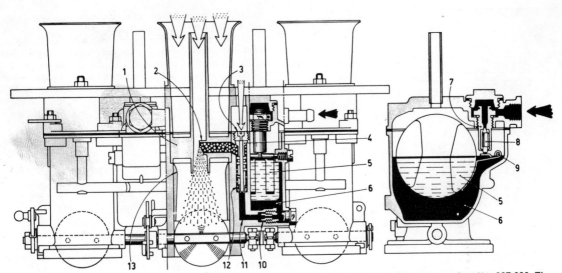

FIG 2:13 Diagrammatic sections through Weber triple-throat carburetter as fitted to engines after No. 907.000. There are two float chambers

Key to Fig 2:13 1 Pre-atomizer 2 Mixture delivery port 3 Air correction jet 4 Emulsion tube 5 Float 6 Float chamber 7 Float needle valve 8 Float valve needle 9 Float pivot 10 Main metering jet 11 Fuel port 12 Emulsion tube well 13 Venturi

Adjusting injection quantity:

Refer to **FIG 2:11**. Remove air filter and throttle shaft connecting link. Earth the body of an electric fuel pump and mount the pump on the blower housing. Disconnect float chamber hose from mechanical fuel pump and connect it to electric pump inlet. Disconnect carburetter hose from mechanical pump and connect to electric pump outlet. Connect terminal 1 of electric pump to terminal 15 on the ignition coil.

Switch on ignition and check that both electric pumps are working. Wire a small graduated test tube as shown in the illustration and hold it under the injection nozzle or tube (see **FIG 2:7**). Move throttle linkage twice from stop to stop and check quantity of fuel collected. Correct quantity should be .40 to .50 cc in summer and .55 to .65 cc in winter (Northern hemisphere). Adjust at the two nuts indicated by the arrow in the bottom righthand corner of **FIG 2:12**. Pump jet size does not affect injection quantity. The quantity must be the same for all carburetters.

Checking float level:

Withdraw mechanical pump hose from float chamber, using a container to catch draining fuel. Push a short piece of clear plastic hose on the float chamber connector and turn it up at right angles so that the open end is well above the joint line. Switch on the ignition and watch the fuel level rising in the plastic tube. When it is steady, measure the distance from the fuel level to the machined underside of the intake duct. The correct figure is 15 to 20 mm (.60 to .79 inch). If level rises above 15 mm the float must be renewed.

Removing individual carburetter:

1 Remove air filter and duct. Detach link connecting throttle actuating shafts.

2 Withdraw vent hose from float chamber bowl. Remove air inlet horns and base plate (six nuts).

3 Release particular carburetter from flange, lift off carburetter and cover the intake to prevent dirt entering.

When installing, clean the flange faces and fit a new gasket. Make sure the gasket does not overlap the inlet duct. Adjust the throttle link so that the throttle closes fully (see 'Throttle valve adjustment'). Adjust the idling speed.

Removing carburetters and inlet duct:

1 Remove air filter and duct. Disconnect ball joints from throttle levers and remove throttle control rod and connecting links.

2 Remove the bellcrank shaft connecting the two banks of carburetters. The righthand joint is solid, but the lefthand joint is mounted on a spring leaf. Pull this outwards to remove the shaft.

3 Disconnect fuel hoses to float chamber and carburetters. Disconnect inlet duct from cylinder head flanges and remove the assembly complete. Cover the inlet ports in the heads. Refit in the reverse sequence. Adjust the idling.

Dismantling and reassembling:

Refer to **FIG 2:1** and remove the cover. Withdraw jet carrier (two screws—white arrow). Unscrew jets and shake out mixing tube. Remove idling mixture adjustment screw. The pre-atomizer can be seen in the same illustration. Unlock and slacken the retaining screw indicated by the lefthand arrow in **FIG 2:12** and lift out the pre-atomizer and venturi. Remove pump rod nuts (bottom righthand arrow in **FIG 2:12**). Remove pump cover (4 screws). Remove diaphragm and spring.

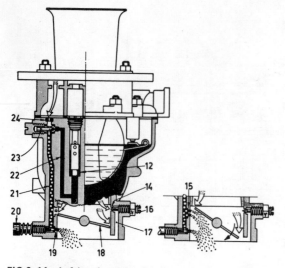

FIG 2:14 Lefthand section shows delivery of idling mixture on Weber carburetter. Righthand view shows additional mixture being delivered by transition ports as throttle starts to open

Key to Fig 2:14   12 Emulsion tube well   14 Passage
15 Transition ports   16 Air adjustment screw   17 Air port
18 Throttle valve   19 Idle mixture discharge port   20 Idle
mixture control screw   21 Delivery port   22 Fuel delivery
port   23 Idle metering jet   24 Idle air bleed

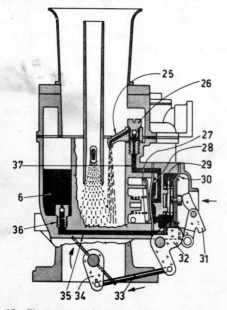

FIG 2:15 Throttle opens and actuates diaphragm pump on Weber carburetter. Pump delivers fuel to discharge nozzle to enrich the mixture

Key to Fig 2:15   6 Float chamber   25 Pump discharge
nozzle   26 Check valve   27 Disc   28 Diaphragm
29 Spring   30 Diaphragm   31 Lever   32 Cam
33 Connecting link   34 Lever   35 Port   36 Inlet
check valve   37 Delivery port

Clean all parts in fuel and pass compressed air through the jets. Do not use needles or wire for cleaning jets as any enlargement will lead to inaccurate metering. Check fit of throttle shaft in body as air leaks will upset performance. Check that throttle disc closes to a light-tight fit. Check diaphragm and renew if cracked or if rivet is loose. Shake body to check that both ball valves are free. The idling mixture screw must have a point which is smooth and not bent. Check sizes of jets against those given in Technical Data.

Main jet:

These must be stamped with the prefix 'X'. In the case of hesitancy or flat spots with carburetters of early type having covers of an older design, try a main jet X125 instead of the X130 jet fitted.

Idle air bleed and metering jet:

The idle air bleed bore is now machined in the jet carrier. The original hole for the idle air bleed is blocked with a plug. Check the tapered seating of idle metering jet g (see FIG 2:7). Renew faulty parts.

Reassembling:

Do this in the reverse order to dismantling. When fitting the jet carrier make sure that the bottom gasket does not obstruct the idle mixture bore. Renew the O-ring at the top if it is deformed or stretched. Tighten the carrier screws alternately and a quarter of a turn at a time so that the gasket is not damaged. Poor sealing at this point causes abnormally high fuel consumption.

Tuning:

If the engine is run without the air filter there is considerable risk of a carburetter fire.

Large variations in altitude call for differing main jets. Change jet calibration by 6 per cent for each 1000 m (3280 feet) variation. As an example, jet size at 400 m (1312 feet) is 125. At 1400 m (4592 feet) it should be 117.5.

Throttle linkage:

Regular lubrication of all joints will make for smooth operation. Place a small quantity of high melting point grease in the ball joint cups. Lubricate all moving joints with engine oil and put a drop or two on each accelerator pump linkage.

To remove and install the linkage under the floor, remove the mat to reveal the opening in the floor panel. Detach the throttle control from the ball joint at the front bellcrank. Withdraw the gearshift lever and fixture. Withdraw handbrake lever. This will leave room for access to the throttle linkage retaining clamps, which can now be removed. From under the transmission, detach the throttle control from the ball joint in the rear bellcrank. Withdraw the control rearwards.

Install in the reverse order, lubricating all ball joints and bellcrank pivots. Tighten ball joint locknuts securely.

2:8 The Weber carburetter

FIG 2:13 is a section through a Weber triple-throat assembly, each of the three carburetters feeding its own cylinder. The assembly is provided with two float chambers supplied by an electric fuel pump. The three views in **FIGS 2:13, 2:14** and **2:15** will help in understanding the operating principles.

During idling, fuel is drawn from well 12 through port 22 to idle metering jet 23 to mix with air from bleed 24 (see **FIG 2:14**). The mixture passes through port 21 to port 19, control screw 20 metering the quantity delivered to the intake. Above throttle valve 18 are two transition ports 15 which will also deliver mixture as the valve starts to open (see righthand view). To equalize air flow into the three carburetters at idling speeds, adjustment screws 16 are provided.

For normal operation, refer to **FIG 2:13**. From float chamber 6, fuel flows through main jet 10 and port 11 to emulsion tube well 12. Mixing with air from jet 3 it flows through holes in emulsion tube 4 and is delivered into pre-atomizer 1 and venturi 13 by way of port 2.

For accelerating, refer to **FIG 2:15**. Opening the throttle causes link 33 to operate cam 32 which presses diaphragm 30 to the left by means of lever 31. Fuel is forced past valve diaphragm 28 through port 37 (one for each carburetter) through opened valve 26 to discharge nozzle 25 and so into the throat of each carburetter to enrich the mixture. Retraction of the pump diaphragm to the right closes the valves and allows fuel to be drawn into the pumping chamber from the float chamber by way of check valve 36. This action takes place when the throttle is closing.

2:9 Servicing Weber carburetter

Adjusting idling:

Follow the instructions given for Solex carburetters in **Section 2:7**. If the intake air flow differs from throat to throat, turn the air adjustment screws 4 one of which is shown on the right in **FIG 2:16**. One idle mixture control screw 5 is shown in the same illustration.

Checking and adjusting float level:

The operation is shown in **FIG 2:16**, the gauge being P.226. Remove plug from float chamber to be checked and fit the gauge. Car must be standing level. Run engine at idling speed, when the fuel level should be between the two marks at the top of the glass. If level is incorrect, remove plug indicated by arrow in **FIG 2:17**, unscrew float needle valve from inside and fit a thicker gasket to raise the level or a thinner one to lower it. If this is not enough, slight bending of the float lever will help.

If the gauge is not available, the following figures may be useful in determining where the level should be. Distance from top of float to top edge of float housing without gasket should be 12.5 to 13.0 mm (.49 to .51 inch). Fuel level, when pump pressure is 3.6 lb/sq in, should be 20.5 to 21.0 mm (.81 to .83 inch) from top edge of housing. Variations of these figures are as follows:

Fuel level 20.75 ± 1 mm (.82 ± .04 inch) for 2000S cars starting with engine number 408.0773 (with Sportomatic, 418.0144). Also for 2000T cars fitted with type 40.IDT.3.C and 40.IDT.3.C1 carburetters and 2000 engines equipped with Exhaust Emission Control.

FIG 2:16 Weber carburetters. Float level gauge P.226 attached to side of float chamber. Level is marked on glass tube

Key to Fig 2:16   1 Main jet carrier   2 Idle metering jet 3 Venturi setscrew   4 Air adjusting screw   5 Idle mixture control screw

FIG 2:17 Top cover of Weber carburetters showing fuel feed detached. Arrow points to plugs over the float needle valves

FIG 2:18   Dismantling details on Weber carburetters

Key to Fig 2:18   1 Air correction jet   2 Accelerator pump check valve   3 Pre-atomizer   4 Float pivot pin

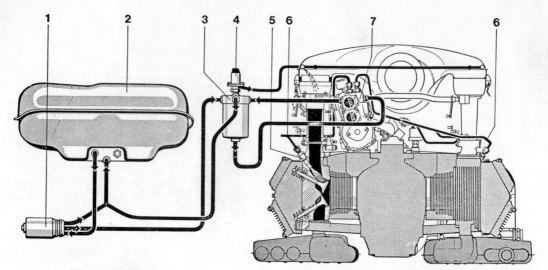

FIG 2:19 Layout of fuel injection system fitted to 1969 models of 911E and 911S cars

Key to Fig 2:19 1 Fuel pump 2 Fuel tank 3 Fuel filter 4 Enrichment solenoid 5 Injector 6 Pipeline to injector
7 Injector pump

Checking pump injection quantity:

This operation will be similar to the one suggested in **Section 2:7** for the Solex carburetter. Note, however, that it is not possible to adjust the pump to alter the quantity injected.

Correct quantity per carburetter per stroke is .80 cc with a permissible variation of ± .20 cc. This variation is reduced to ± .10 cc on 2000S cars starting with engine number 408.0773 (with Sportomatic, 418.0144). On 2000T engines with type 40.IDT.3.C and 40.IDT.3.C1 carburetters the quantity is .50 ± 1 cc per stroke. This also applies to 2000 engines with Exhaust Emission Control.

Removing and refitting carburetters:

1 Remove hoses from air filter and oil filler. Withdraw air filter element. Unclip ducts from carburetters and lift off the air filter assembly.
2 Detach fuel hoses. Disconnect throttle control links from throttle levers.
3 Remove nuts from carburetter flanges and lift off assembly. **Take great care that the spring washers do not fall into the inlet ports.** Cover the ports to exclude dirt.

When refitting the carburetters, use new gaskets on the inlet flanges. Clean the flanges and make sure that the gasket does not overlap the port. Adjust the throttle control so that the throttle valves can be fully closed and adjust the idling speed.

Dismantling carburetters:

1 Remove carburetter top (see **FIG 2:17**). Detach fuel feed assembly, as shown. Remove plugs arrowed and unscrew float needle valves from inside.
2 Refer to **FIG 2:16** and remove main jet carrier 1, air adjustment screw 4, the stop screw adjacent to screw 4, the idle metering jet 2, and the venturi setscrew 3 from each carburetter.

3 Refer to **FIG 2:18,** unscrew air correction jet 1 and withdraw the emulsion tube. If it sticks, push in a tapered drift to gain a hold. Remove check valve and nozzle 2.
4 Withdraw pre-atomizer 3 followed by the venturi (see 13 in **FIG 2:13**). Remove float pivot pin 4 and withdraw float.
5 Remove pump cover (4 nuts). Remove diaphragms, disc, springs and valve (see **FIG 2:15**).

Clean all parts with fuel and compressed air. **Do not push wire or a needle through the jets, as enlargement will affect performance.** Jets are stamped with an identifying number. Correct sizes are given in Technical Data. The idle air bleed is drilled into the body and cannot be renewed. Check fit of throttle valve spindles in body. Excessive wear will allow air to upset the correct mixture. Throttle valve must close to a light-tight fit. Check pump diaphragms and renew if deteriorated. Renew idle and air adjustment screws if tips are deformed or broken.

Reassembling:

Do this in the reverse order of dismantling. Wire the setscrews which secure the venturis. Adjust so that the throttle valves close completely and refit controls so that there is no strain. Adjust for correct idling. Lubricate all ball joints.

2:10 The fuel tank

To remove the tank, work under the car at the front to remove the drain plug, having a container handy to catch the fuel. Detach both fuel lines. Remove spare wheel and padding from front compartment. Pull off the vent hose and the fuel gauge cable. Remove fuel filler hose and after removing three Allen screws, lift the tank up and away.

When refitting the tank, renew the support gasket if damaged. Clear the vent hose with compressed air. Detach fuel line from electric pump, use compressed air to clear the pipes and then reconnect.

2:11 Fault diagnosis (carburetter systems)

(a) Fuel delivery nil or erratic

1 Tank vent blocked
2 Fuel pipes blocked
3 Air leaks on inlet side of pumps
4 Pump valves stuck or faulty
5 Pump diaphragm or spring faulty
6 Blocked pump filter

(b) Electric pump inoperative

1 Faulty electrical connections
2 Contact points dirty or out of adjustment (Hardi)
3 Breakdown of solenoid

(c) Engine will not start with adequate fuel supply and ignition working

1 Check (b)
2 Mechanical fuel pumps not working
3 Engine flooded by repeated throttle opening with engine not running

(d) Uneven idling

1 Faulty ignition
2 Idling speed adjusting screw damaged
3 Jets blocked
4 Sparking plugs fouled
5 Air leaks into inlet duct

(e) Uneven running

1 Check 5 in (d)
2 Mixture too rich or too weak
3 Incorrect idling adjustment, throttles not synchronized
4 Lower gasket of jet carrier not sealing (Solex)
5 Float chamber vent hose blocked

(f) Hesitancy or 'flat spots'

1 Check 4 and 5 in (d) and 3 in (e)
2 Incorrect injection quantity

(g) Engine stalls on sudden throttle closure

1 Check 3 in (e)
2 Throttle damper ineffective (Solex)

2:12 Fuel injection system

This was introduced on 911E and 911S cars, starting with the 1969 models. **FIG 2:19** shows the layout diagrammatically.

The object of the system is to inject an exact quantity of fuel into the desired inlet port to produce correct combustion. Chief advantages are greater power, improved acceleration, easier cold starting and lower fuel consumption.

A pump with six plungers 7 is driven by belt from the lefthand camshaft. Fuel is supplied to the pump by another pump 1, delivery being through a filter 3. The six plungers are operated by a camshaft and they force fuel at a pressure of 220 to 265 lb/sq in into pipes which are connected to injectors 5. Injection is timed so that fuel is discharged from an injector onto an inlet valve just as it begins to open.

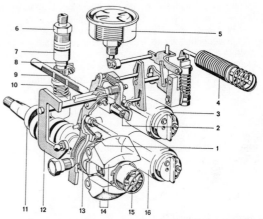

FIG 2:20 Control and compensating units on fuel injection system. These govern fuel injection quantity through the control rack

Key to Fig 2:20   1 Sensor on contoured cam   2 Control rack head   3 Enrichment solenoid   4 Thermostat   5 Barometric cell   6 Check valve   7 Plunger unit   8 Toothed segment   9 Control rack   10 Roller tappet   11 Camshaft   12 Governor control lever   13 Contoured cam   14 Centrifugal governor   15 Idle adjusting screw   16 Shut-off solenoid

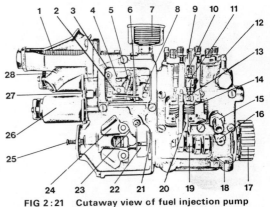

FIG 2:21   Cutaway view of fuel injection pump

Key to Fig 2:21   1 Thermostat   2 Compensating lever   3 Thermostat connecting sleeve   4 Cross-arm   5 Support   6 Guide stud   7 Barometric cell   8 Guide   9 Injector line fitting   10 Check valve   11 Plunger unit   12 Fuel inlet   13 Toothed segment   14 Plunger spring   15 Engine oil return   16 Engine oil inlet   17 Pump drive wheel   18 Support flange   19 Camshaft   20 Roller tappet   21 Contoured cam spring   22 Contoured cam   23 Sensor   24 Centrifugal governor weight   25 Idle speed adjustment   26 Shut-off solenoid   27 Access to control rack head   28 Enrichment solenoid

The throttle valves are connected together and are also linked to the pump control lever. To compensate for changes in air pressure, engine speed and variations in load there is a centrifugal governor connected to the pump control rack, and movement of the rack is also controlled by a barometric cell, a thermostat, an enrichment solenoid and a shut-off solenoid. All these devices work to compensate for the variations and to ensure that the correct quantity of fuel is injected to suit the requirements. The arrangement of the parts is shown in **FIG 2:20**.

Cam 13 is moved axially by governor 14 and turned by the accelerator pedal. Sensor 1 transfers movement to control rack 9 in the injection pump. Barometric cell 5 compensates for changes in ambient air pressure in the same way as an aneroid barometer. Thermostat 4 responds to engine cooling air temperature to enrich the mixture for cold starting. Enrichment solenoid 3 is controlled by time-limit and temperature-limit switches so that it gives a rich mixture for starting, over a 2-second period or for longer at low temperatures. Shut-off solenoid 16 is controlled by a throttle valve microswitch and a rev/min transducer to stop fuel delivery from the injection pump when coasting in gear.

The action of the compensating devices is cumulative and is transferred to the pump rack by connecting levers.

Injection pump:

This is illustrated in **FIG 2:21**. The compensating parts shown in **FIG 2:20** may also be seen in this view, together with the pump camshaft 19, the roller tappets 20,

the injection plungers 11 and toothed segments 13 which engage with the rack to control the volume of fuel injected.

There are six cylinders and plungers 11, the plungers being reciprocated by roller tappets operated by the camshaft. The plungers may be turned by the rack, and as they are provided with cut-off lands, timing of fuel inlet duration to the pumping cylinder is obtained. The plunger land acts as an inlet valve in conjunction with a port in the side of the cylinder. Fuel is forced from the pump cylinders into pipelines connected to the injectors in the engine cylinder heads. At a pressure of 220 to 265 lb/sq in, check valves in the injector nozzles open and fuel is sprayed onto the opening inlet valves.

Servicing fuel injection system:

It will be obvious from the complicated control system and the fact that the mechanical parts are made to a very high standard of precision, that the wisest course in the event of trouble is to take the car to an accredited service station.

CHAPTER 3

THE IGNITION SYSTEM

3 : 1 General description

The ignition system comprises a battery, an ignition coil, a distributor and the sparking plugs. The distributor is driven by a spiral gear on the rear end of the crankshaft (see **Chapter 1**), and cams on its rotating shaft open the points of a contact breaker. At each moment of breaking, high-tension electricity is induced in the coil and this is fed back to the central terminal in the distributor cap. Connected to this terminal is a spring-loaded brush which bears on the brass electrode of a rotor arm at the top end of the distributor shaft. As the shaft revolves, the rotor segment comes opposite each one of six brass terminals in the cap in turn. It does not actually touch the terminals but high-tension electricity is able to jump the small gaps. The terminals are connected by leads to the sparking plugs in the correct firing order (see Technical Data).

The 911T model is fitted with a Marelli distributor, type S112.AX and the other models with a Bosch distributor, type JF.DR6. Automatic centrifugal advance mechanism is incorporated in both types, but the Marelli is unique because the cam weights are not in the usual position below the contact breaker but are housed above it (see **FIG 3 : 1**). If a car is equipped with exhaust emission control the distributor has vacuum control in addition to the centrifugal mechanism (see assembly 34 in **FIG 3 : 4**).

3 : 2 Routine maintenance

Marelli distributor :

Every 6000 miles apply a thin smear of grease to the contact breaker cams. At the same intervals, check the ignition timing (see **Section 3 : 5**) and check the contact breaker gap. To check and adjust the gap, refer to **FIG 3 : 1**. Remove rotor (two screws, lefthand view). Turn crankshaft by means of pulley until a cam has lifted the breaker arm to give the maximum gap between the contact points. Measure the gap with feeler gauges as shown in the righthand view. If gap is not $.4 \pm .03$ mm ($.016 \pm .001$ inch), loosen the front retaining screw of the fixed contact plate, adjust until the gap is correct and re-tighten screw. **After every adjustment, always check the ignition timing** (see **Section 3 : 5**).

Bosch distributor :

Every 6000 miles, remove cap and rotor arm and apply a thin smear of non-corrosive, high temperature grease to the cams (see arrow in lefthand view of **FIG 3 : 2**). Take care no grease gets onto the contact points.

Every 6000 miles check the contact points gap and adjust if necessary. Remove cap and rotor arm and turn crankshaft pulley until a cam has fully raised the breaker arm. Check gap with feeler gauges as shown in righthand

FIG 3:1   Removing rotor arm on Marelli distributor (left). Adjusting gap between contact breaker points (right). Arrow points to distributor securing nut

view of **FIG 3:2**. Correct gap is .40 mm (.016 inch). To adjust gap, loosen screw indicated, insert screwdriver in slot adjacent and twist it between the two pips on the base plate to move the contact plate. On early models, turn the eccentric screw. Tighten screw when gap is correct. **Always check the ignition timing after adjusting the points gap** (see **Section 3:5**).

Distributor cap and contact breaker:

At regular intervals, remove the cap and clean it thoroughly. The inside surfaces must be clean and dry. Check central brush by pressing it in. It should spring out again. Slight erosion of the brass terminals is normal.

If dirty, clean the contact points with fuel on a cloth. Slight corrosion may be rectified with a fine file, but the mating surfaces must be quite flat and must meet squarely. The best cure for contact breaker troubles is to fit a new set.

Sparking plugs and leads:

Check plug gaps every 6000 miles. As Bosch W265.P21 plugs have platinum electrodes, gap adjustment should be unnecessary. Gap should be .35 mm (.014 inch). Check the gap for other makes by referring to Technical Data. Electrodes must be clean and bright and the gap must be adjusted by bending the outer electrode only. Have carbon deposits removed in a sand-blasting machine and then have plugs checked under pressure.

Check sparking plug leads for cracks and deterioration. Insulation failure may sometimes be seen as a bluish discharge when running the engine in the dark.

3:3 Ignition problems

If the engine refuses to fire, check HT (high-tension) lead between centre of distributor cap and ignition coil

for good contact. Pull lead out of cap and hold about 6 mm ($\frac{1}{4}$ inch) from a good earth (not a carburetter). Keep fingers away from end of lead and operate the starter. Sparks should jump the gap.

If no sparks. connect a 12-volt test bulb between terminal 1 on the distributor body and a good earth. Switch on ignition and operate starter. If light goes on and off, the coil primary is in order. If lamp stays alight while engine is turning over, check contact breaker points for dirt or too wide a gap. If lamp does not light, there may be a break in the coil primary or the points may not be opening properly. Check for loose cable connections, earthed wire to distributor and try substituting a coil which is known to work. Make sure contacts close and that breaker spring is not broken.

Failure to trace an ignition fault should lead to a check of the ignition timing and the fuel system, followed by mechanical checks on the engine.

3:4 Removing and refitting distributor

On all types, remove nut and washer indicated by arrow in righthand view of **FIG 3:1**. Do not slacken long clamp bolt or timing will be lost. Lift out distributor. Check gear and shaft for wear. Fit new sealing ring on neck.

To refit, turn crankshaft pulley until Z1 mark is aligned with crankcase joint or mark on blower rim (see **Section 3:5**). Piston of No. 1 cylinder should then be at TDC on the firing stroke. Set rotor arm on distributor so that it points in the direction of the rear edge of the blower while inserting neck of distributor in crankcase. The arm will move as the gears engage. Slacken the long bolt on the split clamp plate and turn the distributor to the left until the contact breaker just opens. The tip of the rotor arm should then be vertically over a notch on the rim of the distributor body. This position is shown in **FIG 3:3**. Check the timing as instructed in the following Section.

3:5 Ignition timing

Marelli:

Having set the contact breaker gap correctly, set the basic ignition timing at TDC on the firing stroke of No. 1 cylinder as described at the start of the preceding Section. Run engine up to operating temperature and connect a stroboscope. Note before starting the engine, that there are two marks on the crankshaft pulley rim to the right of the TDC mark (Z1). These indicate positions 30 deg. and 35 deg. BTDC when aligned with the crankcase joint or mark on blower rim. Gradually increase engine speed and watch the Z1 mark move to the left. At 6000 rev/min the 35 deg. mark should be in-line with the joint or mark.

When the setting is correct at this speed there may be a change in the basic setting but this does not matter. With engine stationary the basic timing may be up to 3 deg. ATDC. Make adjustments by slackening clamp plate bolt and turning distributor.

Bosch:

With correct breaker gap, set basic timing as described in **Section 3:4**. Check the timing at 6000 rev/min as instructed in the preceding notes on the Marelli distributor. For 2000S engines the 30 deg. BTDC mark on the pulley must line up with the crankcase joint or mark on blower rim, and basic timing at a standstill may be a minimum of 5 deg. BTDC. For other 2000 engines except 2000T, the timing should be the same at 6000 rev/min but may be out by a maximum of 5 deg. ATDC at a standstill.

If the car is fitted with exhaust emission control (EECS) it will also be fitted with a Bosch distributor incorporating vacuum control. The basic timing must be carried out with a stroboscope so that it is 3 deg. ATDC at 850 to 950 rev/min. At 6000 rev/min it should be 30 deg. ± 2 deg. BTDC. If the ignition point is not within the tolerances given, the 3 deg. ATDC setting may be altered in the range 2 to 5 deg. ATDC. Make adjustments by slackening the clamp plate bolt and turning the distributor body.

Note that engines from No. 902.029 onwards have a distributor with a basic timing of 5 deg. BTDC. The distributor is marked with a yellow dot or may be stamped 5 deg. v.OT (5 deg. BTDC). This type of distributor may be fitted to earlier engines as a replacement unit.

Pulley marks:

Marks on the crankshaft pulley rim give a timing BTDC when to the right of the Z1 mark (TDC). For 5 deg. BTDC make a mark 5 mm (.197 inch) to the right. Intermediate marks may be set out using similar calculations.

Timing with test lamp:

Basic ignition timing may be carried out using a test lamp between side terminal 1 on the distributor body and an earth. Turn on the ignition switch. Slacken clamp plate bolt and turn distributor clockwise until points are closed.

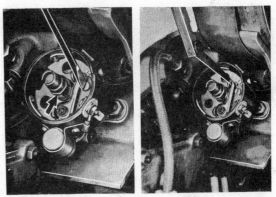

FIG 3:2 Adjusting contact breaker points gap on Bosch distributor. Loosening fixing screw (left) and checking gap with feelers (right)

FIG 3:3 Rotor arm vertically above notch on rim of distributor body to give TDC on No. 1 cylinder

The Z1 pulley mark must be aligned with the crankcase joint or mark on blower rim. Turn distributor slowly in opposite direction until points open and light goes on. Tighten clamp bolt. The rotor arm must be over the distributor body notch as mentioned at the beginning of **Section 3:4** and the timing will then be correct for No. 1 cylinder. Proceed to set the timing with a stroboscope as instructed earlier in this Section.

In all these adjustments, remember that alterations to the points gap will affect the ignition timing.

3:6 Servicing distributor

Marelli:

It is necessary to remove the distributor to renew the contact breaker parts. Detach wire from terminal 1 on side of distributor and also remove cap and plug leads as an assembly. Remove nut holding clamp plate to crankcase

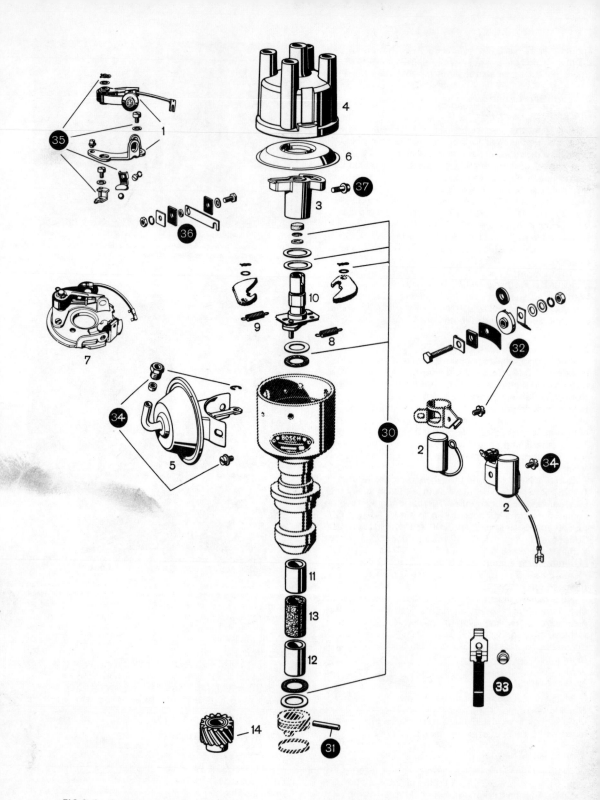

FIG 3:4   Component parts of typical Bosch distributor. Cap 4 should have six sockets for plug leads

and lift distributor away. Do not disturb the long bolt in the clamping plate. Take rotor off (see lefthand view in **FIG 3:1**). Remove breaker set complete with stationary plate. After fitting a new breaker, adjust the gap and then check the ignition timing.

Renew rotor if electrode is badly eroded or if plastic part is cracked. Check action of centrifugal weights and springs, renewing faulty parts.

It is difficult for the normal owner to check the capacitor (condenser) for faults. Symptoms may be poor performance, difficult starting and rapid contact point erosion due to arcing which the capacitor is designed to prevent. Substitution with a new condenser is the quickest and easiest method of checking.

Bosch:

FIG 3:4 is representative of the components of the Bosch distributor fitted to Porsche 911 cars. There may be some variations between early and late models but none which make servicing difficult when following the instructions. Note that the vacuum unit 34 is fitted only to cars with exhaust emission control (EECS).

To renew the contact points, remove the cap 4 and rotor 3 (the cap illustrated is for a four-cylinder engine). Loosen nut of terminal assembly. Remove lock ring from pivot of moving contact arm (part of 1). Lift off arm. Remove screw and lift off fixed contact plate (part of 1). Renew points which are pitted or badly worn. A kit is inexpensive and engine performance will suffer if defective points are overlooked.

Check the distributor cap for dirt and cracks. Black 'tracking' marks on the inside surface may be due to insulation breakdown. Renew cap if brass terminals are eroded, but note that slight erosion is normal. Renew rotor arm if electrode is badly eroded. Check carbon brush in centre of cap. When pressed in it should spring out again.

Check action of centrifugal advance mechanism 8, 9 and 10. Turn rotor arm clockwise till it stops and then release it. If the mechanism is free and the springs in order, the arm should return smartly to its original position.

Dismantling Bosch distributor:

Remove side terminal and screws and lift out contact plate 7. Make a careful note of the exact positions of insulating washers on terminal. Remove vacuum unit if fitted. Lift out camshaft 10 and centrifugal mechanism. Drive out pin 31, pull off gear 14 and push drive shaft out of body after removing any burrs. Note position of metal and fibre thrust washers. **Do not put body in solvent, or self-lubricating qualities of bushes 12 and felt 13 will be impaired.** Have bushes and shaft renewed if worn.

Check condition of gear and thrust washers. Check pins, springs and weights of centrifugal mechanism. Check vacuum unit under suction to see that diaphragm is sound. Renew all faulty parts.

Reassemble in the reverse order of dismantling, making sure that the thrust washers and insulating washers are correctly positioned. Put a drop of oil on the weight pivots and oil the felt pad inside the top end of the camshaft. Put a tiny drop of oil on the contact breaker pivot, but be careful to keep all lubricants from the contact points.

3:7 Sparking plugs

Correct sparking plugs for the various models are listed in Technical Data. Carry out routine maintenance and adjustment as instructed in **Section 3:2**.

To check the appearance of the plugs, remove them as soon as the engine has stopped after running under operating conditions. Do not let the engine idle.

If the deposits at the firing end are white, the plug has been running at a high temperature possibly due to weak mixture. Light tan-coloured deposits indicate the use of the correct grade of plug and good operating conditions. Fluffy black deposits are caused by rich mixture, but if the deposits are wet and black it is a sign of oiling up due to piston or cylinder wear.

3:8 Fault diagnosis

(a) Engine will not fire

1 Battery discharged
2 Contact breaker points dirty, pitted or out of adjustment
3 Distributor cap dirty, cracked or 'tracking'
4 Carbon brush inside distributor not in contact with rotor arm
5 Faulty cables or loose connections in the low-tension circuit
6 Distributor rotor arm cracked
7 Faulty coil or coil lead to distributor
8 Broken contact breaker spring
9 Contact points stuck open
10 Faulty capacitor (condenser)
11 Faulty ignition switch

(b) Engine misfires

1 Check 2, 3, 5 and 7 in (a)
2 Weak contact breaker spring
3 Plug or coil high-tension leads cracked or perished
4 Loose sparking plugs
5 Sparking plug insulation cracked
6 Sparking plug gap incorrect
7 Ignition timing too far advanced or retarded

CHAPTER 4

COOLING, HEATING AND EXHAUST EMISSION CONTROL

4:1 Description of cooling system

The air required for engine cooling is produced by a belt-driven blower (see 7 in **FIG 1:2** in the Engine Chapter). It is propelled forward into a large glass-fibre reinforced plastic cover which extends sideways to carry it to the two banks of cylinders and cylinder heads. The bowed outline of this cover can be seen immediately above the crankcase and cylinders in **FIG 1:1** in the same chapter. After passing down between the fins of the cylinders and heads, some of the air is deflected upwards by shrouds or deflectors as shown in **FIG 1:35**.

4:2 Routine maintenance of cooling system

This is confined to adjustment of the driving belt for the blower and alternator. The method is shown in **FIG 4:1.**

Check tension by pressing belt inwards about midway between the pulleys. Light thumb pressure should deflect it 15 to 20 mm (.60 to .80 inch). A belt which is too tight puts a greater strain on the alternator bearings and is more liable to break. A slack belt may slip, causing overheating problems and lower output from the alternator.

To adjust tension, remove nut from blower pulley shaft. A steel bar with pegs, similar to tool No. P208, can be

used to engage the holes in the pulley flange to hold it still. Remove washer and any spacers which may be fitted. Remove the belt flange.

Removal of spacers from between the pulley flanges will tighten the belt and vice versa. Spacers from between the flanges must be added to those outside so that the total number of washers remains unaltered. A belt which is so stretched or worn that only one spacer remains between the flanges must be renewed. A belt must not run on the bottom of the pulley groove.

Tighten pulley nut to 29 lb ft torque. Check the belt tension. If a new belt is fitted, check the tension after 50 miles of running, as the belt will stretch slightly.

Never remove a belt by levering it over the pulley with a screwdriver. Belts contaminated with oil may be cleaned in a detergent solution and rinsed in water. Any signs of cracking or of frayed edges call for renewal.

4:3 Removing and refitting blower

The blower is mounted on the alternator shaft and the assembly must be removed complete (engine in or out of car). Details of the mounting can be seen in **FIGS 1:2** and **4:2**. Proceed as follows:

 1 Remove screws securing upper air channel. Remove belt (see **Section 4:2**).

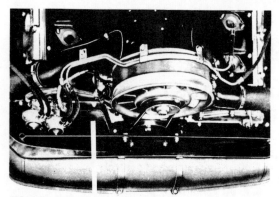

2 Slacken clip surrounding blower housing. Pull housing and alternator to the rear. Mark cables for correct position before detaching from alternator.

3 Refit in the reverse order, making sure that dowel for blower housing is correctly located.

4:4 Removing and refitting covers and deflectors

The arrow in **FIG 4:3** points to the top cover or upper air channel. To remove it, first detach the carburetters and intake pipes (see **Chapter 2**). Next, remove the rear coverplate and the fuel pipes which pass over the blower housing (see **FIG 4:2**). Remove the air hoses to heat exchangers and the hot air ducts on both sides of the engine. Remove the front coverplates (see **FIG 4:3**). Remove the side coverplates.

The deflector plates or shrouds between the cylinders cannot be removed until the camshaft housings are taken off (see **Chapter 1** and **FIG 1:35**). These plates are held in place with spring clips.

When refitting the shrouds, ensure that the spring clips hold them securely. Secure the coverplates so that there are no gaps where air can leak out and reduce cooling efficiency.

4:5 Silencer and heat exchangers

The position of the silencer is shown in **FIG 1:2**. Note retaining clip. To remove silencer, take out the two flange bolts and the bolts from the clips. Check for leaks and deterioration. Refit in reverse order, using a new gasket. Tighten flange bolts gradually and alternately.

To remove the heat exchangers, detach the air intake pipes and the connecting hoses between exchanger and heater control box (see **FIG 4:4**). Remove the heat exchanger securing bolts and the exhaust flange nuts (see **FIG 1:10** in the Engine chapter). Check for damage, distorted flanges or cracks. Refit, using new gaskets and tighten the fixings evenly and alternately.

4:6 Heating system and controls

FIG 4:4 shows the heating system. Fresh air is drawn in by blower 2 and some is diverted through offtake pipes 3 into the casings of heat exchangers 4. The exhaust pipes pass through these casings and the air becomes heated (also see part 20 in **FIG 1:1**). Connecting hoses carry the air to control boxes 8, and then through ducts and air silencers to the various distribution points. The heater controls are so arranged that air still passes through the heat exchangers even though flaps prevent hot air from reaching the car interior (see shutter slots in **FIG 4:5**).

Servicing heater controls (first type):

To remove cables, detach rear ends from control box levers shown in **FIG 4:5**. Remove tunnel cover and release gearlever mounting (3 screws). Remove heater control lever knob and lift off gearlever. Release control lever bracket (2 screws), ease lever forward and pull cables out of tunnel (see **FIG 4:6**).

When refitting, pass cable through correct hole in lever until the bend is reached. The greased cables must pass through the larger (lower) aperture. They must not cross. Fit the lever mounting and push the lever to the closed position (right forward). Attach the rear ends of the cables to the control box levers and check that flaps work smoothly and open and close to their fullest extent. Refit the gearlever.

Lever adjustment (first type):

Refer to **FIG 4:7**. The lefthand view shows the friction adjustment by means of nut 8. To adjust, hold bracket in a vice as shown in righthand view. Tighten nut to 50 cm/kg or 3.6 lb ft torque and slacken off one turn.

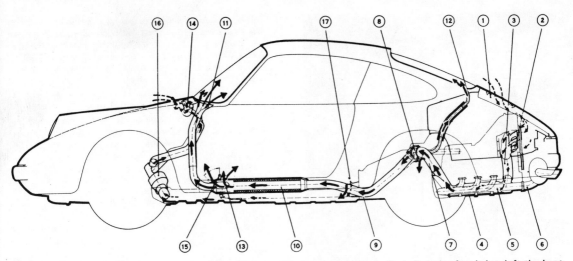

FIG 4:4 How heated air is supplied to the car interior. The heavier arrows indicate hot air after it has left the heat exchangers

Key to Fig 4:4   1 Slots in rear engine hood   2 Cooling air blower   3 Offtake pipes   4 Heat exchangers   5 Exhaust pipes   6 Silencer   7 Connecting hoses   8 Heat control box   9 Heater pipe   10 Air silencer   11 Windshield defroster nozzle   12 Rear window defroster nozzle   13 Sliding valves   14 Fresh air unit   15 Pivoted lever   16 Self-powered heater   17 Air intake for self-powered heater

Attach a spring balance to the inner hole in the lever and pull at right angles. Lever should not start to move until the pull is 10 ± 1 kg (22 ± 2.2 lb). Adjust by turning nut.

Servicing heater control (second type):

From 1968 models onwards, the heater control lever is fitted to the handbrake mounting (see **FIG 4:8**). The small lever is a hand throttle control. To remove the rear end of the control cables, refer to the instructions for the earlier type. Remove tunnel cover and handbrake lever boot. Release handbrake mounting from tunnel. Lift mounting and release spring clip on lower end of handbrake lever so that the pin through the equalizer bar may be removed. Pull the heater cables out of the guide tubes and control lever.

Check friction of control lever as described for the earlier type. Friction faces must be dry and free from grease. Fit cable, and grease with multi-purpose lithium-based lubricant. Make sure cables do not cross and insert longer cable in lefthand tube. Refit handbrake equalizer bar so that cables are correctly positioned. Tighten handbrake mountings to 2.5 mkg (18 lb ft). Refit rear ends of cables as described earlier. Do not forget to install the dust caps for the guide tubes. Check action of flaps.

4:7 The exhaust emission control system

A diagrammatic representation of the system is given in **FIG 4:9**. Known as 'EECS', it must, by law, be fitted to cars operating in America. The principle is that unburnt gases in the exhaust are injected with air from a pump. The oxygen in the air causes after-burning of the gases which considerably reduces the poisonous pollutants which would otherwise pass out into the atmosphere.

A pump 2, is belt-driven from one of the camshafts. Air is delivered from the pump to a regulating control valve 3 for each bank of cylinders. The valves incorporate a pressure

relief valve and a check valve, the relief valve releasing excess air back to atmosphere. The check valve prevents exhaust gas flowing back into the air supply hoses if the pump stops working, probably through a broken belt. At conditions of high negative pressure in the induction system due to closed throttles and a steep down-grade, the mixture is liable to be excessively rich. To overcome this there is a dashpot compensator 10 which opens the throttles slightly in such circumstances.

The distributor 11 is fitted with a vacuum control unit so that a retarded ignition at low speeds calls for increased throttle opening to give a better mixture during deceleration.

Routine maintenance:

Check belt tension. It should yield about 10 mm ($\frac{1}{2}$ inch) when pressed inwards at a point midway between the pulleys. Adjust by loosening the mounting bolt on the

FIG 4:5 The rear end of a heater control cable, showing connection to lever for control box valve. Shutter slots are open when heated air is not required in the car interior

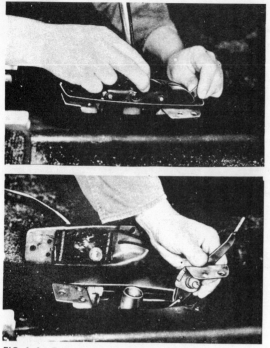

FIG 4:6 Removing the gearlever mounting plate (top view). Lower view shows heater control bracket

righthand side of the pump and the bolt on the lefthand side as shown in **FIG 4:10**. Lift pump by hand to tighten belt. Do not use force or the mounting may be deformed. Tighten the two bolts to a torque of 4 mkg (29 lb ft). Check hose connections. Always slacken off the adjustment before removing a belt.

Checking vacuum control unit of distributor:

Turn the crankshaft pulley until the Z1 mark is visible. This represents TDC when aligned with the mark on the blower housing. Make another mark to the left of TDC which corresponds to an angle of 3 deg. ATC.

Run the engine at idling speed and use a stroboscope to flash the pulley. The 3 deg. ATC mark should align with the mark on the blower housing. There is a permissible tolerance of between 2 and 5 deg. ATC. When checked at 6000 rev/min the ignition timing should be 30 deg. $\pm$ 2 deg. BTC. If adjustment at idling speed is not satisfactory, correct the timing at 6000 rev/min within the tolerance of $\pm$ 2 deg.

After setting the ignition timing, adjust the idler speed and check the adjustment of the throttle valve compensator (see later).

Ignition timing:

Check contact breaker gap and make sure the dwell angle is 38 $\pm$ 3 deg. Run engine up to temperature and connect a stroboscope to No. 1 sparking plug lead. Loosen distributor clamping plate so that distributor can be turned by hand. Run engine at 6000 rev/min and flash

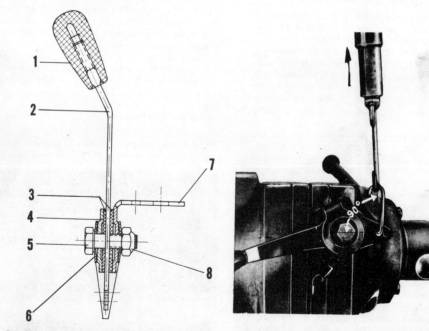

FIG 4:7 Section through frictional mounting of heater control lever (left). Righthand view shows spring balance checking friction setting. Adjustment is made at nut 8

Key to Fig 4:7   1 Knob   2 Control lever (lefthand drive)   3 Friction disc   4 Shim   5 Pivot bolt   6 Cup spring   7 Bracket   8 Nut

the crankshaft pulley. Turn the distributor until the 30 deg. BTC mark on the pulley rim lines up with the mark on the blower housing. Tighten clamp plate and check timing.

Removing and refitting air pump:

1 Detach hoses from pump.
2 Remove bolts attaching pump to mounting.
3 Remove belt and lift pump away.

The pump must not be dismantled. Turn the pulley and check that the pump turns freely in an anticlockwise direction. A new pump may squeak a little when turned, and there may be slight drag, but this is not important.

Refit the pump in the reverse sequence and tension the belt as explained at the beginning of 'Routine maintenance'.

Removing and refitting regulating valve:

Refer to **FIG 4:11**, disconnect the hose, remove the flange bolts and lift the assembly away from the engine rear shield. Remove the two long through-bolts and separate the three valve parts.

Check the condition of the flowback and pressure relief valves. Renew worn parts. Renew the rubber diaphragm in the flowback check valve if the edges are torn

FIG 4:8   Later type of handbrake mounting for heater control lever. The shorter lever is for throttle control

or frayed. Use new gaskets when reassembling, fitting the valve housings so that their arrows point outwards, with the pressure relief valves pointing downwards.

When refitting the valve assembly, fit gaskets under the flanges, and O-rings on the relief valve nozzles.

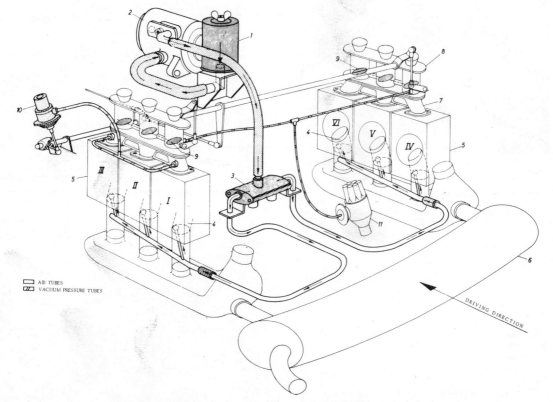

FIG 4:9   Diagrammatic layout of the exhaust emission control system

Key to Fig 4:9   1 Air filter   2 Air pump   3 Regulator (pressure relief and check valves)   4 Exhaust port   5 Cylinder head
6 Silencer   7 Inlet manifold   8 Carburetters   9 Throttle valve   10 Compensator dashpot   11 Distributor

FIG 4:10 The slotted adjustment for tensioning the air pump belt on the EECS system

FIG 4:11 EECS regulating valve showing mounting flanges

Removing and refitting pressure lines:

Remove regulating valve as just instructed. Remove heat exchanger hoses and then remove the heat exchangers. At the exhaust ports, unscrew the unions as shown in **FIG 4:12**, withdraw the connecting pipes and then unscrew the injector bodies.

Refit the bodies with new gaskets. Check condition of pipes and then fit them so that they cannot chafe against other parts. Check hoses for leaktight fitting.

Removing and installing camshaft pulley:

1 Remove engine transverse support and silencer. Remove regulating valve from rear shield (see earlier section).

2 Remove rear shield and pump belt. Do not lever belt over pulley flanges but slacken pump mounting bolts.

3 Remove retaining bolt and draw pulley off camshaft extension.

When refitting the parts in the reverse order, make sure the belt is correctly tensioned (see 'Routine maintenance').

Removing and fitting pulley bearing:

This is mounted in the lefthand camshaft chain cover. Remove the pulley as just explained, remove the retaining nuts and withdraw the bearing cover. Use a puller to draw the bearing off the camshaft, after removing the chain cover.

Clean the parts and check condition of bearing when unlubricated. Check the oil seal in the cover and renew if leaking. Oil sealing lip after fitting in cover. Refit bearing on camshaft after lubricating.

Fit chain cover on a new gasket. Fit bearing cover on a good gasket. Refit the pulley and tension the belt correctly.

Servicing throttle valve compensator and vacuum pipes:

Remove hose from compensator (10 in **FIG 4:9**). Detach connecting rod ball joint socket, release compensator from mounting bracket and lift away.

The vacuum lines are a push fit on the connections. The pipe from the compensator goes to a T-piece with branches to intake ports of cylinders 1 and 3. Branches from cylinders 1 and 4 go to a T-piece which is connected to the distributor vacuum control unit. Check that pipes are in sound condition and not chafed through.

FIG 4:12 Removing pressure pipe from exhaust port connection

FIG 4:13 Throttle valve compensator showing return lag adjusting screw (top arrow). At idling speed there must be slight clearance between levers (lower arrow)

Adjusting compensator and linkage:

Before embarking on any adjustments, check that the ignition timing and carburetter idling are correctly set. Run the engine up to operating temperature and then check the compensator adjustment as follows:

Shut the throttle quickly from an engine speed of 3000 rev/min. Engine speed should then fall to around 1000 rev/min within 4 to 6 seconds. If this is not so, loosen the side screw which locks the adjusting screw indicated by the top arrow in **FIG 4 :13**. Turn the adjusting screw right in.

Accelerate the engine quickly and shut off to draw the compensator rod up into the device and check the engine speed at once. It should be 2000 to 2200 rev/min. If speed is greater, lengthen the rod, if it is lower, shorten the rod, but make sure there is always slight clearance between the levers as indicated by the lower arrow when the engine is idling again.

Now adjust the time lag taken for the engine speed to drop. It must lie between 4 and 6 seconds, so turn the adjusting screw to the left to reduce the lag and to the right to increase it. In case of difficulty, check that the compensator is not sticking when the engine oil temperature is at least 200°F, or the indicator needle is in the green sector. Keeping the time lag to the upper limit will reduce exhaust back-firing to a minimum.

Testing the EECS system:

1 Check ignition timing and compensator adjustment. Adjust carburetters.
2 Remove hose connecting air pump to regulating valve.
3 Connect exhaust gas analyzer and check carbon monoxide content at idle speed. It should be approximately 4.5 per cent.
4 Reconnect the pump hose, run the engine at idling speed and check for carbon monoxide. The figure should be approximately 1 to 1.5 per cent.

4 : 8 Fault diagnosis

(a) Engine overheats

1 Blower belt slipping
2 Cooling air leaking from cover joints
3 Crankcase, oil cooler and cylinder fins caked with dirt
4 Carburetters out of tune, ignition wrongly timed
5 Exhaust system blocked
6 Air deflectors or shrouds wrongly fitted

(b) Heating system ineffective

1 Check 1 in (a)
2 Control cables broken or out of adjustment
3 Control box valves stuck
4 Hoses disconnected or leaking

CHAPTER 5

THE CLUTCH

5:1 General description

The clutch is of the single dry-plate variety incorporating a diaphragm spring (see **FIG 5:1**). The cover 1 is bolted to the front face of the flywheel 6 and carries diaphragm spring 4 on pins and fulcrum rings. The outer edge of the spring bears on pressure plate 2 and spring pressure traps driven plate 3 between the faces of the flywheel and the pressure plate. The driven plate is splined to the gearbox input shaft 7 and thus transmits drive from the flywheel to the gearbox. When the clutch pedal is depressed, release bearing 5 presses on the diaphragm spring. As the spring becomes dished the outer edge moves in the opposite direction by reason of the fulcrum rings. In consequence, pressure on the pressure plate is relieved, the driven plate is no longer trapped and there is no drive from the flywheel to the input shaft and gearbox. The dark shaded parts of the driven plate are friction linings which are riveted in place. The hub of the plate incorporates shock-absorbing springs to eliminate snatch.

5:2 Routine maintenance

Accurate setting of free play at the clutch pedal is essential. The amount of play before the clutch starts to disengage must be 20 to 25 mm ($\frac{3}{4}$ to 1 inch). Too little clearance may cause clutch slip and too much may cause rapid wear of the gearbox synchronizing cones.

Clearance may be adjusted at either end of the clutch cable. The top view in **FIG 5:2** shows the location of the adjustment at the release lever where it protrudes from the transmission casing. Loosen the locknut and turn the adjusting nut until pedal pad free play is correct. When satisfied, tighten the locknut. See 'Removing release bearing' (**Section 5:7**) for details of free play when pedal is fitted with a return spring.

The adjustment at the clutch pedal is shown in the lower view of **FIG 5:2**. Turn back the mat and rubber cover at the front end of the floor tunnel. Loosen locknut, disengage spring clip and withdraw clevis pin. Turn clevis and fit pin to check pedal pad free play. Do not let cable end protrude in clevis fork. Tighten locknut, make sure spring clip is secure and smear cable threads with grease.

After adjusting, check the pedal travel. Run the car until the gearbox is at operating temperature, depress the clutch pedal fully, and after a short pause, engage reverse gear. This should happen silently. If this is not so it will be necessary to move the pedal stop shown in **FIG 5:3**.

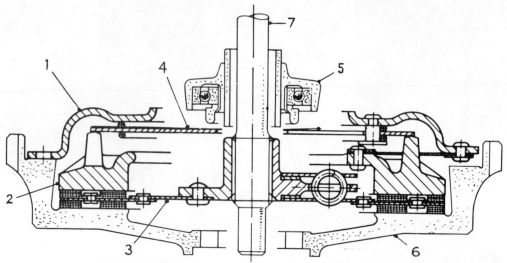

FIG 5:1　Section through clutch, flywheel and releasing bearing

Key to Fig 5:1　1 Cover　2 Pressure plate　3 Driven plate　4 Diaphragm spring　5 Release bearing　6 Flywheel　7 Input shaft

After removing the rubber mats, slacken the two socket-head screws and slide the stop up or down as required. Tighten the screws and check engagement of reverse gear again.

5:3　Removing and refitting clutch cable

At the front end of the floor tunnel, peel back the mats and tunnel cover. Loosen clevis locknut and release spring clip to remove clevis pin (see lower view of **FIG 5:2**). Unscrew clevis and locknut. Take hold of the rear end of the cable at the release lever (see top view in **FIG 5:2**) and pull the cable out of its guide. Check condition of cable, guide and rubber bellows.

Before refitting, smear cable with grease and push into place from the rear. Fit release lever nut and locknut, connect clevis at front end and set the clearance (see **Section 5:2**).

FIG 5:2　Clutch cable adjusting nut and locknut at release lever (top). Lower view shows adjustment of cable at pedal shaft

FIG 5:3　Location of adjustable stop used to set clutch pedal travel

FIG 5:4　Clutch cover assembly. Top arrow points to inner ends of diaphragm spring leaves which take thrust of release bearing. Pressure plate face indicated by lower arrow

5:4 Removing and inspecting clutch

Removing:

Remove the engine and separate from gearbox (see **Chapter 1**). Do not let weight of transmission hang on input shaft and keep it square to prevent damage to clutch driven plate.

Release clutch cover from flywheel (six bolts). Loosen bolts diagonally a turn at a time to release the spring pressure and to avoid distorting the cover. Lift off cover assembly and driven plate.

Inspecting:

Clean the parts and examine for wear or damage. Refer to **FIG 5:4** and check spring leaves for scoring by the release bearing (top arrow). Scores up to .30 mm (.011 inch) in depth are permissible.

Check face of pressure plate (lower arrow). Cracks, deep scores, burn marks or uneven wear call for renewal. Note that the clutch must be renewed as an assembly and there is no point in dismantling it by removing the rivets. Use a straightedge and feelers to check the flatness of the pressure plate face. Concavity up to .30 mm (.011 inch) is permissible. Check all rivets for security and check the cover and springs for cracks. Examine the fulcrum rings and rivet heads where they contact the diaphragm spring. If worn, renew clutch. Put molybdenum disulphide grease on fulcrum rings where they contact the diaphragm spring.

5:5 Clutch driven plate

Examine friction linings. Renew plate if linings are worn, broken or contaminated with oil. Thickness of plate should be 10.1 —.40 mm (.40 —.015 inch) as shown at

FIG 5:6   Clutch secured to flywheel (left). Dowel pins and dummy input shaft used to centre clutch when refitting (right)

FIG 5:7   Top arrows indicate clearance between clutch release lever and gearbox housing with lever pulled in direction of lower arrow

'A' in **FIG 5:5**. Renew plate if thickness is much less than 9 mm (.354 inch).

Mount plate on a mandrel between centres and check runout with a dial gauge (see **FIG 5:5**). Maximum permissible runout is .60 mm (.023 inch). It will be noticed that the steel disc is divided into leaves and the linings are riveted to these alternately. The leaves are bowed and offset to provide a cushioning effect and the offsetting must be evenly balanced. Compressed thickness of the plate should be 9.20 ± .20 mm (.362 ± .007 inch) and the wear limit is 8 to 7.80 mm (.314 to .307 inch).

Check hub splines for wear. Plate should slide freely on input shaft without undue play. Check shock-absorbing springs for wear and breakage.

The linings may have a high polish and be perfectly capable of transmitting power. If the grain of the lining material is visible the linings are good, but if the linings are a dark brown, with an opaque glaze, they are probably contaminated with burnt oil and the plate must be renewed. It is not advisable to try riveting linings into place. Renew the whole plate.

5:6 Refitting clutch

It is assumed that the clutch face of the flywheel has been checked for cracks, scoring and wear. Details for the restoration of a worn surface have been given in **Chapter 1**.

FIG 5:5   Driven plate spun on mandrel between centres to check runout with dial gauge. 'A' is the uncompressed thickness over linings

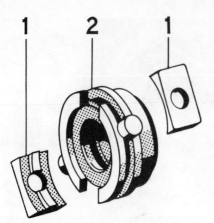

FIG 5:8 Later type of clutch release bearing showing plastic guides 1 and bearing 2

FIG 5:9 Releasing clutch withdrawal fork. Allen key is loosening dowel pin

It will be evident from an examination of the clutch section in **FIG 5:1** that the driven plate hub must be truly centred in the flywheel or the gearbox input shaft will not be able to pass through the hub splines so that the pilot or spigot will enter the bushing in the flywheel boss. Centralizing is assured by using a mandrel which may be the rear end of an old input shaft or, for a one-off job, a wooden dowel turned so that the smaller diameter is a snug fit in the flywheel bush and the larger diameter is a good fit in the driven plate splined hub.

Fit the driven plate, using the temporary mandrel. One can be seen in use in the righthand view of **FIG 5:6**. About 2 cc of molybdenum disulphide grease should be pressed into the flywheel bushing before fitting the mandrel. Fit the clutch cover assembly to the flywheel using centralizing pins as shown. Fit the bolts and tighten them diagonally a turn at a time so that the cover is not distorted. Use spring washers and tighten to a torque of 3.5 mkg (25 lb ft).

Remove the mandrel, apply a smear of grease to the input shaft splines and pilot and refit the transmission to the engine as explained in **Chapter 1** under the heading 'Refitting engine' in **Section 1:3**. Finally, check the clutch release lever setting as shown in **FIG 5:7**. Pull

lever in direction of arrow. Distance between lever and gearbox housing must be at least 20 mm (.80 inch) as indicated by top arrows. Adjust clearance as in **Section 5:2**.

5:7 Servicing release bearing and fork

The bearing is part 5 in **FIG 5:1**. Note, however, that a new release bearing No. 901.116.081.11 was fitted as follows:

911 from 12th January, 1967
911S from beginning of production

The new bearing may be used as a replacement for the original type. It is essential to fit plastic guides No. 901.116.825.11 to the new-type bearing, as shown in **FIG 5:8**. Use fine emerycloth on the plastic guides if the bearing is not a free fit in the release fork.

Removing release bearing:

With transmission detached from engine, release socket-head bolt as shown in **FIG 5:9** and remove release lever and bearing, after unhooking return spring. This spring is not fitted to models with the modified release bearing and it will be found that there is a spring fitted to the clutch pedal shaft to keep the pedal pressed towards the toe board. In this case the clutch pedal free play is checked by pulling the pedal away from the toe board.

Servicing release fork and bearing:

The fork is carried on a ballpin as shown in **FIG 5:10**, the earlier version being on the left. This plain-shanked pin was cemented into the housing and was fitted up to transmission number 102082 or 222706. Clean the parts and check ballpin and bush for wear.

Do not use solvents on the release bearing, as it is packed with grease. Renew the bearing if dirt has entered or if it sounds noisy when turned.

Refitting release fork and bearing:

If screwed ballpin was removed, refit it using a good sealing washer and tighten to a torque of 2.1 to 2.3 mkg (15 to 16½ lb ft). Smear molybdenum disulphide grease in the ballpin bush and on the rubbing surfaces of the release bearing. Refit the bearing and fork and tighten the socket-head bolt to a torque of 1.0 mkg (7 lb ft).

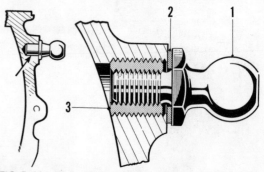

FIG 5:10 Plain shank of early withdrawal lever ballpin (left). Later type of screwed ballpin (right)

Key to Fig 5:10   1 Ballpin   2 Sealing washer
3 Threaded insert in housing

5:8 Fault diagnosis

(a) Noisy clutch

1 Worn pilot bush in flywheel boss
2 Worn release bearing
3 Broken springs in driven plate hub
4 Broken driven plate disc or linings

(b) Clutch judder

1 Defective engine and transmission mountings
2 Pressure plate face worn and uneven
3 Diaphragm spring distorted
4 Driven plate disc distorted
5 Grease or oil on linings

(c) Dragging or incomplete release

1 Excessive clutch clearance
2 Driven plate or input shaft running out of true
3 Driven plate segments or linings unevenly set
4 Input shaft spigot bearing tight
5 Stiffness of clutch pedal, cable or release mechanism
6 Sticky linings
7 Distorted clutch cover or pressure plate

(d) Slipping

1 See 3 and 5 in (b)
2 Lack of free play in clutch pedal
3 Linings burned or broken, contact faces defective

CHAPTER 6

THE TRANSMISSION

6:1 General description

To simplify instructions, the transmission system has been divided into two sections, this chapter dealing with the gearbox and final drive gears. **Chapter 7** covers the rear axles, universal joints, rear hubs and suspension.

Servicing details will be given for fourspeed and five-speed gearboxes with synchromesh engagement of all forward gears, for the optional ZF self-locking differential unit and for the Sportomatic transmission. The instructions for the fivespeed gearbox will be given in full and most of these are applicable to the fourspeed box, any differences for the latter being given in **Section 6:14**. The Sportomatic transmission is described in **Section 6:15**.

The fivespeed transmission is shown in **FIG 6:1**, housing 18 being bolted to the engine to form the power unit. **This unit can be removed or installed only as an assembly.** The housing is a tunnel which contains the input shaft 19 and pinion shaft 5, the pinion engaging with the crownwheel or ring gear which is bolted to differential carrier 12. Gears A, B, C, D and E are in constant mesh with companion gears on the pinion shaft and one gear of each pair is free to revolve on needle roller bearings. When a gear is selected, synchronizing device 6 to 9 speeds up or slows down the particular gears until sliding teeth can be engaged and the freely-revolving gear can be locked to its shaft to complete the drive. Front cover 2 encloses the first-speed gears, but gear A also drives a pair of gears on a layshaft. These drive large gear 20 when it is moved to the left, to provide reverse gear.

911T models from 1968 onwards have a simplified differential unit. **It is important to check this when fitting an exchange unit, as the simplified type must be used only with LOEBRO half-axles.**

6:2 Routine maintenance

Just forward of the ribbed differential cover on the left-hand side of the transmission housing there are two plugs. The lower one is a drain plug and the upper one is a filler plug. Drain the oil while it is hot, doing this every 6000 miles. Clean the magnetic drain plug free from adhering steel particles and refit it. Refill to the bottom of the filler

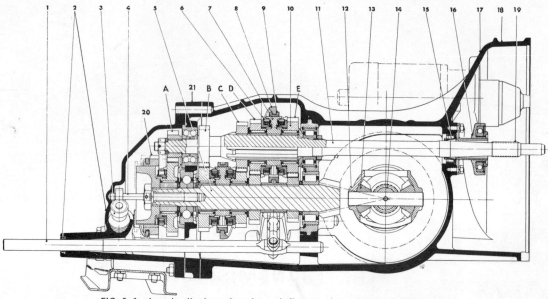

FIG 6:1 Longitudinal section through fivespeed gearbox and differential

Key to Fig 6:1   1 Shift rod   2 Front cover and oil seal   3 Tachometer driven gear   4 Tachometer drive gear   5 Pinion shaft   6 Synchronizing ring   7 Spider   8 Shift fork   9 Sliding sleeve   10 Fifth-speed gear   11 Input shaft   12 Differential carrier   13 Spider gear   14 Side gearshaft   15 Oil seal   16/17 Clutch release bearing   18 Housing   19 Clutch plate splines   20 Pinion shaft gear for first-speed and reverse   21 Intermediate plate   A First-speed fixed gear   B Second-speed fixed gear   C Third-speed fixed gear   D Fourth-speed free-running gear   E Fifth-speed free-running gear

plug hole with SAE.90 Hypoid transmission oil. Approximate capacity is 2.5 litres ($4\frac{1}{2}$ Imp pints or 5 US pints). Tighten both plugs to a torque of 2 to $2\frac{1}{2}$ mkg ($14\frac{1}{2}$ to 18 lb ft).

Maintenance recommendations for the Sportomatic transmission are given in **Section 6:16**.

6:3 Transmission removal

Fourspeed and fivespeed transmission:

To remove the complete power unit from the car, refer to **Chapter 1**. Note that the differential assembly may be removed without detaching the complete unit (see **Sections 6:4** and **6:8**), but if adjustment or renewal of parts is intended it is best to remove the entire power unit.

Sportomatic transmission:

Use the removal instructions in **Chapter 1** but note a few extra details. Remove the vacuum hose from the reservoir. Adjacent to the lefthand bank of carburetters is the control valve. Withdraw the rubber cap, remove the splitpin and pull off the wire connector (see **FIG 6:29**). Detach B+ cable from connector mounted just above coil and remove connectors from bypass switch.

After lowering the power unit a little, detach cables from temperature switch and temperature gauge sensor which are adjacent to the vacuum servo cylinder (see **FIG 6:30**).

6:4 Dismantling fivespeed transmission

Servicing the Porsche transmission demands a high degree of mechanical skill and the use of many special

tools not normally available. The relative positions of the pinion and crownwheel (ring gear) must be set with great accuracy if the gears are to operate silently. Any error may lead to rapid tooth wear and noisy running which will call for expensive renewals.

Due to manufacturing tolerances, renewal of such parts as the housing, the differential carrier, the intermediate plate, the pinion shaft and its bearings and the crownwheel will upset the relative positions just mentioned and it will be necessary to go through the whole procedure for meshing the drive gears. It is, of course, possible to dismantle and reassemble the transmission without the need for adjustment, provided that all shims and spacers are refitted in their original positions. It is also possible to renew parts which obviously have no effect upon the meshing of the drive gears.

The following instructions are therefore given primarily to help those who have access to the necessary tools and precision measuring equipment.

1 Drain oil and remove starter. Prise up flange caps as shown in **FIG 6:2**. Hold input shaft splines securely and engage fifth gear. Remove bolts and withdraw flanges.

2 Remove side cover and withdraw differential assembly. Remove support from front cover 2 (see **FIG 6:1**). Remove front cover with care as reverse gears may fall out.

3 Remove selector fork screw (top arrow in **FIG 6:3**). Remove gear and fork.

4 Engage fifth-speed and lock pinion with tool P37. Remove bolt A from pinion shaft (see **FIG 6:3**). Drive out locking pin from nut B, remove nut and first-speed gear.

5 Select neutral. From underside of housing remove plate and guide fork shown in **FIG 6:4**. Pull out inner shift rod through rear acess hole. Insert screwdriver in guide fork hole and select fifth-speed. **Gears cannot be withdrawn or inserted unless transmission is in this position.**

6 Tap intermediate plate with soft-faced hammer and detach it complete with gears. **Check gasket thickness for correct reassembly.** Hold plate in a vice with soft jaws and prise off spider wheel C (see **FIG 6:3**). Remove first-speed gear and needle bearing from pinion shaft. Shift into neutral.

7 Remove plug and detent spring (top view in **FIG 6:5**). Withdraw selector shaft and detent ball for first and reverse gear (see **FIG 6:18**). Mark forks to avoid confusion and remove shafts, forks and detents (see lower view in **FIG 6:5** and also **FIG 6:18**).

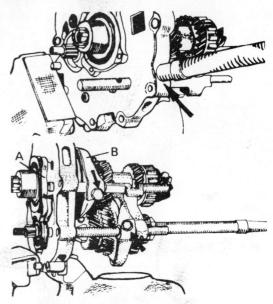

FIG 6:5 Five-speed gearbox. Removing detent plug for selector shaft (top view). Arrows indicate selector fork screws (bottom view), where A is the bearing retaining plate and B is the fork for second and third gear

FIG 6:2 Prising out caps from universal joint flanges

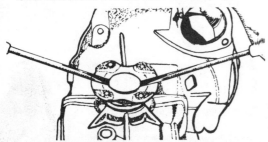

FIG 6:3 Five-speed gearbox. Arrow indicates selector fork retaining screw

Key to Fig 6:3
B Castle nut on input shaft spider wheel

A Pinion shaft bolt
C First and reverse-speed

FIG 6:4 Guide fork for inner shift rod partially removed

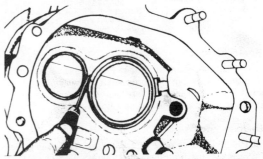

FIG 6:6 Prising out front spring retainer (circlip) for pinion shaft bearing

8 Tap dowels forward and remove throttle linkage. Place intermediate plate under a press with gears downwards and press out input and pinion shafts simultaneously. Balls may fall out of input shaft bearing. Service intermediate plate as in **Section 6:6**. Prise out circlips from centre web as in **FIG 6:6**.

9 Heat housing to 120°C (248°F) and tap out bearing races one at a time using tool P254 and a soft-faced hammer.

Clean the parts and check for damage, cracks or wear. Tooth breakage and subsequent jamming may cause housing cracks and possible damage to bearing bores. Check bearings when clean and dry. Service the various assemblies according to the instructions in the following Sections.

6:5 Servicing the input shaft

Details of the shaft and its components are given in **FIG 6:7**. These may be compared with the shaft for the fourspeed box by referring to **FIG 6:25**.

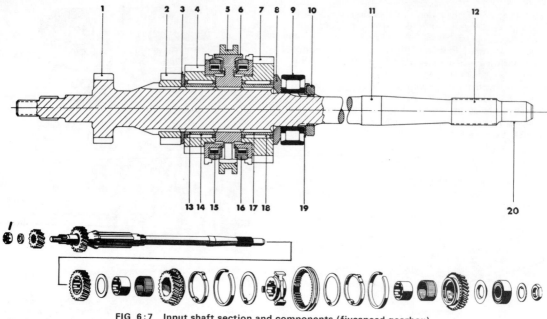

FIG 6:7   Input shaft section and components (fivespeed gearbox)

Key to Fig 6:7   1 Input shaft (with fixed gear for second-speed)   2 Gear of third-speed (fixed)   3 Thrust washer
4 Gear of fourth-speed (free-running)   5 Sliding sleeve   6 Spider   7 Gear of fifth-speed (free-running)   8 Thrust washer (5.9 mm)
9 Roller bearing   10 Nut   11 Oil seal race   12 Splined end for clutch plate   13 Needle bearing inner race
14 Needle bearing cage   15 Brake band   16 Synchronizing ring   17 Needle bearing inner race   18 Needle bearing cage
19 Nut lockplate   20 Spigot for flywheel bearing

Removal:

It is not necessary to remove the differential assembly in order to take out the input shaft. Having pressed the shaft out of the intermediate plate as described in the preceding Section, proceed as follows:

Dismantling:

1 Unlock and remove nut 10 (see **FIG 6:7**) after checking runout. Press roller bearing 9 off shaft. Mark needle bearing cages for position and pull all components off shaft.
2 The inner half of the front bearing race is hard against gear 1. Drift it away a little and use a puller to remove it, taking care not to damage the gear.

Inspection:

Clean parts and check for wear or damage. Runout must be checked before shaft is dismantled because tightening nut 10 may alter it. Assemble bearings on shaft and mount in V-blocks. Check runout of pilot spigot 20. Maximum permissible is .10 mm (.004 inch). Excessive runout up to .30 mm (.012 inch) may be corrected cold under a press, using tools VW.405 and VW.406.

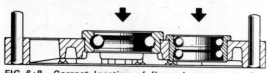

FIG 6:8   Correct location of flanged outer races for bearings in intermediate plate

Check spigot for wear. Check clutch plate splines for radial play. Oil seal race 11 must be smooth and unmarked. Running surfaces of gears and bearings must be unworn and check parts which must be a press fit on the shaft. Gear 1 is integral with the shaft. If worn, renew shaft after checking mating numbers. Also check numbers when renewing gears or bearings. Check synchromesh parts for wear and renew parts, particularly if gearchanging has been noisy.

Reassembling:

Fit all components dry. Gear 2 has its small collar facing the shaft flange. Follow up with thrust washer 3 and inner race 13. Fit cage 14, gear 4 and spider 6. **Used bearing cages must be fitted in original positions.** Fit sleeve 5 followed by bearing 17 and 18 and gear 7. Fit thrust washer 8 and roller bearing 9 with cover ring of cage facing towards the clutch plate splines. Press bearing into place using a tubular extension to avoid damaging the threads at the front end of the shaft. Fit new lockplate 19 with inner tab in the groove in the shaft and under the inner race of the bearing. Oil face and threads of nut and fit with spherical part uppermost. Tighten to 10 to 12 mkg (72 to 86 lb ft). Bend up locking tab. Check mating numbers then press inner half of front bearing race into place.

6:6 Servicing intermediate plate

Dismantling:

Unlock four bolt heads inside plate, remove bolts and lift off bearing retaining plate A (see **FIG 6:5**). Heat intermediate plate to 120°C (248°F) and press out the

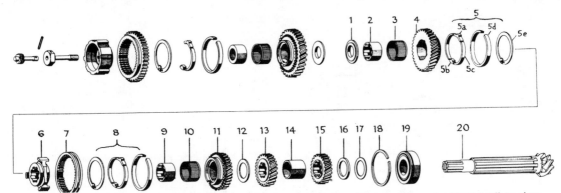

FIG 6:9 Components of pinion shaft (fivespeed gearbox). Numbered items are to rear of intermediate plate

Key to Fig 6:9   1 Thrust washer (6.6 mm)   2 Needle bearing inner race   3 Needle bearing cage   4 Second-speed gear
(free-running)   5 Synchronizing assembly   5a Energizer   5b Stop   5c Brake band   5d Synchronizing ring   5e Retainer
6 Spider   7 Sliding sleeve   8 Synchronizing assembly   9 Needle bearing inner race   10 Needle bearing   11 Third-speed
gear (free-running)   12 Thrust washer   13 Fourth-speed gear (fixed)   14 Spacer bush   15 Fifth-speed gear (fixed)
16 Spacer   17 Shim   18 Retaining ring   19 Roller bearing   20 Pinion shaft

bearing outer races. There are bushings in the holes for the detents and springs (see **FIG 6:18**). These may be withdrawn with tool P.66a and new ones fitted with tool P.262.

Reassembling:

Clean the parts and check the bearings when unlubricated. Heat the plate as before and fit the bearing races as shown in **FIG 6:8**. Use grease to fit any loose balls. Fit the retaining plate and bolts, using new lockplates. Tighten to 2.5 mkg (18 lb ft) and bend up locktabs.

When fitting new detent bushings, drive the long one up to the collar of tool P.262. Drive the short one to the second mark on the tool. Drive the middle-length one to the first mark. **Check that no bush protrudes into a selector shaft bore.**

6:7 Servicing pinion shaft

FIG 6:9 shows the components of the shaft, the parts which are not numbered being in front of the intermediate plate.

Dismantling:

Place the shaft, pinion downwards under a press, using tool P.225 as an abutment to the roller bearing so that the shaft may be pushed through the gear and bearing assemblies. **Mark the positions of the needle bearing cages for correct reassembly and take great care of the shims 17 as they control the endwise location of the pinion.**

Inspection:

After cleaning, look for wear and damage. **Note mating numbers when renewing gears and bearings.** Check shaft for condition of splines and pinion for worn, cracked or broken teeth. Check synchromesh parts for wear, particularly if gearchanging has been noisy. Dismantle these by removing retaining plate 5e with circlip pliers. Make a note of the positions of the bands 5c, energizers 5a and stops 5b. When installed, diameter of ring 5d should be 76.30 mm ± .18 mm (3.004 inch ± .007 inch).

Reassembling:

Remember that the pinion and crownwheel (ring gear) are a matched pair and are marked as such (see **FIG 6:12**). If no parts are renewed which affect the endwise location of the pinion shaft, then there is no problem in reassembling, but otherwise refer to the instructions which follow after these.

1 All parts must be fitted to the pinion shaft in a dry state. Press roller bearing into place with thin coverplate of cage facing away from the pinion. Fit shims 17 as removed or as calculated under 'Pinion shaft shims'.

2 Fit spacer 16. Fit fifth-speed gear 15 with small collar facing away from pinion. Fit spacer bush 14, followed by fourth-speed gear 13 with collar against the bush.

3 Fit thrust washer 12 and needle bearing inner race 9. Fit bearing cage 10. Reassemble synchromesh parts and fit third-speed gear 11 followed by spider 6. **Always fit used needle bearing cages in their original positions.**

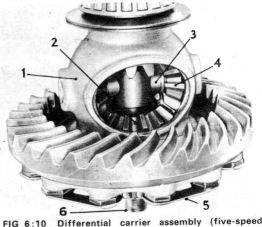

FIG 6:10 Differential carrier assembly (five-speed gearbox)

Key to Fig 6:10   1 Carrier   2 Side gear
3 Spider gearshaft   4 Pinion   5 Lockplate
6 Side gearshaft

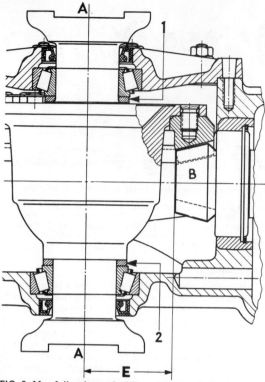

FIG 6:11 Adjusting relative positions of pinion and crownwheel (ring gear). A-A is centreline of differential assembly, B is the pinion and E is the adjustment value. 1 is spacer S1 and 2 is spacer S2

4 Fit inner race 2, bearing cage 3 and sliding sleeve 7. Fit gear 4. Fit bevelled thrust washer 1 with wide face against needle bearing. Follow up with the thin spacer but note that starting with transmission No. 100.407 the washer and spacer were replaced by a single washer 6.60 mm (.26 inch) thick. Using a tubular drift, press on the inner half race for the front bearing. This must be marked with the mating number without the letter X.

Pinion shaft shims:

Preliminary adjustment of the meshing of the pinion with the crownwheel is necessary if parts have been renewed which affect the position of the pinion with respect to the intermediate plate. The plate controls the endwise location of the pinion because the rear roller bearing permits axial movement of the pinion shaft. Final adjustment is made by using gaskets under the intermediate plate after accurate measurement of distance E in **FIG 6:11** (see **Section 6:9**).

Refer to **FIG 6:12** and note that designed dimension R is 63.50 mm (2.50 inch). Manufacturing tolerances make it impossible to set every pinion face to this dimension and any variation is marked at 1 (lefthand view) as a + or − value. 2 is a mating number which must be the same as that on the crownwheel.

The deviation is in $\frac{1}{100}$ mm. Take +4 as an example and call it +.04 mm. Add this to the designed dimension

R and the result is 63.54 mm, which becomes dimension E.

The makers suggest a basic approximation of 64.70 mm as a starting point. Take value E away from this and the answer is 1.16 mm, which is the thickness of shims required (see 17 in **FIG 6:9**). These are made .25, .30 and .40 mm thick. Do not use the earlier thickness of .10 and .15 mm. Calculate the required thickness to the nearest .05 mm, either up or down. Thus 1.16 mm becomes 1.15 mm by using three shims .30 mm thick and one .25 mm thick.

6:8 Overhauling and setting differential

Withdraw the differential unit as described early in **Section 6:4**. If this is done with the transmission in the car, first detach both rear axle halfshafts at the differential flanges. Also detach the clutch cable and the rear throttle linkage. The unit is shown in **FIG 6:10**. See end of **Section 6:1** for 911T differential details. Dismantle as follows:

1 Remove roller bearings with a puller. **Take careful note of spacers.** Inside shaft 6 is a pin which secures the spider gearshaft 3. Drive out this pin and drift out the spider shaft.
2 Remove gears from inside carrier 1. Unlock tabs of plates 5, unscrew bolts and remove crownwheel (ring gear).

Check inside of carrier for wear of gear seats. Check bearings when dry. Renew carrier if worn or if inner races of bearings are not a good fit. Renew complete bearing including outer race as a set. Check gear teeth and spherical seats. Check shafts and side gear splines as well as axle joint flanges.

Side bearings are preloaded by selection of spacers S1 and S2 in **FIG 6:11**, but note that diaphragm springs were used instead of spacer S2 on transmissions up to No. 100.268. **Gear backlash is adjusted by spacer S1.** For the springs to be effective the inner race of the bearing must be free to move on the carrier trunnion. Do not use the diapragm springs on replacement carriers but fit spacers S1 and S2. However, if a carrier with diaphragm springs is being modified to use spacers only, put a packing ring 5 mm (.197 inch) thick under spacer S2.

Reassembling:

Reverse the dismantling procedure, coating bearing surfaces with molybdenum disulphide compound. Make sure to set the locking pin hole in the spider gearshaft so that it lines up with the hole in the longer side gearshaft, then drive the rollpin up to the stop using Tool No. P.257/1. Tighten crownwheel bolts to 9.5 to 10 mkg (69 to 72 lb ft). Tap new lockplates into bolt grooves, squeeze open end inwards with pliers and bend down tabs. Do not forget to fit the spacers before pressing on the bearing inner races.

If new outer races are fitted in the housing or side cover, heat the housings to 120°C or 248°F and drive in the races with a drift.

The crownwheel must be readjusted if a new carrier or a new housing is fitted.

Setting differential position:

Refer to **FIG 6:11**. Fit spacers under side bearings, S1 being 3.5 mm (.138 inch) thick and S2 being 3.0 mm (.118 inch) thick. Insert unit in housing and fit cover

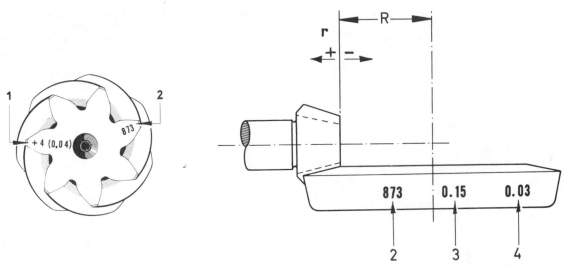

FIG 6:12 Typical pinion and crownwheel (ring gear) markings for use when adjusting relative positions of gears

Key to Fig 6:12   **R** Designed value of 63.50 mm (five-speed) and 54.50 mm (Sportomatic)   **r** Plus or minus deviation from **R** shown in $\frac{1}{100}$ mm (+4) or in mm (+.04)   **1** Deviation r   **2** Mating number   **3** Gear backlash   **4** Deviation from T-value (+ or —mm)

without oil seal. Use a gasket .20 mm (.008 inch) thick and just tighten two opposite nuts. Check gap under cover flange with feelers. Gap for bearing preload should be .15 mm (.006 inch). If gap is, say, .40 mm (.016 inch) when it should be .15 mm (.006 inch), spacer S1 must be replaced with one which is .25 mm (.01 inch) thinner.

Tighten side cover nuts to 2.5 mkg (18 lb ft). Insert axle flange and tighten bolt a little. Check differential drag with a rotating torque measuring device. The pinion must not be engaged and there must be no oil seal in the side cover. Torque to move differential unit must be 18 to 24 cmkg (15.6 to 20.8 lb in). If incorrect, adjust by fitting a different thickness of spacer.

Withdraw unit, remove side bearings and measure spacer thickness at four equidistant points. Determine total thickness of spacers S1 and S2 and say that it is 6.25 mm (.246 inch). To prepare for final adjustment of crownwheel and pinion meshing, spacer S1 must be .10 mm (.004 inch) thinner and spacer S2 the same amount thicker, the total thickness being unaltered. Thus, spacer S1 must be 3.025 mm (.119 inch) thick and spacer S2 must be 3.225 mm (.127 inch) thick. Spacers come in thicknesses from 2.5 to 3.5 mm (.098 to .138 inch) in steps of .10 mm (.004 inch) and there is a .25 mm (.01 inch) washer also available, so that adjustments to the nearest .05 mm (.002 inch) are possible. Round off thickness to the nearest available spacer thickness but make sure that the total thickness of S1 + S2 remains unaltered. As an example, S1 + S2 = 3.025 + 3.225 = 6.25 mm. When rounded off S1 + S2 = 3.0 + 3.25 = 6.25 mm.

Permissible variation in spacer thickness (measured at four points) is .02 mm (.0008 inch). Remove all burrs from spacer edges.

6:9 Adjusting pinion shaft setting and backlash

Preliminary adjustments have been outlined in **Sections 6:7** and **6:8**.

Adjusting pinion shaft:

Fit intermediate plate, gears and selector shafts into housing without a paper gasket. Put spacers on four opposite studs and tighten nuts diagonally to secure plate. Tighten shaft bolt to 11 to 12 mkg (79 to 86 lb ft). Put carrier P.258 on the setting plate (see **FIG 6:13**) and secure the dial gauge so that small pointer is on 1 and large pointer on 0, giving a preload of 1 mm (.04 inch). Fit dummy carrier and side bearings into housing with axial preload of .10 mm (.004 inch) when cover is secured. Use differential spacers if necessary to ensure that carrier has no end play. A notch on the face of the carrier indicates the position of the gauge plunger. Turn carrier until plunger is at right angles to the face of the pinion and note highest reading. Now follows an example of the calculations.

Side of dummy carrier is marked with dimension from centre line to surface for setting plate. Setting plate is marked with dimension from surface to recess for gauge plunger. Add together and say that result is 53.98 mm + 9.52 mm = 63.50 mm (2.5 inch). If gauge reading differs in clockwise direction, subtract the difference. For

FIG 6:13 Dummy carrier P.258 for setting pinion relative to differential assembly centreline. Dial gauge is adjusted to a preload of 1 mm, using a setting plate

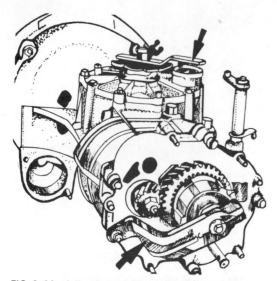

FIG 6:14 Adjusting backlash of crownwheel (ring gear). Top arrow shows dial gauge holder P.259 bolted to axle flange. Bottom arrow points to tool P.259 (part of) which locks pinion shaft against turning

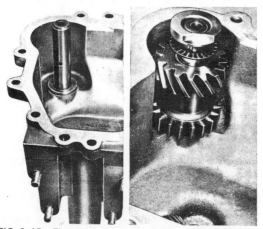

FIG 6:15 Five-speed gearbox. Reverse gearshaft installed with oil hole downwards (lefthand view) and reverse gears fitted, with needle bearing and thrust washer (righthand view)

example, small pointer between 1 and 2, large one at .24 mm. Subtract .24 mm from gauge setting of 63.50 mm and answer is 63.26 mm. If value E (see **FIG 6:11** and **Section 6:7**) is 63.54 mm then pinion is too near and as difference between 63.54 mm and 63.26 mm is .28 mm, that is the thickness of gasket required under the intermediate plate.

If gauge reading differs in anticlockwise direction, add the difference. For example, small pointer between 1 and 0, large one at .08 mm. Add .08 mm to gauge setting of 63.50 mm and result is 63.58 mm. If, for example, value E is 63.68 mm, that figure minus 63.58 mm gives .10 mm, which is the thickness of gasket required.

Paper gaskets for the intermediate plate are available in thicknesses of .10, .15 and .20 mm (.004, .006 and .008

inch). Total thickness may lie between .10 and .50 mm (.004 and .02 inch). If calculations prove that gaskets must be thicker than .50 mm then pinion shaft must be dismantled and further adjustment made to shims 17 (see **FIG 6:9**).

When determining the thickness of gaskets, round off second figure decimal fractions as follows. Make 3 and over into 5 and 7 and over into 10. Thus .28 mm becomes .30 mm.

After the intermediate plate has been installed on the correct gaskets, check value E again. Deviations of ± .03 mm (.001 inch) are permissible.

Adjusting backlash:

Refer to **FIG 6:14**. Build up the transmission with the required gaskets and spacers. Secure the intermediate plate as described in the preceding instructions. Check backlash when securing the side cover on a .20 mm (.008 inch) paper gasket, as there must always be some play between the drive gears. **Jamming of the gears is not permissible**. Tighten nuts to 2.5 mkg (18 lb ft). Fit anchoring tool P.259 to the pinion shaft bolt as shown. Insert the axle flange, fit dial gauge holder P.259 to flange and tighten bolt (top arrow). Fit dial gauge so that its plunger contacts the bottom of the clutch cable bracket. Move holder from stop to stop to determine backlash. Make four checks by turning the crownwheel through 90 deg. each time. Backlash must not differ by more than .05 mm (.002 inch) between each measuring point. The correct figure is etched on the crownwheel (see 3 in **FIG 6:12**), but a backlash of .12 to .18 mm (.005 to .007 inch) is permissible.

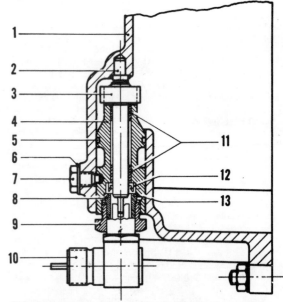

FIG 6:16 Components of tachometer drive as fitted to gearbox front cover

Key to Fig 6:16   1 Front cover   2 Thrust stud
3 Shaft and gear   4 Body   5 O-ring   6 Spring ring
7 Setscrew   8 Elbow drive sleeve   9 Coupling nut
10 Elbow drive   11 Bushes   12 Oil seal   13 Centring disc

Errors may be rectified by adjustment of spacers S1 and S2 (see **Section 6:8**) but total thickness of spacers must not be altered.

6:10 Servicing front cover

Remove front cover as in **Section 6:4** and collect the thrust washer, axial thrust needle bearing, reverse gears and bearings. Remove screw 7 and withdraw tachometer drive (see **FIG 6:16**). If reverse gearshaft needs renewal, drive out retaining pin, heat cover to 120°C or 248°F and drive shaft inward. Press bronze thrust washer off shaft. Check cover for cracks or damage, clean up joint faces. Check gears, shaft and bearings for wear or damage. Renew oil seal for inner shift rod if defective.

To dismantle tachometer drive, hold body 4 between soft jaws in a vice, unscrew nut 9 and pull out drive 10 and centring disc 13 (see **FIG 6:16**). Pull out shaft 3. Renew shaft, bushes or oil seal if defective. Check thrust stud 2 in cover. This is a press fit. Check condition of gears. If the gear which extends from the pinion shaft bolt is worn, it may be removed by driving out the cross-pin (see part 4 in **FIG 6:1**).

When refitting the drive in the body, orientate it so that the cable connection and the locating hole for the set-screw are pointing in the same direction. Insert assembly in cover so that hole lines up with setscrew orifice, insert screw and tighten to 2.5 mkg (18 lb ft). If pinion shaft bolt was removed, tighten to 11 to 12 mkg (79 to 86 lb ft).

Reassembling:

Check that mating numbers of gears are correct. Heat cover to 120°C or 248°F and refit shaft with oil hole pointing down (see lefthand view in **FIG 6:15**). Fit retaining pin. Heat bronze washer to same temperature and fit to shaft, pressing it firmly against cover. Fit bearing cages and spacer bush. Fit gears, thrust needle bearing and washer (see righthand view in **FIG 6:15**).

Fitting cover:

Fit a new .20 mm (.008 inch) paper gasket. Pull reverse gear assembly and thrust washer as near to the end of the shaft as possible. Feed cover into place, making sure that curved recess in thrust washer fits over outer race of ball-bearing. Tighten nuts to 2.5 mkg (18 lb ft).

6:11 Reassembling transmission

Reverse the dismantling procedure. Lubricate the assemblies as required. Heat the housing to 120°C or 248°F when fitting the outer races of the two roller bearings into the central web. Make sure spring rings are correctly seated. If the clutch release bearing guide was

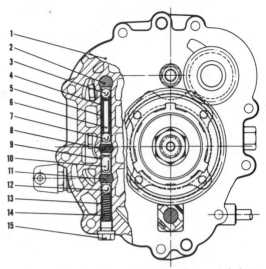

FIG 6:18 Section through detent components in intermediate plate

Key to Fig 6:18
1 Intermediate plate
2 Fourth and fifth selector shaft   3 Ball   4 Detent bush
5 Detent spring of second and fifth-speed   6 Detent pin
7 Ball   8 Second and third selector shaft
9 Detent bush   10 Detent pin   11 First and reverse selector shaft   12 Ball   13 Detent bush
14 Detent spring for reverse   15 Plug

FIG 6:17 Five-speed gearbox. Correct position of single brake band in first-speed synchronizer

FIG 6:19 Arrows in top view show where clearance of 2 to 3 mm must exist. Lower view shows tool P.260 supporting the shafts for selector fork adjustment

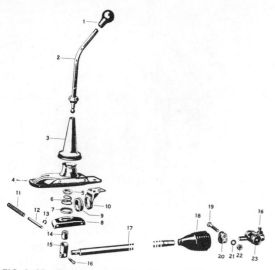

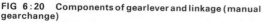

FIG 6:20 Components of gearlever and linkage (manual gearchange)

Key to Fig 6:20   1 Gearlever knob   2 Gearlever
3 Boot   4 Base   5 Spring seat   6 Spring
7 Spring seat   8 Stop plate   9 Guide bush
10 Guide bracket   11 Stop plate thrust spring
12 Guide pin   13 Retainer   14 Ball socket
15 Shift rod joint   16 Tapered screw   17 Shift rod
18 Boot   19 Bolt   20 Clamp   21 Lockwasher   22 Nut
23 Shift rod coupling

removed from the rear face of the housing for attention to the input shaft oil seal, refit it. Note that this seal may be renewed without dismantling the transmission, by prising it out with a screwdriver, taking care not to damage the bore or the running surface of the shaft. Put sealer on the outer circumference of the seal, and oil the lip. Drive seal into place with tool VW.244b.

With front bearing inner races in place, fit both shaft and gear assemblies to the intermediate plate. Use a tubular drift to fit outer halves of inner races, the one for the pinion shaft being marked X. **Make sure mating numbers match.** Insert plate and shaft assemblies into housing, fit spacers to four studs and tighten nuts lightly in diagonal sequence with fifth-speed engaged.

Fit first-speed gear and spacer washer to input shaft. Tighten nut to 6 to 6.5 mkg (43 to 47 lb ft). Secure nut with rollpin. Fit pinion shaft thrust washer with small collar facing bearing. Fit needle bearing race, followed by needle bearing and large helical gear. Make sure only one brake band is fitted to the synchronizing unit as shown in **FIG 6:17**. Fit spider wheel for sliding gear, oil pressure face of bolt and tighten to 11 to 12 mkg (80 to 86 lb ft) while holding input shaft at clutch end with tool P.37. Remove intermediate plate and hold in soft jaws in a vice.

Fit selector shafts and forks. Fit fork 8 (see **FIG 6:1**) and push shaft through until it enters plate. The shaft must be complete with shift arm secured by rollpin. Slightly tighten fork screw on spring washer. Refer to **FIG 6:18** for details of the selector detents and springs. Fit ball 3, stick pin 6 in spring 5 with grease and drop into bore. Fit ball 7.

Fit second and third-speed fork and push its shaft into place with shaft 2 in the neutral position. Press down ball

7 when inserting the shaft in the plate. Slightly tighten fork screw on a spring washer. Push shaft into neutral. Fit detent 10 followed by first and reverse shaft 11 and fit ball 12 with spring 14. Tighten plug to 2.5 mkg (18 lb ft).

Fit gear 20 and fork (see **FIG 6:1**). Slightly tighten fork screw. For help in recognizing the detent springs, the short one should have a free length of 29.2 mm (1.15 inch) with a minimum length of 28.2 mm (1.11 inch). Long spring should be 38.5 mm (1.52 inch) with a minimum of 37.3 mm (1.47 inch).

Take up all free play of sliding gear for first-speed and reverse, pressing it (in neutral) in the direction of forward travel of the car. Put plasticine on gear teeth adjacent to reverse gear and push the transmission cover into place to check that there is at least 1 mm (.04 inch) clearance between the teeth of the two gears under conditions which bring them closest together. Check that selector shaft control forks for first and reverse have a side clearance of 2 to 3 mm (.08 to .12 inch) with those for second and third-speed (see lefthand arrow in top view of **FIG 6:19**). Tighten first and reverse selector fork screw to 2.5 mkg (18 lb ft).

It is not possible to set the remaining forks accurately without supporting the shafts with tool P.260 as shown in the lower view of **FIG 6:19**. Adjust the position of second and third and fourth and fifth-speed forks so that the sliding sleeves are exactly central between the synchronizing rings. After a shift test, tighten the fork screws to 2.5 mkg (18 lb ft), making sure that the control forks clear each other by 2 to 3 mm (.08 to .12 inch) as shown by righthand arrow in top view of **FIG 6:19**.

Take shift rod 1 (see **FIG 6:1**) and assemble the shift lever and pin, making sure the pin and hole tapers are correct. Fit cotterpin.

Insert shift rod into housing and install the intermediate plate and gears, fitting the correct gaskets under the plate as determined during the drive gear meshing adjustments carried out in **Sections 6:7, 6:8** and **6:9**. It is essential to select fifth-speed for this operation and care must be taken not to damage the input shaft oil seal. Shift back into neutral. Set shift lever between selector control forks and pushrod into rear bore. Put on a new gasket and install the guide fork (see **FIG 6:4**), locating the lever in the fork correctly. Fit front cover.

Starting with transmission No. 100.100 there is a breather fitted to the differential section of the transmission housing. If there is no breather pipe or ventilation labyrinth in the front cover which is being fitted as a replacement it is necessary to fit a breather. The hole in the breather must point forward at an angle of 45 deg. from the transmission centre line.

If the reversing light switch is removed, make sure, when refitting it, that the operating pin is fitted with the rounded end entering first.

6:12 Gearshift mechanism

This is illustrated in **FIG 6:20**. Early gearlever knobs were screwed on, but from 21st March 1967 they were pressed into place. The later type of knob has the gearshift pattern marked on it. To remove the pressed-on type, make a steel fork from 6 mm ($\frac{1}{4}$ inch) flat bar, the slot being 15.5 mm ($\frac{5}{8}$ inch) wide to accommodate the lever. Slip

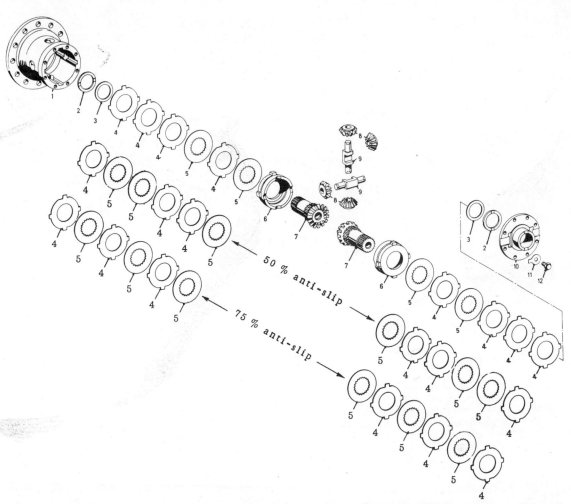

FIG 6:21 Components of ZF self-locking differential with standard assembly of plates and discs in top row. Plate and disc assemblies for 50 per cent and 75 per cent anti-slip effectiveness are also shown

Key to Fig 6:21   1 Differential carrier   2 Thrust washer (non-ferrous)   3 Thrust washer (ferrous)   4 Friction plate   5 Friction disc   6 Side gear ring   7 Side gear   8 Spider gear   9 Spider shaft   10 Differential cover   11 Lockplate   12 Bolt

this under the knob and drive it upwards by striking the bar with a hammer.

With gearlever and heater knobs removed, lift off boot 3 and tunnel cover and release base 4. Remove tunnel cover in rear compartment (4 screws), push boot 18 forward, loosen clamp bolt 19 and drive rod 17 off coupling 23. Pull off clamp and boot. Cut locking wire, unscrew square-headed screw 16 and remove socket 15. With transmission unit removed, gearshift rod may be pulled out rearwards.

Installation:

Refit in the reverse order. Tighten screw 16 to 1.5 mkg (11 lb ft). Coat working faces of coupling 23 with lithium grease. Tighten bolts for gearlever base to 2.5 mkg (18 lb ft). Tighten bolts securing guide bracket 10 to 1.0 mkg (7 lb ft). Adjust linkage as described later.

Overhauling gearlever base:

Remove plastic socket 14 from lever. Remove retainers 13 and push one pin out halfway. Take care that spring 11 does not jump out. Put a cloth round the base and prise the free end of the spring out. Remove the second spring in the same way. Remove stop plate 8. Remove parts 5, 6 and 7. Withdraw lever and clean all parts. Renew worn or defective items.

Reassemble by coating working surfaces with lithium grease and snapping seat 5 into the spring. Insert lever in base and put one retainer on each guide pin. Fit stop plate and partly insert pins. Thread springs over pins. Grind a pilot stub on an old screwdriver so that it will enter the first coils of the spring and compress each spring until it can be inserted in the plate. Fit guide pins and retainers. Coat all parts with lithium grease and drive on ball socket 14.

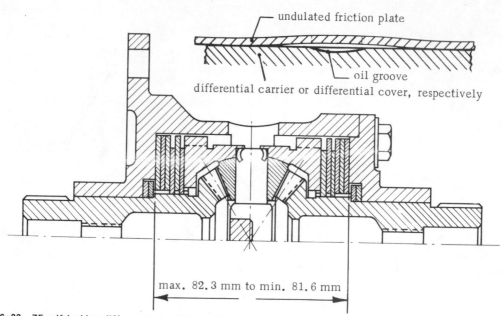

undulated friction plate

oil groove

differential carrier or differential cover, respectively

max. 82.3 mm to min. 81.6 mm

FIG 6:22 ZF self locking differential. In differentials with preloaded disc and plate assemblies, install as in top view. Under 100 kg (220 lb) pressure, check installed length of retarder assembly (lower view)

Adjusting linkage:

Through aperture in tunnel, loosen bolt 19. Put gearlever in neutral and press it to the right as far as it will go. With transmission in neutral, move coupling 23 as far to the left as it will go and tighten the clamp bolt to 2.5 mkg (18 lb ft), using a serrated lockwasher under the nut.

Try all gears and check for play in the linkage. Gearlever play should be the same in all gears in every direction.

Fitting gearlever knob:

There is a locking ring inside the later type of press fit knob. This may be hooked out. Fit a new ring by driving it down until it seats in place. Mark travel depth of knob on lever, select third-speed and drive knob into place with

FIG 6:23 Four-speed gearbox. Single brake band A must be fitted as shown when assembling first-speed synchronizer. This is the opposite of the five-speed arrangement

a block of wood suitably recessed to accommodate the top face of the knob. Check that knob has reached the mark.

6:13 Servicing ZF differential

The components are shown in **FIG 6:21**. Note the additional views of friction disc assemblies for 50 per cent and 75 per cent non-slip effectiveness. These were introduced from 6th March, 1967, the 75 per cent assembly being used for sporting events.

With ordinary differential assemblies, if one wheel is held stationary the other will spin helplessly. In the ZF self-locking assembly this effect is largely eliminated so that the greater the need the greater the torque. Examine **FIG 6:21** and note the squared-off ends of spider shafts 9. These engage angled recesses in side gear rings 6 which are driven by the crownwheel carrier. Driving force thus tends to press both side rings outwards so that they exert a compressive effect on the friction discs and plates. As the discs are splined to the axle shafts, the greater the compression through high torque, the more the assembly is virtually locked together, so that one-sided wheelspin is impossible.

Recommended lubricant is Shell Transmission Oil S.1747.A. In other countries the correct grades are—Australia, Shell SCL Gear Oil 90, Canada, Shell HDR Gear Oil 90 and USA, Shell HDR Gear Oil 90 EP.

Dismantling:

1 Unlock and remove bolts 12. Remove cover 10 (see **FIG 6:21**). Lift side gear 7 together with associated parts out of carrier 1.
2 Lift out spider gears and shafts 8 and 9. Lift out the opposite side gear and friction assembly. **In both cases, do not confuse the locations of the discs and plates 4 and 5. Clean all parts.**

Inspecting:

Check carrier and cover thrust faces for wear and scoring. Check plate grooves for wear. Side gear rings must slide freely in carrier. The locating tabs and thrust faces must not be worn or grooved. Thrust washer faces must be smooth and unworn. Friction discs must slide freely on side gear splines. Check plates for worn tabs and spline teeth.

Check dimension indicated in **FIG 6:22** by assembling all internal parts between the carrier and its cover and putting them under a load of 100 kg (220 lb) in a press. Tolerance lies between a maximum of 82.3 mm (3.24 inch) and a minimum of 81.6 mm (3.213 inch). Renew worn parts which reduce overall length below the minimum.

Reassembling:

Fit non-ferrous thrust washer 2 with machined recess downwards. Fit steel washer 3, then plates and discs in order of removal, starting and finishing with a plate. Differentials fitted with pre-loaded disc and plate assemblies must have the undulated plate fitted first and last, and so arranged that a space exists between the oil groove in the carrier and the cover and the bow in the plate as shown by the insert in the illustration. Check that plates and discs are correctly assembled (see **FIGS 6:21** and **6:22**).

Continue assembling the side gear, spider shafts and gears, and second side gear and the second set of plates and discs. Fit the steel washer followed by the non-ferrous one with the groove facing upwards. Secure the cover, tightening the bolts on new lockplates to a torque of 2.5 mkg or 18 lb ft. Turn up locking tabs.

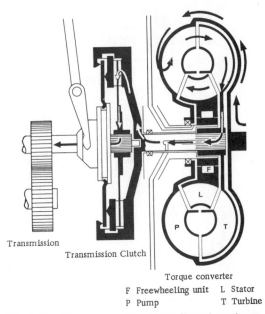

Transmission
Transmission Clutch

Torque converter
F Freewheeling unit   L Stator
P Pump   T Turbine

FIG 6:24 Diagram showing power flow through converter and clutch in Sportomatic transmission

The assembled differential must turn freely under a torque of 1 to 1.5 mkg (7.2 to 10.8 lb ft) without binding.

Note that slight noises may be heard when driving through sharp curves under power. These are inherent in the design and are not the result of defects.

Note also that the ZF self-locking differential must always be used in conjunction with NADELLA halfshafts.

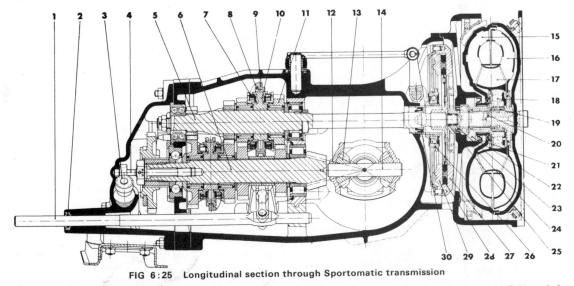

FIG 6:25 Longitudinal section through Sportomatic transmission

Key to Fig 6:25   1 Selector shaft   2 Oil seal   3 Speedometer gearshaft   4 Speedometer drive gear   5 Input shaft
6 Pinion shaft   7 Synchronizing ring   8 Sliding sleeve   9 Selector fork   10 Spider   11 Fourth-speed gear   12 Differential case
13 Pinion gear   14 Pinion gearshaft   15 Pump   16 Turbine   17 Stator   18 Freewheeling unit   19 Turbine shaft bush
20 Oil restrictor in turbine shaft   21 Oil seal   22 Freewheeling unit support   23 Clutch pilot needle bearing   24 Oil seal
25 O-ring   26 Clutch release bearing   27 Clutch carrier and turbine shaft   28 Clutch plate   29 Clutch pressure plate
30 Oil seal

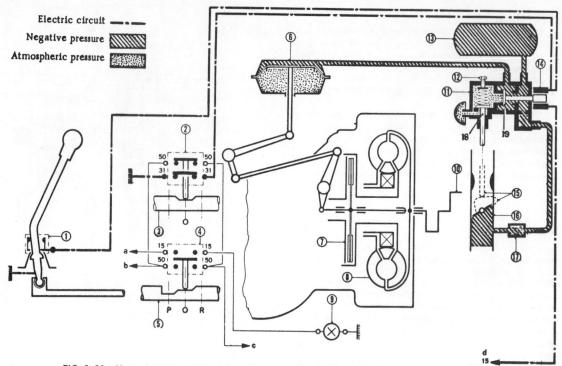

Electric circuit — · — · —
Negative pressure ▨
Atmospheric pressure ▨

FIG 6:26 How clutch is disengaged when gearlever is moved on Sportomatic transmission

Key to Fig 6:26   1 Microswitch in gearlever   2 Bypass switch   3 Gear selector shaft   4 Reverse light switch and 'park' position contact   5 Shift rod P and R   6 Vacuum servo unit   7 Transmission clutch   8 Torque converter   9 Reverse light   10 Crankshaft   11 Control valve   12 Adjusting screw   13 Vacuum reservoir   14 Electric solenoid switch   15 Cam and plunger   16 Inlet manifold   17 Check valve   18 Auxiliary valve   19 Main valve   **a** Wire from fuse 1   **b** Wire from ignition switch   **c** Wire to starter terminal 50   **d** Wire to intermediate fuse 8/15 A

FIG 6:27 Sportomatic transmission. Separating torque converter housing from transmission

Key to Fig 6:27   1 Mounting stud   2 Intermediate lever   3 Clevis   4 Servo unit   5 Clutch rod

6:14 The fourspeed transmission

When servicing this transmission, follow the instructions for the five-speed type. For reference purposes it will be found that the Sportomatic fourspeed gearbox closely resembles the manual box and **FIGS 6:25** and **6:35** may be useful.

As first-speed is inside the gearbox, the front cover accommodates reverse gear only. Due to reversed action the synchronizing parts for first-speed gear must be fitted the opposite way round (see **FIG 6:23**). Note that there is only one brake band A. This gear occupies the position taken by gear 4 in **FIG 6:9**. Use the same torque values and adjustment data as those given for the five-speed transmission.

6:15 Sportomatic description

FIG 6:25 is a sectional view of the Sportomatic transmission showing the torque converter 15, 16 and 17 which is driven by the engine. The torque converter casing is filled with oil and fan blades on pump unit 15 cause a power transfer to blades on turbine 16 through the inertia of the oil. Power from the turbine is transmitted to the gearbox through a normal single-plate clutch 27, 28 and 29. This clutch is used for gearchanging, being operated by a vacuum-servo unit. This unit (6 in **FIG 6:26**) is connected to a control valve 11 which is electrically operated when a microswitch on the gearlever is closed.

The switch closes as soon as the gearlever is moved for gear selection. Releasing the lever, after a gearshift, opens the switch, the control valve allows atmospheric pressure to break down the pull of the vacuum servo unit and the clutch re-engages. Rapid accelerator opening causes a still more rapid engagement of the clutch, the throttle spindle carrying a cam which operates a plunger to open an auxiliary valve in the control unit (see parts 15 and 18 in **FIG 6:26**).

A pump driven from the lefthand camshaft keeps the converter filled with oil and promotes cooling by oil circulation. The oil is drawn from the main oil tank, the outlet from the tank being 30 mm higher than that for engine oil circulation to ensure that a leaking converter will not cause failure of engine lubrication. To prevent excessive temperature rise under adverse conditions there is an oil temperature gauge and a red warning light on the instrument panel. When the gauge shows 145°C (295°F) the lamp will light up and the driver must drop down into a lower gear to reduce oil temperature.

6:16 Routine maintenance (Sportomatic)

Lubrication:

Follow the recommendations in **Section 6:2** for the gearbox and differential. Check the oil level in the tank by means of the dipstick. Do this with the engine running. Top-up with oil to the specification given in **Chapter 1**. Change oil at the intervals recommended in the same chapter, the quantity being 9 litres (19 US pints or 15.8 Imp pints). After an overhaul, when it is necessary to fill the torque converter and the oil pipes, fill up with 11.5 litres (24 US pints or 20¼ Imp pints). The converter must be filled with oil before checking the level by dipstick. If there is any doubt about this, detach the oil return pipe from the converter at the tank, run the engine and check that oil flows from the pipe.

Clutch free play:

Check this every 6000 miles. Raise the car and open throttle fully to depressurize vacuum servo unit. Push clutch intermediate lever 2 towards righthand rear wheel (see **FIG 6:27**). Free play at this point should be at least 5 mm (.20 inch). If play is less, readjust as follows:
1 Remove power unit (see **Section 6:3**). Remove clevis pin from fork 3.
2 Pull actuating rod of vacuum servo unit 4 right out to stop. Push intermediate lever 2 towards servo unit as far as possible.
3 The holes in the fork must be farther away from the servo unit than the hole in the intermediate lever by 10 to 12 mm (.40 to .47 inch). Refit the clevis pin, using a new splitpin. Tighten locknut on rod. Check control valve adjustment then refit power unit.

Control valve adjustment:

Do this every 6000 miles or when required as in preceding notes. Control linkage and engine idling speed must be correctly adjusted first.

Upshift on acceleration is adjusted as follows:

1 Refer to **FIG 6:28**. Clearance at 3 must be 1.5 mm (.06 inch) when the throttles are set for idling. Cam 6 must be fully returned.

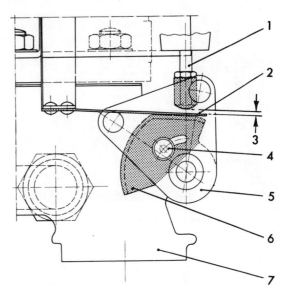

FIG 6:28 On Sportomatic transmission there must be correct clearance between control valve plunger and drag spring

Key to Fig 6:28 1 Control valve plunger 2 Drag spring 3 Correct clearance of 1.5 mm (.059 inch) 4 Socket-head bolt 5 Plate on throttle cross-shaft 6 Cam 7 Inlet manifold

FIG 6:29 Control valve for Sportomatic transmission. White arrow points to cover over adjusting screw, black arrow to splitpin securing cable connector

2 Put a 3 mm (.12 inch) shim under the lefthand idling stop screw (see **Chapter 2**). Adjust cam so that drag spring just touches control valve plunger 1.
3 Remove shim. In this position the original clearance of 1.5 mm may be different but a minimum clearance of 1.0 mm (.04 inch) must be maintained.

Downshift on deceleration is adjusted as follows:

1 Drive the car or run it on a roller stand. As a rough guide on a standing vehicle, set the handbrake, let the engine idle and engage a gear. Time lag between releasing gearlever and perceptible impact of engagement must be .30 to .50 seconds.

FIG 6:30 Sportomatic transmission. Cable connections for temperature switch and temperature gauge sensor

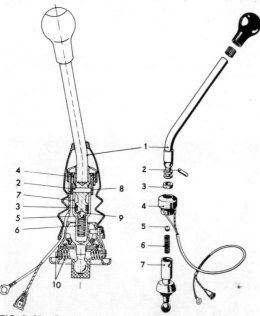

FIG 6:31 Details of the Sportomatic gearlever and microswitch

Key to Fig 6:31   1 Gearlever   2 Retaining pin
3 Stop ring   4 Microswitch   5 Ball   6 Spring
7 Gearlever lower part   8 Position of switch when engaged
with pin   9 Parts to be lightly lubricated   10 Spring and
guide pin

2 Check under driving conditions by running at 4500 rev/min in 'D'. Take foot off throttle and shift down to 'L'. Clutch should engage without time lag, but the rear wheels must not lock. If necessary, adjust time lag as follows:

3 Remove air cleaners. Remove plastic cover over control valve adjusting screw (white arrow in **FIG 6:29**). Turn screw in to give a softer delayed clutch engagement. Turn screw anticlockwise to give a harder and more instantaneous clutch engagement. Do not turn more than $\frac{1}{4}$ to $\frac{1}{2}$ a turn at a time. Refit cover and air cleaners.

Cleaning maintenance:

There is an air filter for the control valve at the end opposite to the electrical connections (see **FIG 6:29**). Clean this every 6000 miles.

Clean electrical contacts in gearlever switch and re-adjust if necessary. Do this every 6000 miles (see **Section 6:21**).

6:17 Driving hints (Sportomatic)

Gearshift symbols are: P (Parking lock), R (Reverse), L (Low gear for steep hills), D (for city driving), D3 (for moderate highway speeds), D4 (for high-speed motorways).

Engine will not start unless gearlever is at P. Use hand throttle for idling when engine is cold. Start off in D or use L on steep hills. Shift up by taking foot off throttle, moving gearlever and taking hand away. **Do not shift down when engine rev/min are very high or engine may be overspeeded.**

If oil temperature warning light goes on, shift to a lower gear.

Gear may remain engaged for brief stops. To park, move gearlever to P when car has stopped moving. Pull on handbrake.

6:18 Removal and installation (Sportomatic)

Removal of the power unit is covered in **Section 6:3**. When refitting the assembly, make sure the heating ducts are not jammed. The best plan is to slide these into place on the heat exchanger outlets just before the power unit reaches its final position. Tighten engine and transmission support bolts to 9.5 mkg (69 lb ft). Half-axle flanges must be free from grease. Hollow side of serrated washers must face the baseplates and tighten the Allen bolts to 4.3 mkg (31 lb ft).

6:19 Separating and refitting transmission (Sportomatic)

Just to the rear of the vacuum servo unit is the temperature sensor (see **FIG 6:30**). The electrical cables have been detached. Now detach the oil hose and the pressure pipe. Loosen the oil hose clamp. Detach the vacuum hose from the servo unit.

Unhook and withdraw the rear throttle control rod. Through the large apertures in the housing, remove the angled 12-point bolts which secure the torque converter to the coupling plate. Remove bolts and nuts joining engine to transmission. As units are separated, take care that the torque converter remains in its housing. A short length of flat steel strip may be bolted to one of the housing bolt holes to keep the torque converter in place.

When refitting the engine to the transmission, use a torque of 4.7 mkg (34 lb ft) on the attaching nuts and bolts. The 12-point bolts for securing the torque converter to the coupling plate must be tightened to 2.4 to 2.6 mkg (17 to 19 lb ft). Set the clutch free play as described in **Section 6:16**.

6:20 Servicing control valve and sensors (Sportomatic)

Control valve:

A faulty valve must be renewed. To remove it, detach battery leads. Remove air cleaner assembly after detaching oil tank breather hose and small hose for breather valve.

Withdraw rubber cap from valve, remove splitpin (see black arrow in **FIG 6:29**) and pull off wire connector.

Detach hoses from valve and release bracket from carburetter.

When fitting a control valve, coat sliding surface of cam and drag spring with molybdenum disulphide grease. Adjust valve as in **Section 6:16**. Make sure cable connector is well seated. Re-drill splitpin hole if necessary.

Temperature switch and gauge sensor:

These are shown in **FIG 6:30**. They may be removed without taking the power unit out of the car by following the instructions for removing the engine and transmission as described in **Chapter 1** and **Section 6:3** up to the point where the unit is lowered a little. The switch and sensor are then accessible from above. Pull cables off and remove.

When refitting, heat and quench the copper gaskets to anneal them. Tighten switch and sensor to 4.5 to 5.0 mkg (33 to 36 lb ft). Tighten engine mounting bolts to 9.5 mkg (69 lb ft).

6:21 Servicing gearlever and microswitch (Sportomatic)

Refer to **FIG 6:31**. Remove and refit microswitch as follows:

1 Lift rubber boot and remove tunnel covering. Release base flange from tunnel and lift slightly.
2 Detach microswitch cables in tunnel and lift away lever and base.
3 Drive off gearlever knob as described at the start of **Section 6:12**. Pull boot and switch off lever.

Clean dirty switch contacts or renew switch. Reassemble by pushing switch on lever with split facing forward. Push far enough to engage pin 2. Check contact gap with lever in neutral position. Gap must be .30 to .40 mm (.012 to .016 inch). Alter by bending outer contact tabs. Fit switch top and dust boot. Refit knob as described in **Section 6:12**. Connect cable connectors and fit assembly to tunnel. Earth lead from switch goes under front lefthand bolt. Tighten 8 mm bolts to 2.5 mkg (18 lb ft) and 6 mm bolts to 1.0 mkg (7.2 lb ft).

Overhauling gearlever base:

Apart from the microswitch, the rest of the assembly resembles that for the manual gearbox lever, so refer to **Section 6:12** for instructions. Having fitted the plastic ball socket to the lever, lightly grease stop ring 3 and push onto lever. Grease spring 6 and insert in lower part 7, grease ball and lever and insert in lower part. Fit retaining pin 2. It must enter easily to prevent switch malfunctioning. Install switch and knob.

6:22 Servicing torque converter and clutch (Sportomatic)

Removing:

With engine detached from transmission as described in **Section 6:19**, withdraw torque converter. **Oil will run out.** Cover converter to keep out dirt. Remove external and internal nuts securing converter housing to transmission casing. Release front end of clutch rod 5 from intermediate lever 2 (see **FIG 6:27**). Part housing from casing while disengaging clutch release bearing from fork.

FIG 6:32 Sportomatic transmission. Removing freewheel support from clutch carrier plate

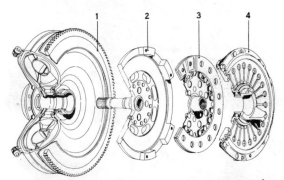

FIG 6:33 Clutch and torque converter components for Sportomatic transmission

Key to Fig 6:33
2 Turbine shaft and clutch carrier plate
4 Clutch pressure plate
1 Torque converter
3 Clutch driven plate

Remove socket-head bolts from clutch pressure plate flange, loosening them a turn at a time diagonally to prevent distortion. Withdraw pressure plate, noting that release bearing may fall out. Remove clutch driven plate. Remove socket-head bolts from freewheel support, fit two long bolts in opposite holes and drive out support with oil seal (see **FIG 6:32**).

Remove circlip from turbine shaft 2 in **FIG 6:33**. Support housing on blocks and drive out turbine shaft. Using a punch at alternating points, drive out shaft bearing and push out oil seal.

Inspecting converter and clutch:

Refer to **Chapter 5** for instructions on checking clutch condition but note that minimum thickness over linings (uncompressed) is 5.5 mm (.217 inch). Also, lateral run-out must not exceed .50 mm (.02 inch).

Torque converters cannot be repaired, so renew one which is damaged.

Check clutch face of turbine shaft and carrier assembly. Renew assembly if heavily scored. Check needle bearing and inspect hub seat and oil passage. Bearing is part 23 in **FIG 6:25**. If worn, needle bearing and oil seal may be extracted with a puller and a new bearing driven in with tool P361. The oil seal is fitted with tool P362. Grease

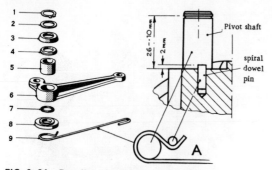

FIG 6:34 Details of clutch intermediate lever for Sportomatic transmission. Upper view on right shows correct assembly of pin and pivot, lower view A shows correct installation of spring

Key to Fig 6:34   1 Lock ring   2 Washer   3 Grommet
4 Spacer   5 Bush   6 Intermediate lever   7 O-ring
8 Thrust ring   9 Spring

bearing with molybdenum disulphide grease, using it sparingly so that clutch plate cannot be contaminated.

Check ballbearing in housing when dry after cleaning. To fit a new bearing, heat housing to 120°C or 248°F. and drive it in with tool P359. Renew the smaller oil seal by driving in with tool P359. Oil the sealing lip.

Check freewheel support and turbine shaft bushing for wear. Check oil passages. A defective support must be renewed as an assembly, complete with bushing and sealing sleeve (see 22 in **FIG 6:25**).

Reassembling:

Secure the freewheel support with three bolts and drive in the turbine shaft using tool P362. Remove bolts and support and fit circlip on shaft. Refit freewheel support, tightening socket-head bolts diagonally to 1.4 mkg (10 lb ft). Fit new O-rings to bolts. Refit seal and oil lip.

Centre clutch driven plate with a suitable mandrel (see **Chapter 5**). Lightly coat both sides of diaphragm spring segments with molybdenum disulphide grease and work release bearing in diagonally from inside. Fit clutch pressure plate, tightening bolts diagonally a turn at a time to 1.4 mkg (10 lb ft). Make sure plate is seating on dowels and release bearing is free.

Refitting:

Use molybdenum disulphide grease to coat contact faces of clutch release fork and bearing, also pilot at rear end of gearbox input shaft. Fit engine mounting bolt and spring washer into housing adjacent to temperature sensor body. **Vacuum servo unit prevents fitting bolt later on.** Bring mounting flanges together while guiding clutch release bearing into fork. Tighten large nuts to 4.0 mkg (29 lb ft) and smaller nuts to 2.2 mkg (16 lb ft).

Torque converter must hold a small quantity of oil during assembly. Put about .50 litres of engine oil in a new converter. The equivalent is 1 US pint and slightly less than 1 Imp pint. Slide converter on freewheel support and turbine shaft. Refit engine to transmission.

6:23 Servicing clutch controls (Sportomatic)

Intermediate lever:

Components of the lever are shown in **FIG 6:34**. To remove lever, detach clutch rod and actuating rod clevis. Remove circlip 1, washer 2, grommet 3, spacer 4 and lever 6. Lift off O-ring 7, thrust ring 8 and spring 9.

Renew pivot shaft and bush 5 if worn. Renew lever if eyes are worn. To remove and refit shaft and dowel pin, heat housing to 120°C or 248°F. Install to dimensions given on right in **FIG 6:34**. Coat shaft with molybdenum disulphide grease. Fit spring as shown at A. Fit thrust ring with cavity over dowel pin and end of spring. Fit O-ring, lever and remaining parts. Install circlip.

Clutch fork:

Detach rear end of clutch rod 5 from release fork lever (see **FIG 6:27**). Fork is carried on shaft located in transmission casing, holes being covered on outside by caps. Prise out caps with two screwdrivers. Drive out rollpin securing fork to shaft. Drift out the shaft and remove fork and washers.

If worn, renew the shaft bushes, driving them below the outer surface so that the caps may be refitted. Reassemble the fork and shaft so that the holes for the rollpin are aligned. Fit the rollpin. Use molybdenum disulphide grease on shaft and bushes.

6:24 Overhauling gearbox (Sportomatic)

Apart from the parking lock shown in **FIG 6:36**, the gearbox is much the same as the manual fourspeed box. Sectional views in **FIGS 6:25** and **6:35** will be found useful, and a comparison with the fivespeed manual box shown in **FIG 6:1** will reveal how closely the components behind the intermediate plate resemble each other. Reading **Section 6:14** will show how the parts in front of the intermediate plate differ.

Servicing the fourspeed gearbox and differential unit may be carried out by following the instructions in **Sections 6:4** to **6:11**. Any differences which call for changes in procedure will be covered in the rest of this section.

Initial dismantling:

1 Release clutch intermediate lever from vacuum servo clevis (see **FIG 6:27**). Release servo unit and bracket from transmission casing.

2 Remove transmission front support. Remove parking lock cap screw just above tachometer elbow drive. Withdraw spring and ball. Remove bypass switch.

3 Remove front cover. Refer to **FIG 6:36** and remove parking lockpin and ball from reverse selector fork 1. Remove circlip 6 and pull off reverse sliding gear 5 and fork. Detach springs and lift off parking lock lever and pawl 2.

4 Select fourth-speed by turning selector rod clockwise and pulling it out. Fit tool P37 to splines at rear end of input shaft to prevent turning and unscrew bolt 3. Remove splined muff.

5 Remove rollpin 4 and unscrew castle nut. Remove reversing light switch and actuating pin. Remove selector shaft guide fork and continue with removal of intermediate plate as in **Section 6:4**. Carry on dismantling as instructed for the fivespeed transmission.

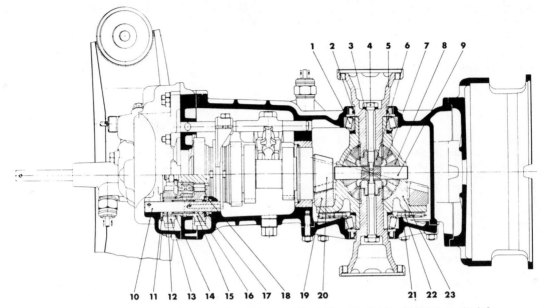

FIG 6:35   Plan view of Sportomatic gearbox and final drive, the front end being on the left

Key to Fig 6:35   1 Side bearing   2 Oil seal   3 Washer   4 Bolt   5 Axle flange   6 Threaded piece   7 Side gear
8 Pinion gear   9 Pinion gearshaft   10 Reverse gearshaft   11 Thrust washer   12 Caged needle bearing   13 Gear for reverse
14 Retaining ring   15 Gear for reverse   16 Caged needle bearing   17 Thrust needle bearing   18 Thrust ring
19 Ring gear (crownwheel)   20 Pinion shaft   21 Transmission side cover   22 Bolt   23 Differential case

Pinion shaft:

Note, when servicing the pinion shaft according to **Section 6:7**, that the dimension R (see **FIG 6:12**) is not 63.50 mm but 54.50 mm (2.146 inch). The method of calculating the spacer thickness remains the same.

Input shaft:

As can be seen from part 5 in **FIG 6:25**, the gear for first-speed is splined to the shaft and is mounted to the rear of the intermediate plate, the shaft carrying no gear in front of the plate as it does in the fivespeed box. The gear may be pressed off the shaft together with the inner race half of the ballbearing. When refitting gear, its small collar faces outward.

When identifying the gears, remember that there is one speed less, so that what is called a second-speed gear in the fivespeed transmission is the first-speed gear in the fourspeed gearbox, and so on.

Adjusting pinion shaft setting and backlash:

Follow the instructions in **Section 6:9** but remember that dimension R in **FIG 6:12** is not 63.50 mm but 54.50 mm (2.146 inch) in the Sportomatic transmission. This does not, however, affect the method of making the adjustments. In the case of backlash the dial gauge is mounted on the axle flange as shown in **FIG 6:14** but the gauge plunger must be fitted with an angular sensor which is offset. This is made to bear on a projecting fin on the front one of the two lowest ribs on the side cover.

Overhauling differential:

The method given in **Section 6:8** may be followed, but note that there is no rollpin to secure the spider shaft. Reference to part 4 in **FIG 6:35** will show that the shaft is secured by short projections on the flange bolts. Make sure the hole in the shaft is correctly aligned when assembling. Note the use of threaded blocks 6 and spring retainers. These must be inserted in the side gears before the spider shaft is fitted.

FIG 6:36   Sportomatic transmission. Parking lock and reverse gears

Key to Fig 6:36   1 Reverse selector fork
2 Parking lever and pawl   3 Pinion shaft bolt   4 Roll pin
5 Reverse sliding gear   6 Circlip

Servicing intermediate plate:

Follow the instructions in **Section 6:6** but start by drawing off the front reverse gear with a puller. This will break the retaining ring (see parts 13 and 14 in **FIG 6:35**). **Make sure broken ring is removed.**

When reassembling, push gear 15 into place from inside. Fit a new retaining ring in the groove in the splines on the outside of the plate. Fit gear 13 while squeezing the ring with pliers. Tap gear into place.

Servicing front cover:

Follow the instructions in **Section 6:10**. Refer to **FIG 6:35** and note that reverse gear 13 may, in some cases, touch the reverse sliding gear. Starting with transmissions 4180176 and 3180261 respectively, a spacer was fitted between the cover and the bronze washer 11. Do not forget to fit this spacer.

Before refitting cover, grease the parking lockpin and insert in selector fork bore, followed by the ball. With cover installed, refit parking lock ball and spring and tighten plug to 3.5 to 4.0 mkg (25 to 30 lb ft).

Those transmissions which are fitted with the spacer just mentioned must have the axial play of the reverse gear checked. Select reverse by turning selector rod to the left and pulling out. If reverse gear binds, fit a second gasket under the cover flange.

Reassembling transmission:

Follow the instructions in **Section 6:11** but remember that when they mention engaging fifth-speed gear, convert this to fourth-speed gear, and to the other gears where applicable. Note the following variations:

1 When intermediate plate is installed, put washer on input shaft with bevel outwards and tighten nut to 9.0 to 11.0 mkg (65 to 80 lb ft). Lock rear end of input shaft against turning, using tool P37. After fitting roll-pin, push splined muff onto pinion shaft with inner splines facing outwards. Fit and tighten pinion shaft bolt.

2 The selector rod detent spring lengths are 38.5 mm (1.52 inch) for first and fourth-speed gears and 37.3 mm (1.47 inch) for reverse gear and parking lock.

3 Having tightened the selector fork screws and checked clearance between control forks, insert the detent pin with fork rod for gears 1 and 2 in neutral (see part 8 in **FIG 6:18**). Insert rod for reverse and parking lock (part 11). Make sure detent pin is still in place.

4 Grease and fit thrust bearing 17 in **FIG 6:35** with needles facing reverse gear 15.

5 When fitting the intermediate plate and gear assembly, pull out the selector rod for reverse and parking lock until it rests against the plate. With plate installed, push rod into housing bore (neutral position) and fit detent ball and spring, followed by screwed plug. Test-shift to check that detent pin is still in place.

6 After fitting the guide fork (see **FIG 6:4**), slide reverse gear fork and gear onto selector rod and pinion shaft and fit circlip to rod (see **FIG 6:36**). Grease and insert parking lock pin in selector rod and fork, followed by the ball. Fit parking lock lever and pawl and connect springs. Fit front cover and check reverse gear (see 'Servicing front cover').

6:25 Fault diagnosis (manual gearbox)

(a) Difficulty in changing gear

1 Bent or worn gearshift mechanism
2 Shift rod coupling wrongly set
3 Faulty or worn synchronizing mechanism
4 Faulty clutch or release bearing
5 Stiffness of clutch pedal, cable or release mechanism
6 Input shaft spigot bearing tight
7 Excessive clutch clearance
8 Faulty selector rod detent or springs

(b) Noisy gearchanging

1 Check 3 to 7 in (a)
2 Wrong grade of transmission oil

(c) Slipping out of gear

1 Check 8 in (a)
2 Excessive end float of free-running gears
3 Worn synchronizing teeth
4 Selector fork wrongly positioned
5 Gearshift mechanism worn
6 Worn bearings

(d) Noisy transmission

1 Check 2 and 6 in (c)
2 Incorrect or insufficient lubricant
3 Worn drive gears and differential
4 Insufficient preload on differential bearings
5 Drive gears incorrectly meshed

6:26 Fault diagnosis (Sportomatic)

(a) Clutch slip

1 Oily linings
2 Defective clutch or operating linkage

(b) Clutch slips after gearshift

1 Control valve out of adjustment

(c) Too fast or slow clutch engagement after downshift

1 Control valve needs adjusting

(d) Clutch will not disengage

1 Clutch linkage wrongly adjusted
2 Leaking hoses or vacuum reservoir, blocked hoses
3 Defective servo unit
4 Defective bearing for input shaft spigot
5 Control valve solenoid faulty, break in circuit
6 Dirty gearlever switch contacts, poor earthing

(e) Engine dies on gearshifting, idling cannot be adjusted

1 Check 2 and 3 in (d)
2 Leaking check valves in inlet manifold

(f) Clutch not engaging after downshift, engages too rapidly on opening throttle

1 Gearshift switch contacts sticking or shorted
2 Shortcircuited wire between switch and solenoid
3 Sticking solenoid in control valve

(g) Car leaps when gearlever is released with engine idling and gear engaged

1 Idling speed too high
2 Control valve wrongly adjusted

(h) High-pitched whine from converter

1 Too little oil in converter
2 Oil pressure too low
3 Loss of oil through pump hub of converter
4 Converter seams leaking

(i) Poor acceleration from good engine and transmission system

1 Defective torque converter
   To check this, apply handbrake, select D4 and open throttle. Speed should be 2400 to 2800 rev/min. Keep temperature below red section on dial.

CHAPTER 7

REAR AXLE AND SUSPENSION

7:1 General description

The layout of the system is shown in **FIG 7:1**, each independent suspension unit consisting of a radius arm 1 bolted at the rear end to the flange of control arm 3. The front end of the radius arm is coupled to the outer splined end of torsion bar 2, the inner end of the bar being fixed.

Triangulated control of the suspension is maintained by arm 3, the inner end being pivoted in a bracket on the body. Drive from the transmission is taken through half-shaft 4, each shaft being provided with two universal joints. Telescopic hydraulic dampers 5 are fitted and each incorporates a rubber buffer which supplements the torsion bar springing. Eccentric bolts 6 and 7 permit adjustments to camber and wheel tracking.

Starting with 1968 models, 911T (Sportomatic), 911L and 911S cars had ventilated brake discs, new rear hubs with spacer rings and a wider track. Stabilizer (anti-roll) bars were standard on the 911S, and from 1968 models onwards the bar was optional on all types.

There is no routine maintenance required on the rear axle or suspension system.

7:2 Damper maintenance

BOGE dampers are standard on 911T, 911L and all Targa models. Koni dampers are standard on 911S cars and are optional on all other types except Targa models. From 1968 models onwards the rubber buffer has 9 rings instead of 8. A section through the standard damper is given in **FIG 7:2**. Adjust Koni dampers as instructed in **Chapter 8**.

Removing, testing and refitting damper:

Do this with car standing on its wheels. Alternatively, if car is jacked up, lift radius arm with special tool P.289 or lift outer end of control arm with a jack. In engine compartment, remove cap and self-locking nut from top of damper (see **FIG 7:3**). Damper rod may be held with spanner on flats. Release lower end of damper from control arm.

Clean damper. If heavily coated with oily dirt the damper may need renewal. Hold damper vertically in a vice and reciprocate top end several times to fill cylinder 11 with fluid (see **FIG 7:2**). Press top end in and out through full strokes to check resistance. If excessive free play is evident at any point, damper must be renewed. Check condition of rubber buffer 6. Fit buffer with 9 rings to 1968 models onwards. Do not try to dismantle damper further. **Adjustment or topping up is not possible.**

When reassembling top cover 8, make sure that stop disc 9 is fitted so that its grooves face downwards. Fit the rubber buffer dry.

FIG 7:1 Layout of rear suspension system (left). Eccentric adjusters for camber and tracking (right)

Key to Fig 7:1 1 Radius arm 2 Torsion bar 3 Control arm 4 Halfshaft 5 Telescopic damper 6 Camber adjustment 7 Tracking adjustment

Refit damper in reverse order, tightening lower bolt to 7.5 mkg (54 lb ft). Renew rubber grommets 3 if deteriorated and tighten nut until they are partially compressed.

7:3 Servicing axle halfshafts

'Nadella' and 'LÖBRO' halfshafts are shown in **FIG 7:4**. Cars with ZF self-locking differential must be fitted with 'Nadella' shafts. 911 and 911S cars are fitted with either type on an alternative basis, but after the introduction of the 1968 models, 911T cars are fitted with a simplified differential which must be assembled with 'LÖBRO' shafts.

Removing halfshafts:

1 Raise car and remove rear wheels. Remove splitpin and axle nut. Hub flange may be held against turning with tool P.36b and the nut unscrewed with tools P.296, P.44a and P.42a.
2 Remove socket-head bolts from halfshaft flanges and remove shaft.

'Nadella' halfshafts:

Check the joints for wear. If slack and worn, renew complete shaft, which is available on an exchange basis.

'LÖBRO' halfshafts:

To dismantle, remove clips from dust boots and circlips from shaft ends (see **FIG 7:4**). Withdraw joints from shaft.

Clean all parts and check for wear. When reassembling, fit new dust boots. Slide wire retainer and joint onto shaft and secure with circlip. Fill joint with 70 gm (2½ oz) of multipurpose molybdenum disulphide grease. Any that will not go in the joint and boot should be placed in the flange side. Clean flange and boot free from grease at large end and stick boot to flange with EC.750M.2G51 compound (Minnesota Mining and Manfg. Co). To fit clips, drill 2 mm ($\frac{3}{32}$ inch) holes at each end and draw together with pliers as shown in **FIG 7:5**. Bend tab over and tap down flat.

Refitting halfshafts:

1 Put new gasket ring 11 on halfshaft stub, lightly oil splines and insert stub in wheel hub (see **FIG 7:6**). Flange faces on halfshaft must be free from grease.
2 'LÖBRO' halfshafts must be secured with socket-head bolts marked either 130-140 or 12K on the head or on the side. Tighten to 4.3 mkg (31 lb ft) on Schnorr washers that have their hollow sides facing the base plate.
3 'Nadella' halfshafts must be secured with socket-head bolts tightened to 4.7 mkg (34 lb ft).
4 Tighten outer nut to 30 to 35 mkg (217 to 253 lb ft) and fit a new splitpin.

7:4 Removing control arm:

Refer to **FIG 7:6**.
1 Raise car, remove rear wheels. Remove shrouds 5 from behind brake discs.
2 Block brake pedal in slightly depressed position and remove fluid line from caliper (see **Chapter 10**). Remove caliper.
3 Remove two screws adjacent to wheel studs and pull off brake disc. Remove outer axle shaft nut (2nd paragraph in **Section 7:3**). Release halfshaft (see **Section 7:3**).
4 Use a drift to drive out hub 4 from the rear, taking care not to damage seal 9. Remove splitpin and nut from handbrake cable and pull cable out from behind (see **Chapter 10**).

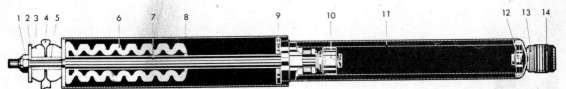

FIG 7:2   Section through rear damper, the top end being on the left

Key to Fig 7:2   1 Self-locking nut   2 Washer   3 Grommets   4 Seat in vehicle   5 Grommet bush   6 Rubber buffer
7 Plunger rod   8 Cover tube   9 Stop disc   10 Plunger   11 Cylinder   12 Check valve   13 Grommet   14 Grommet bush

5 From brake shoe side remove 4 bolts and withdraw brake carrier plate 6. Lift radius arm to relieve tension on damper and remove lower bolt. Tool P.289 engages arm and has a hook and long bolt to lift the arm against torsion bar pressure (see **FIG 7:8**).

6 At inner end of control arm 12, remove self-locking nut from mounting bolt and drive out bolt while tilting arm slightly so that it clears the transmission. It may be necessary to slacken the transmission carrier bolts. Remove the control arm.

7:5 Servicing and refitting control arm

Refer to **FIG 7:6**. Remove inner race of roller bearing 8, move spacer tube 7 out of the way and drift out ball-bearing 2. Remove tube. Using suitable mandrel and support tube, press out roller bearing and oil seal.

Check alignment of control arm on gauge P.295. A bent arm must be renewed. The bushes at the inner end are called Flanblocs and removal entails destruction. New Flanblocs must be pressed in up to the stop.

Check both bearings for roughness when unlubricated. Check spacer tube for wear or damage. Renew oil seals if leakage has been troublesome and check running surfaces for seal lips. These must be polished and free from scoring.

Reassemble by pressing in roller bearing up to stop. Press in oil seal 9 with lip facing inwards. Fit spacer tube so that wider face is at roller bearing end as in illustration. Pack hub and bearings with 40 gm (1½ oz) of multi-purpose lithium grease. Renew seal 3 in brake carrier plate using tool P.294.

When refitting control arm, move it about to ease insertion of mounting bolt. There is a washer under the bolt head as well as under the nut. **Do not tighten nut at this stage.** Connect radius arm to control arm and tighten retaining bolts to 9 mkg (65 lb ft). Tighten camber eccentric bolt to 6 mkg (43 lb ft) and tracking eccentric bolt to 5 mkg (36 lb ft) (see parts 6 and 7 in **FIG 7:1**).

Fit damper bolt and tighten to 7.5 mkg (54 lb ft). Stick a new O-ring in the groove round the outer race of the ballbearing, fit the brake carrier plate and tighten bolts to 2.5 mkg (18 lb ft).

Fit handbrake cable and tighten nut until splitpin hole is visible, then fit a new pin. Check that expander is correctly seated (see **Chapter 10**).

Put a new gasket 11 on the axle stub. With a plastic mallet, drive the hub into place. Support the hub flange and drive in the inner race for the roller bearing. Fit axle stub and halfshaft, tightening flange bolts as specified in **Section 7:3**. Tighten axle nut to 30 to 35 mkg (217 to 253 lb ft) and lock with a new splitpin. Tighten brake caliper bolts to 6 mkg (43 lb ft). Tighten bolts for disc shrouds to 2.5 mkg (18 lb ft).

FIG 7:3   Undoing top fixing of damper inside engine compartment

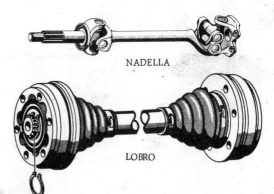

NADELLA

LOBRO

FIG 7:4   The two types of halfshaft which are fitted

Bleed the brake system (see **Chapter 10**). Adjust wheel tracking and camber (see **Section 7:10**). Tighten control arm mounting bolt to 12 mkg (86½ lb ft) when car is standing on its wheels.

7:6 Removing and refitting torsion bar

1 Raise car and remove rear wheel. Lift radius arm and remove lower bolt from damper mounting (see 2nd paragraph, **Section 7:2**).

2 Release radius arm from control arm flange. Remove cover bolts and withdraw single spacer (see **FIG 7:8**). Pry off cover with two screwdrivers.

3 Remove radius arm tensioner (part 'A' in **FIG 7:8**). Remove body plug from side and withdraw radius arm.

4 Pull out torsion bar taking care not to damage its protective coating.

A broken bar is removed by withdrawing opposite bar and pushing out parts with a steel rod. **Do not attempt to identify the bar by scratches or centre-punch marks.**

FIG 7:5 Drawing ends of clip together when securing boot on LOBRO halfshaft

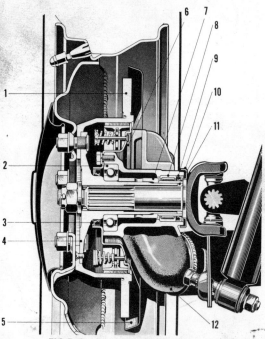

FIG 7:6 Section through rear hub

Key to Fig 7:6   1 Brake disc   2 Ballbearing
3 Oil seal   4 Wheel hub   5 Disc shroud   6 Brake carrier
plate   7 Spacer tube   8 Roller bearing   9 Oil seal   10 Dust
cap   11 Gasket ring   12 Control arm, left

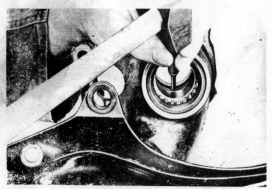

FIG 7:7 Driving outer ballbearing from hub on control arm

Check rubber support for deterioration. Check torsion bar for cracks, rust or worn splines. Renew if necessary. Ends of bars are stamped 'R' for righthand side and 'L' for lefthand side. **They are pre-stressed and must not be interchanged.**

When refitting, coat bar and splines with multipurpose lithium grease. Adjust as instructed in **Section 7:7**. Coat rubber support with rubber grease and fit it. Refit radius arm and cover and start the three bolts which can be reached. Lift the radius arm until the fourth bolt and spacer can be fitted. Tighten bolts to 4.7 mkg (34 lb ft). Refit to control arm as in **Section 7:5**. Adjust wheel tracking and camber as in **Section 7:10**.

7:7 Adjusting torsion bar

The car must be standing level. Check with a spirit level on door sill. Radius arm must be hanging free and detached from the control arm. Check angle of radius arm with clinometer placed along the top edge.

Correct angle for all 911 models is 36 deg. prior to 1968 models. After introduction of 1968 models, angle was changed to 39 deg. and this angle may be used for setting earlier models. Adjustment is by vernier splines on torsion bar. There are 40 splines at the inner end and 44 at the outer end. If bar is turned one spline onwards at the inner end, change in angle is 9 deg. If radius arm is reset in the opposite direction by one spline the change is 8 deg. 10 min. The total movement of the radius arm is thus only 50 min. which is the minimum readjustment possible. Adjust to the nearest degree. After completing assembly of control arm, adjust rear wheel tracking and camber as described in **Section 7:10**.

7:8 Modified radius arm

At chassis serial numbers 305.101.S (911S) and 307.325 (911), the radius arms were fitted with rubber bushes which were vulcanized in place. As the seats in the transverse support tubes had to be enlarged to take these new arms, the modified arms cannot be fitted to cars before the quoted numbers.

7:9 Stabilizer (anti-roll) bar

On 911S cars the stabilizer bar is standard equipment, original diameter being 16 mm. At introduction of 1968 models diameter was reduced to 15 mm. The 15 mm bar is optional on all types, but from 1968 models onwards the optional bar may be either 15 mm or 16 mm in diameter.

The transverse bar is mounted in brackets just forward of the control arms, the outer ends being connected by shackles to ball-studs on the arms. To remove the bar, prise the upper eyes of the shackles off the ball-studs with a large screwdriver. Remove the bearing caps (4 bolts) and lift away the bar. Check the rubber bearing bushes for wear. Place the bar on a flat surface and check that the ends lie in the same plane. Look for cracks and rust which may lead to premature failure. Check shackle bushes and fit new ones dry, making sure they are the right size for the bar diameter. There are grommets in the upper eyes and these may be renewed by lightly lubricating new ones and pressing them in with a vice. When installing the shackles make sure that they are correctly angled to point as shown in **FIG 7:9**. Lubricate grommets with molybdenum disulphide grease.

To refit bar, reverse the dismantling procedure, pressing the upper eyes of the shackles into place with a screwdriver.

7:10 Rear wheel alignment

Checking alignment must be carried out in association with front wheel alignment, the total effect giving the best road-holding and cornering characteristics to the car. It is desirable to have the checking and setting made on accurate equipment and with the car properly prepared. The fuel tank must be full and the spare wheel fitted. All parts of the suspension must be in good mechanical condition and adjustment. Wheel rims must not runout excessively, tyres must not be unevenly worn and they must be correctly inflated. It is assumed that the rear torsion bars are correctly set as described in **Section 7:7**.

Refer to **FIG 7:1** and slacken the eccentric bolt nuts 6 and 7 and the retaining nuts, one of which can be seen to the left of the eccentric bolts. Turn the tracking and camber eccentrics until correct values are obtained on the equipment. Before 1968 models, camber was —55' to —1 deg. 35' and from 1968 models onwards it was —30' to 1 deg. 10', with a maximum deviation between left and right of 20'. Latest setting may be used for earlier models. Correct tracking is a toe-in of 0' ± 10'.

When installing camber eccentric make sure it points downwards so that there is adequate clearance for adjustment. If it is found that the eccentric binds at one end or the other of the slot, turn it round through 180 deg. After adjustment, tighten the nuts.

7:11 Height adjustment

Refer to **FIG 7:10**. Have car correctly prepared as in **Section 7:10** and standing on level ground. Bounce car at rear several times to allow suspension to settle naturally. Note that dimension 'b' cannot be measured because torsion bar is eccentrically mounted in bush and cover. 'b1' is measured after the following calculations. Measure wheel centre height 'a' and add 12 mm (.47 inch) to give value 'b'. Subtract from this figure half the diameter of the radius arm cover (30 mm or 1.18 inch). The result is 'b1'.

Measured height 'b1' must not differ from calculated height by more than ±5 mm (.197 inch), and height difference between righthand and lefthand side must not exceed 8 mm (.315 inch). If correct setting cannot be obtained, check height adjustment of front suspension and rear torsion bar adjustment.

7:12 Fault diagnosis

(a) Noise from axle

1 Worn wheel bearings
2 Worn universal joints
3 Worn axle splines
4 Loose axle nut
5 Damper mountings defective

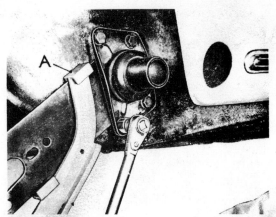

FIG 7:8 Removing radius arm cover. Arm is raised by special tool P.289, indicated at 'A'

FIG 7:9 Stabilizer bar, showing correct angle for top eyes on shackles

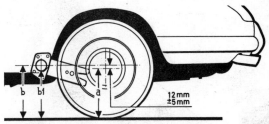

FIG 7:10 Checking rear height adjustment on all models

6 Broken stabilizer bar, faulty mountings
7 Loose radius arm or control arm
8 Control arm pivot mounting worn
9 Worn torsion bar splines or bushes
10 Brake backplate loose

(b) Excessive backlash

1 Check 2, 3 and 4 in (a)

(c) Poor handling, bad road-holding

1 Check 6, 7, 8 and 9 in (a)
2 Torsion bars 'settled' or broken
3 Radius arm setting incorrect
4 Incorrect wheel alignment
5 Incorrect height adjustment
6 Dampers inoperative, rubber buffers worn
7 Faulty transmission mountings

CHAPTER 8

FRONT SUSPENSION

8:1 General description

FIG 8:1 shows the earlier type of suspension system using torsion bar springing. Each control arm 9 houses a torsion bar in the longitudinal tube. Strut 1 incorporates a telescopic damper. At the lower end of the strut is the stub axle and a steering lever. A ball joint 3 couples the bottom end of the strut to the control arm, while the top of the strut is secured to the body. Except on standard 911 cars there is a stabilizer bar 5 to prevent excessive rolling. 1968 models have modified control arms (see **Section 8:9**).

Starting with 1969 models, 911E and 911T Lux cars are fitted with self-levelling suspension struts. These were optional on 911T and 911S cars. The suspension layout remains the same but there are no torsion bars. The control arms or wishbones have rubber bushes at the inner ends and a new type of ball joint. There is no stabilizer bar. **FIG 8:2** is a section through the strut showing the gas chambers and oil chambers which perform the suspension, damping and self-levelling functions. Gas in the high pressure chamber is isolated from the oil by a diaphragm shown as a thick black line. Oil and gas are not separated in the low pressure chamber. Gas pressure acting on the piston rod area takes

90 per cent of the weight of the empty car. Pump rod 12 forms a hydraulic pump in conjunction with piston rod 11.

Road bumps cause the pump to transfer oil through valves 7 and 9 from the low pressure cylinder to the high pressure cylinder. The pressurized gas is further compressed, which raises the car to a predetermined level. The pump action also acts as a damper. At a predetermined height, port 5 is cleared by the damping piston and normal suspension movements continue, the ports being too small to affect them. The pump rod is reduced in diameter higher up so that no pumping can take place. This prevents excessive raising of the suspension.

The struts will bring the car up to normal level within 300 to 1500 yards on smooth roads and much shorter distances on rough roads. The level remains constant if the load is not altered after parking.

Servicing self-levelling suspension:

It is most important to check ground clearance during servicing operations. If the car is lifted so that the wheels are clear of the ground, pressure in the struts is equalized. When the car is lowered the strut will then support only the basic load and the car will drop below the normal static load position.

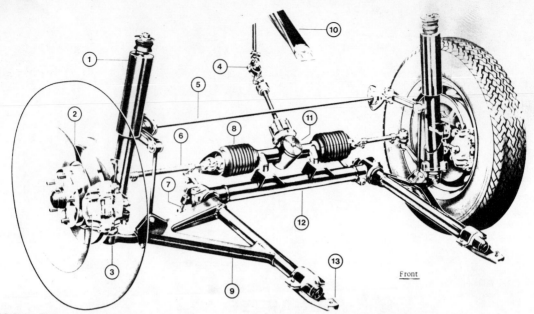

FIG 8:1 The suspension layout prior to the introduction of the 1968 models. FIG 8:9 shows the control arm and cross-member details for later cars

Key to Fig 8:1   1 Damper strut   1 Brake disc   3 Ball joint   4 Universal joint   5 Stabilizer   6 Steering tie rod
7 Adjusting screw   8 Bellows   9 Transverse control arm   10 Steering post   11 Steering gear assembly   12 Reinforcing
crossmember   13 Bearing support

As there are no height adjusters on this system, wheel alignment must be entrusted to a Porsche Service Station. The agent must also be consulted if the strut gives trouble.

8:2 Routine maintenance

There are no lubrication points, but the front hubs must be filled with fresh grease at major overhauls.

At every 6000 miles check tightness of wheel nuts, check tyre pressures and check wheel alignment and balance. At the same mileages check the wheelbearings for play. Adjust as described in **Section 8:4.**

8:3 Servicing damper strut

Removing:

1 Raise car and remove front wheels. Remove shroud 1 from behind brake disc 2 (see **FIG 8:3**). Block brake pedal in slightly depressed position and remove fluid line from caliper (see **Chapter 10**). Detach line from bracket, pull out hose and withdraw line and retaining spring.

2 Remove brake caliper. Prise cap 6 off hub. Loosen socket-head screw and remove nut 7 with washer 8. Pull off hub 3. Remove brake carrier (4 bolts and lock-plates).

3 Release outer end of steering tie-rod from lever 12 using tool VW.266h. Remove bolts from outer end of control arm (2 castle nuts). Inside luggage compartment, release top end of damper strut (see **FIG 8:4**).

Dismantling:

1 Remove shield 8 and buffer (see **FIG 8:5**). Remove steering lever and ball joint 15. Take care of bush.

2 Release ball from lever (castle nut) and press it out. Drive distance ring off stub (see 10 in **FIG 8:3**).

Checking strut:

Alignment of the damper and stub axle is checked on special tool P.286. Renew the strut if the outside is covered in oily dirt. Hold strut vertically in a vice and pump it a few times. Then give long full strokes up and down and check for free play at any point. Excessive free play calls for strut renewal.

Koni adjustable dampers are standard on 911S cars and are optional on other models except Targa. To adjust outside car, mount vertically, press top end right down and turn gently to left until lugs engage inside damper and mark position. Check damper action by pumping top end up and down. If more damping is needed, press down and engage lugs at mark and then turn top tube to left for harder setting and to the right for a softer setting. Make sure both dampers have the same setting. To adjust Koni dampers when installed in car, raise front end and remove wheels. Hold up control arm with a jack and remove nut from top end of strut (inside luggage compartment). Adjust as just described. When finished, fit top nut on a new safety plate with tab upwards. Tighten nut to 8 mkg (58 lb ft).

Checking steering lever and ball joint:

Check the lever on special tool P.284. **Never try to straighten a bent lever.** Renew the ball joint if it moves freely and if play can be felt. There must be slight drag when the stud is moved. Renew the rubber boot if defective.

Assembling and refitting strut:

Do this in the reverse order. Fit O-ring R32-2.5 on axle when installing ring 10 (see **FIG 8:3**). Heat ring to 150°C (300°F) and push into place.

Fill rubber boots on new ball joints with 6.5g (.20 oz) of multipurpose molybdenum disulphide grease. **Taper of ball stud must be grease-free.** Tighten stud nut to 4.5 mkg (32½ lb ft). Use new lockplates and tighten steering lever bolts to 4.7 mkg (34 lb ft). Fit rubber buffer dry. Fit top nut of strut on a new safety plate with tab upwards. Tighten nut to 8 mkg (58 lb ft).

Use following torques on fixings:

Ball joint to control arm nuts 7.5 mkg (54 lb ft). Use washers and new splitpins. Tie rod ball joint nut 4.5 mkg

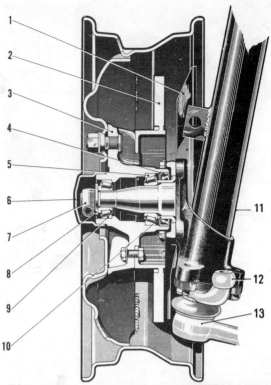

FIG 8:3   Section through front hub, showing bearings and seal

Key to Fig 8:3   1 Cover shroud   2 Brake disc   3 Hub
4 Seal   5 Taper roller bearing   6 Cap   7 Clamping nut
8 Washer   9 Taper roller bearing   10 Distance ring
11 Damper strut   12 Steering lever   13 Ball joint

(32½ lb ft) using new splitpin. Brake carrier plate bolts on new lockplates 4.7 mkg (34 lb ft). Caliper bolts on spring washers 7 mkg (50½ lb ft). Gland nut for brake pipe at caliper 2 mkg (14½ lb ft). Shroud bolts 2.5 mkg (18 lb ft).

Adjust wheel bearings as in **Section 8:4.** Bleed brakes as in **Chapter 10.** Check wheel alignment as in **Section 8:11.**

8:4   Servicing and adjusting hub bearings

Removing:

Do first two operations in **Section 8:3** but do not remove carrier. Press out outer races of bearings and inner oil seal using appropriate tools and spacer tube. If the brake disc is in the way, remove it after marking position. Removal of bearings is easier if hub is heated to 120° to 150°C or 250° to 300°F.

Checking:

Clean out old grease from hub and check flange for cracks, distortion or loose studs. Clean bearings and check in dry state. Renew if rough, but note that renewed parts must be of same make if mixed with original parts. Various makes of bearing have been fitted, such as SKF, FAG or Timken. **Do not mix parts of one make with those of another.**

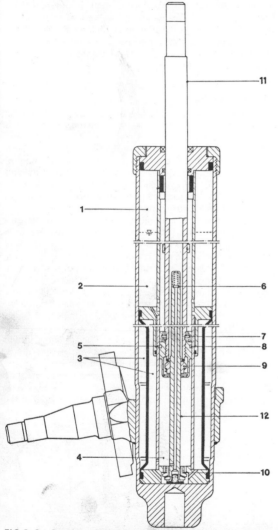

FIG 8:2   Section through the self-levelling hydro-pneumatic suspension strut fitted to 1969 models onwards. Standard on 911E cars, it was optional on 911T and 911S models

Key to Fig 8:2   1 Low pressure chamber   2 Low pressure cylinder   3 High pressure chamber   4 High pressure, or damping cylinder   5 Relief port orifice
6 Overload valve   7 Suction valve   8 Piston ring seal
9 Pressure valve   10 Damping valve   11 Piston rod
12 Pump rod

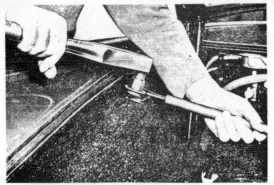

FIG 8:4 Releasing top end of damper strut

Reassembling:

Heat hub to 120° to 150°C (250° to 300°F) and press in outer race of inner bearing. Insert inner race and press in oil seal until flush with hub. Fit outer race of outer bearing.

Refit brake disc with marks aligned and fit bolts from inside. Tighten nuts on spring washers to 2.3 mkg (16½ lb ft). Fill hub with 50 cc or 43g (3 cu in or 1½ oz) of multipurpose lithium grease, pressing it well into bearings. Smear grease on both lips of oil seal. Refit hub to axle stub.

Tighten clamping nut to about 1.5 mkg (10.8 lb ft) while turning hub to seat the rollers in their races. Slacken nut until it is possible to turn the washer 8 in FIG 8:3 with a screwdriver (see FIG 8:6). There must be no free play in the bearings. Lock nut by tightening socket-head screw to 2.5 mkg (18 lb ft). Check that adjustment is still correct.

Coat nut and washer with lithium grease. Fit cap without filling with grease. Fit caliper, tightening bolts on spring washers to 7 mkg (50½ lb ft). Tighten gland nut of brake pipe at caliper to 2 mkg (14½ lb ft). Bleed the brakes.

8:5 Servicing control arms (1st type)

These are part 9 (see FIG 8:1). Remove as follows:
1 Remove undershield below crossmember 12. Slacken torsion bar adjusting screw 7.

2 ~~Release ball joint 3 from end of control arm (two bolts).~~ Remove bearing support and cap 13 (3 bolts). Torsion bar lies inside control arm tube.
3 At front end, remove dust cap and circlip and drive torsion bar forward and out. Loosen socket-head bolt just forward of adjusting screw 7 and pull and turn control arm until it is free. The adjusting lever may be driven out with a punch, taking care not to damage the splines.

Checking:

Note that the bearing block at the rear end cannot be removed without damaging the arm. Renew the parts as a pair. Check arm for distortion on fixture P.288. Check rubber bush for deterioration. Check torsion bar for cracks, worn splines or rust. **Rust pitting may lead to premature failure.**

Reassembling:

A new bearing block (Flanbloc) may be pressed onto a new control arm. Apply grease to mating surfaces, fit Flanbloc spacer to smaller journal of control arm, chamfered side first, and press Flanbloc into place. Refit rear end of control arm into crossmember. Set control arm so that it hangs down at 10 deg. to the horizontal and tighten the Flanbloc socket-head bolt to 4.7 mkg (34 lb ft). **This is important to prevent unequal torsion on the Flanbloc during suspension movements.**

Coat torsion bar and splines with lithium grease and insert at front end of control arm tube. Fit circlip and dust cap. End of torsion bar is marked 'R' for righthand side and 'L' for lefthand side. **Do not transpose.**

Coat front bush with rubber grease and fit to control arm with flange against face of arm. Install bracket and cap with radiused faces coinciding. Fit front bolt finger tight, check that bush is not trapped between the bracket and cap and fit remaining two bolts. Tighten to 4.7 mkg (34 lb ft).

Fit ball joint arm to outer end of control arm. Tighten nuts to 7.5 mkg (54 lb ft). Use washers and new splitpins.

To fit torsion bar adjusting lever at rear end, turn the adjusting screw right back. Smear lever with graphite grease. With damper strut attached, hook a long bar over the control arm and press it down to the full extent of the

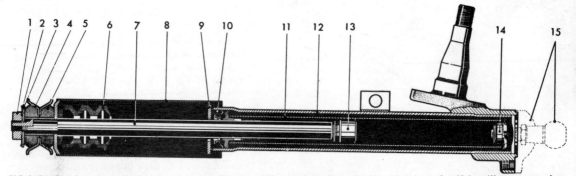

FIG 8:5 Section through the damper strut fitted to all models before the introduction of self-levelling suspension

Key to Fig 8:5   1 Hexagon nut   2 Safety plate   3 Washer   4 Bracket (on vehicle)   5 Rubber bush   6 Rubber buffer   7 Piston rod   8 Shielding tube   9 Stop disc   10 Oil seal   11 Cylinder   12 Strut tube   13 Piston   14 Bottom valve   15 Steering lever and ball

damper strut. Push lever into place on torsion bar, leaving minimum clearance at the adjusting point. Fit circlip and dust cover. Adjust front height as in **Section 8:10** and check wheel alignment as in **Section 8:11**.

8:6 Servicing crossmember (1st type)

Removing:

Crossmember is part 12 in **FIG 8:1**. To remove after control arms have been taken off, release rear ends of braces from body (see **FIG 8:7**). Release steering gearbox from both brackets on crossmember. Loosen bolts, tap crossmember off studs, remove bolts and crossmember.

Checking:

Make up two steel tubes as in **FIG 8:8** (lefthand view). Fit into crossmember housings as in central view and tighten Flanbloc clamping bolts. Check dimensions 'A' and 'B'. Maximum deviation from parallel must not be more than 2 mm (.08 inch). Place assembly on flat plate as in righthand view and check for twist. With one tube in full contact with plate, other tube must not be clear of plate at either end by more than 2 mm (.08 inch).

Check steering gearbox mounting brackets for cracks and distortion.

Refitting:

Ensure that crossmember is correctly seated on the aligning studs, then tighten fixing bolts to 9 mkg (65 lb ft). Fit braces so that they are not strained (see **FIG 8:7**). Tighten nuts to 6.5 mkg (47 lb ft) and bolts to 4.7 mkg (34 lb ft).

8:7 Removing torsion bar (1st type)

Follow the instructions in operations 1, 2 and 3 in **Section 8:5** but do not detach the strut ball joint from the control arm or disturb the control arm mounting beyond removing the front bearing bracket and cap (see 13 in **FIG 8:1**). Refit torsion bars as described under 'Reassembling' in **Section 8:5**.

8:8 The stabilizer bar

Removing:

The bar is part 5 in **FIG 8:1**. At outer ends of bar, loosen lever clamp bolts and pull levers off squared ends of bar. Release support flanges from body (3 bolts), apply penetrating oil to support and rubber bush on one side and prise off with screwdrivers. Pull out stabilizer bar from other end. Press off rubber bush. Remove tie rods. Check all rubber bushes and renew if necessary. Check bar for rust, cracks or distortion. Squared ends must lie in same plane.

FIG 8:6 Checking adjustment of front hub bearings by turning thrust washer with a screwdriver

FIG 8:7 Adjust crossmember braces so that they fit body location without strain. Bolt has been removed from body fixing point

Refitting:

During installation, treat the bushes with rubber grease. Lightly attach support flanges and centre the bar. Tighten bolts to 2.5 mkg (18 lb ft). Fit levers so that about 1 mm (.04 inch) of squared end of bar protrudes. Fit tie rods, tightening bolts to 2.5 mkg (18 lb ft).

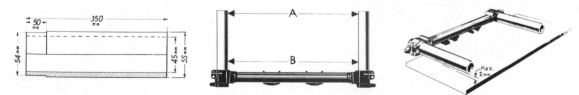

FIG 8:8 Methods of checking crossmember, showing dimensions of tubes (left). Check dimensions 'A' and 'B' to test for parallelism (centre). Check for twist on a flat plate (right)

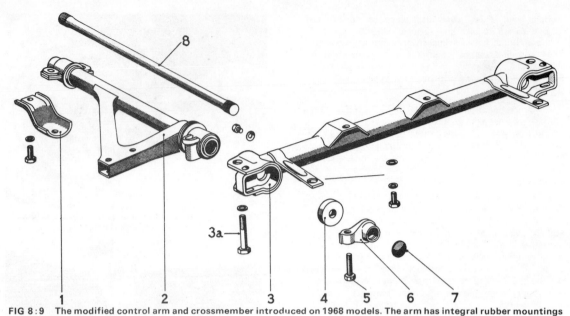

FIG 8:9   The modified control arm and crossmember introduced on 1968 models. The arm has integral rubber mountings

Key to Fig 8:9   1 Cover bracket   2 Transverse control arm (left)   3 Crossmember   3a Crossmember bolt   4 OWA-seal
5 Adjusting screw   6 Adjusting lever   7 End cap   8 Torsion bar

Stabilizer bars:

These are not fitted to 911 cars. Until the 1968 models were introduced, the standard bar for 911L models was 13 mm (.512 inch) diameter and for 911S models it was 14 mm (.55 inch) diameter. For 1968 models onwards these diameters were changed to 11 mm (.433 inch) and 15 mm (.59 inch) respectively. Optional diameters for models up to 1968 are 11, 14 and 15 mm (.435, .55 and .59 inch). For 1968 models onwards, optional diameters are 13, 14 and 15 mm (.512, .55 and .59 inch).

8:9 Modifications on 1968 models

The redesigned control arm and crossmember are shown in **FIG 8:9**, the arm having integral rubber mountings. The track was increased to 1367 mm (53.82 inch) with modified hubs having grease caps without expansion slots to prevent loss of grease. Standard stabilizer bar diameter on 911L cars (except USA) is 11 mm (.433 inch) and for 911L (USA) and 911S cars it is 15 mm (.59 inch). **It is essential to make sure that the mounting rubbers are the correct size for the stabilizer bar.**

Servicing control arm:

1 Unscrew torsion bar adjusting screw 5 in **FIG 8:9**. Release damper strut from outer end of control arm 2 (2 bolts and castle nuts).
2 Pull off lever 6 and remove OWA seal 4. Remove crossmember bolt 3a.
3 Remove bracket 1. Press control arm 2 and torsion bar 8 out of the crossmember 3. If both control arms are to be removed, first remove one arm and replace the crossmember bolt to keep the member in place.

Check control arm rubber mountings for wear or deterioration. Defects call for renewal of the complete control arm. Check torsion bar for damaged splines, chipped paint, rust or cracks. **Deep rust pitting may lead to premature failure.** Have control arm checked for distortion on fixture P.288, first driving out the plug at the splined end. To fit a new plug, insert with bulge outwards and partially flatten with a punch.

Refitting control arm:

1 Torsion bars are marked on the end 'L' for lefthand and 'R' for righthand. **Do not interchange.** Coat bar lightly with lithium grease and insert into control arm.
2 Insert arm and bar assembly into crossmember and tighten front mounting bracket bolts to 4.7 mkg (34 lb ft). Tighten crossmember bolt to 9 mkg (65 lb ft).
3 Fit damper strut ball joint arm into control arm and tighten castle nuts to 7.5 mkg (54 lb ft). Fit new split-pins.
4 Fit OWA seal on torsion bar and into outer recess in crossmember. See that the end cap is fitted to the adjusting lever. Press the control arm down as far as possible, using a long lever, and fit the adjusting lever. Engage the splines to give the maximum clearance for adjustment, coat the adjusting screw with molybdenum disulphide grease and fit it without tightening. Fit cover bracket and tighten bolts to 4.7 mkg (34 lb ft).
5 Adjust front height as described in **Section 8:10** and have the wheel alignment checked on optical equipment.

Servicing torsion bar:

To remove a bar, remove the adjusting screw 5 in **FIG 8:9**. Pull lever off bar and remove seal 4. Remove cover bracket 1. Taking care not to damage splines, drive torsion bar forwards and out. Refit bar as described in the preceding instructions for the control arm.

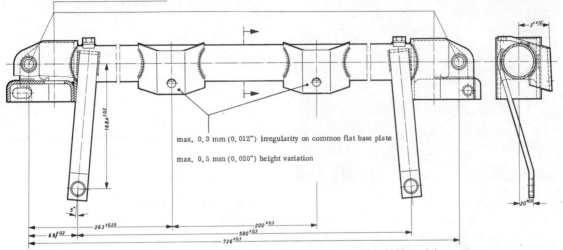

converging angle of 4 axes, max. 20'

max. 0.3 mm (0.012") irregularity on common flat base plate

max. 0.5 mm (0.020") height variation

FIG 8:10 Dimensional checks on the crossmember for 1968 models

The crossmember:

Checking points for correct alignment are shown in **FIG 8:10.** To remove crossmember, remove control arm as described earlier. Detach undershield and steering gearbox, remove crossmember bolts and withdraw it. Check crossmember against dimensions given, placing it on a flat surface to test for distortion. Check for cracks and damage.

When refitting, make sure crossmember seats properly on body studs. Tighten steering gearbox bolts to 4.7 mkg (34 lb ft) using new spring washers. Refit the control arm.

8:10 Height adjustment (not for cars with self-levelling suspension)

Prepare the car as described in **Section 7:10** of the preceding chapter. Mark the centre of the hub caps. Bounce the front end of the car several times and allow it to rise by itself on the rebound from the last depression. Measure height 'A' from level ground to wheel centre (see righthand view in **FIG 8:11**). Measure height 'B' from ground to torsion bar centre. The centre will be visible if the dust cover is removed from the adjusting lever. Turn the torsion bar adjusting screw (see part 7 in **FIG 8:1**) until the value 'B' is 108 ± 5 mm ($4.25 \pm .20$ inch) less than 'A'. Check both sides and bounce car again for a further check on dimensions. Although permissible deviation is given as ± 5 mm (.20 inch) the difference between the heights of both sides must not exceed 5 mm.

8:11 Wheel alignment

Refer to **Chapter 9** for details of toe-in adjustment.

Camber angle and steering axis inclination are shown in the lefthand view of **FIG 8:11**. Camber is the angle the wheel makes to the vertical. Steering axis inclination is the angle of the damper strut to the vertical.

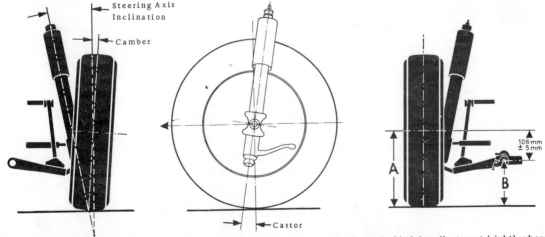

FIG 8:11 Checking steering angles for wheel alignment (left and centre). Method of height adjustment (right) where 'A' is wheel centre height and 'B' the height of the torsion bar centre at the adjusting lever end

FIG 8:12 Releasing top end of damper strut to adjust camber and castor angles

Castor angle is shown by the central view in **FIG 8:11**. The centre line of the damper strut meets the ground ahead of the point of tyre contact to give a self-centring effect.

Adjusting camber:

Note that castor and camber cannot be adjusted on cars up to chassis No. 302.694, on chassis No. 302.736 or on chassis No. 302.805. Any errors on these cars must be corrected by checking the suspension parts and damper strut mountings for distortion and renewing faulty components.

To adjust camber (see lefthand view in **FIG 8:11**), pull away the carpet in the luggage compartment to reveal the three retaining screws which permit damper strut adjustment (see **FIG 8:12**). Remove sealing compound from pressure plates and dished ring and then mark round the plates to register their positions. Loosen the socket-head screws. Re-position the dished ring sideways to alter the camber angle. Moving it 1 mm (.04 inch) makes an alteration of 6' to the angle of the damper strut. Correct angle is $0 \pm 20'$ with a permissible deviation between left and right of 20'.

Adjusting castor:

Read the comments on certain cars at the start of 'Adjusting camber'. Follow the instructions for loosening the top fixing of the damper strut but instead of moving the dished ring sideways for adjustment, move it fore and aft. Correct castor angle is 6 deg. $45' \pm 45'$ with a maximum deviation between left and right of 30'. Tighten retaining screws to 4.7 mkg (34 lb ft). Apply a non-hardening sealer and stick the carpet back into place.

8:12 Fault diagnosis

(a) Wheel wobble

1 Unbalanced wheels and tyres
2 Worn steering ball joints
3 Incorrect steering angles
4 Weak or incorrectly set torsion bar
5 Worn hub bearings

(b) Erratic steering

1 Check (a)
2 Bent suspension components
3 Worn ball joints and control arm mountings
4 Uneven tyre wear or pressures
5 Defective damper strut

(c) Excessive pitching, rolling or 'bottoming'

1 Check 4 in (a) and 5 in (b)
2 Buffer rubbers missing or faulty
3 Broken stabilizer bar or tie rod

(d) Rattles

1 Check 3 in (b) and 3 in (c)
2 Loose damper strut mountings
3 Loose crossmember or control arm mountings

CHAPTER 9

THE STEERING

9:1 General description

Reference to **FIG 8:1** in the preceding Chapter shows that the steering gearbox assembly 11 is mounted on two brackets forming part of crossmember 12. The steering pinion shaft is connected by universal joint 4 to a relay shaft which is connected by another universal joint to the steering wheel shaft at the top of post 10. The pinion engages a rack in the steering gear housing as shown in **FIG 9:15**. The outer ends of the rack are coupled by tie rods and joints 6 to the steering levers attached to damper struts 1. A modified rack and pinion assembly was introduced at the same time as the self-levelling suspension fitted to some 1969 models.

9:2 Routine maintenance

As the steering gearbox is packed with a special grease at the time of manufacture, or after a complete overhaul, there is no provision for subsequent extra lubrication. The same applies to the universal joints and ball joints in the steering system. There is no need for routine adjustment at any point.

9:3 Removing and refitting steering wheel

Removal:

1 Disconnect battery. Release horn button by turning anticlockwise and then pull out the contact pin.
2 Unscrew wheel retaining nut. Mark relative positions of wheel and shaft and withdraw wheel, taking care of the bearing support ring and spring (see **FIG 9:1**).

Refitting:

1 Fit spring and support ring on wheel hub. Set road wheels straightahead and install steering wheel, aligning marks made before dismantling. In the correct position the return striker must point towards the flasher switch and the wheel spokes must be horizontal.
2 Tighten wheel nut to 8 mkg (58 lb ft) using a spring washer under nut. Check flasher return striker for correct operation.
3 Lightly grease the horn contact ring, insert the contact pin and fit the horn button, turning it clockwise until it is locked.

FIG 9:1 Support ring and spring correctly located on steering wheel hub

FIG 9:2 Prising up prong of spring clip when removing intermediate shaft cover (top). Removing heater pump bolts (bottom)

9:4 Servicing switch and steering shafts

Removal:

1 Disconnect battery. Remove luggage compartment carpet and lift access flap. If fitted, detach auxiliary heater duct from steering column post.

2 Refer to top view in **FIG 9:2** and pry up a prong of the spring clip as shown. Remove clips and cover over intermediate shaft.

3 Remove heater pump bolts (lower view in **FIG 9:2**). Lay pump to one side.

4 Release the lower clamping bolts in each of the two universal joints. One joint is shown as part 4 in **FIG 8:1**. Note large bush just below it. Release cap from this bush as shown in **FIG 9:3** and pull the lower universal joint off the shaft. Withdraw the intermediate shaft and lower joint out of the upper universal joint.

5 Remove the steering wheel (see **Section 9:3**). If car is fitted with a steering lock, remove cover, drill out the bolts indicated by the arrows in **FIG 9:4** and remove the lock and spacer without disconnecting the cables. Remove the light switch alongside and let it hang on the cables.

6 Loosen socket-head bolt in clamp which secures the switch assembly (see **FIG 9:5**). Turn clamp lugs downwards and pull out locking pin with pointed-nosed pliers (see **FIG 9:10**). Detach cable connectors, marking the cables for correct reassembly.

7 Switch assembly is now free and may be pulled away, complete with upper shaft and universal joint. Feed cables through instrument panel. Inside luggage compartment, unlock and remove two bolts securing lower end of steering post. Squirt glycerine under the grommet and twist the post to remove it.

Inspection:

Check cables and connections. Check condition of grommet. Test universal joints for play and renew them if worn. If it is necessary to remove the upper shaft proceed as follows:

Servicing upper shaft:

1 Remove universal joint (see **FIG 9:6**). From same end of post extension prise out spring ring and remove washer, seal and second seal retainer.

2 Remove socket-head bolts and drive post extension out of switch assembly (see **FIG 9:7**). From lower end of shaft remove bearing circlip and drive out shaft.

3 Remove bearing circlip and drive out bearing at lower end. At top end, tap out column bearing with a blunt screwdriver, working from side to side to keep it square.

Inspecting upper shaft and bearings:

Check both bearings and renew if worn or rough in action. Check shaft splines.

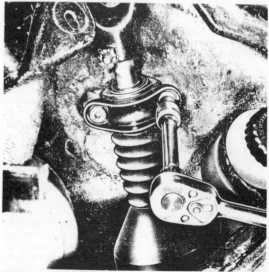

FIG 9:3 Removing cap from bush on lower steering shaft

Reassembling:

Fit top bearing as shown in **FIG 9:8**. Pack both bearings with multipurpose lithium-based grease before installation. Refit shaft after fitting and securing lower bearing. Push post extension into switch assembly and align it so that the hole for the steering lock is central (see **FIG 9:9**). Set relative positions so that post extension is 7 mm (.28 inch) below face of switch assembly (see **FIG 9:9**). Tighten socket-head bolts to 2.5 mkg (18 lb ft). Fit universal joint using a new bolt. Fit a 'Schnorr' lockwasher under the nut, tighten to 3.5 mkg (25 lb ft) and fit a new splitpin.

Refit steering post, lightly tightening bolts at lower end on washers and a lockplate. Fit retaining clamp so that the threaded lug is on the right. Coat sealing ring on steering post extension with assembly paste such as Conti-Fix and push the switch assembly into place, at the same time guiding the cables through the instrument panel. Fit the steering lock, insert the protecting plate and lightly tighten the new shear bolts.

Refit locking pin between lugs of clamp (see **FIG 9:10**). Turn clamp anticlockwise, fit socket-head bolt and spring washer and tighten to 2.5 mkg (18 lb ft). At this point, check clearance between switch assembly and instrument panel. It should be about 2 mm (.08 inch). If necessary, move steering post. Tighten bolts at lower end of steering post to 2.5 mkg (18 lb ft). Turn up tabs on lockplate.

Tighten steering lock bolts until heads break off. Refit intermediate shaft and universal joints using new bolts and 'Schnorr' lockwashers under the nuts. Tighten to 3.5 mkg (25 lb ft) and fit new splitpins. Refit cap over bush on lower shaft, put spring washers on socket-head bolts and tighten to 2.5 mkg (18 lb ft).

9:5 The intermediate shaft and universal joints

This is the angled shaft which connects the lower shaft to the steering wheel shaft by means of two universal joints. When dismantled, check shaft and splines for damage. Joints must have no play.

If necessary, fit new dowel pins. Install the ring seal and then drive in the dowels with the grooves entering first. Tap the universal joint into place so that the dowel engages the slot in the joint as shown in **FIG 9:11**. Always fit a new bolt, place a 'Schnorr' lockwasher under the nut and tighten to 3.5 mkg (25 lb ft). Fit a new splitpin.

FIG 9:5 Slackening bolt in clamp which retains switch assembly

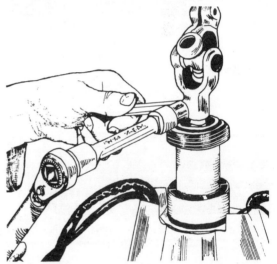

FIG 9:6 Removing universal joint from upper shaft

Modified universal joints:

Early joints were fitted to their respective shafts without splines. Starting with chassis Nos. 305.101, 354.001 and 458.101, the internally-splined universal joints mate with splined shafts. These are not interchangeable with joints and shafts without splines. When fitting splined joints it is also necessary to fit splined shafts.

When installing splined joints, push them onto the shafts to the point where the bolts will enter freely. Tighten to 2.5 mkg (18 lb ft).

9:6 The steering coupling

This joins the lower steering shaft to the pinion shaft flange next to the steering gearbox as can be seen in **FIG 9:12**. Remove the coupling and lower shaft by unlocking and unscrewing the bolts as shown. The flexible part of the coupling is provided with recessed holes (see **FIG 9:13**). **Make sure, when fitting the coupling, that it is the recessed holes which contact the pinion and lower shaft flanges.**

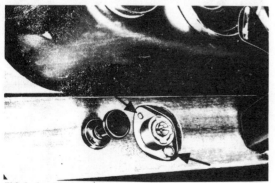

FIG 9:4 Arrows show position of shearing bolts for steering lock. Light switch is to left of lock

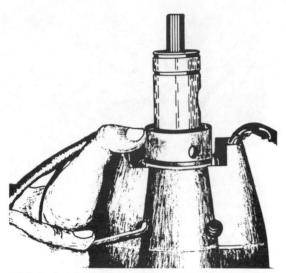

FIG 9:7 Releasing steering post extension from switch assembly

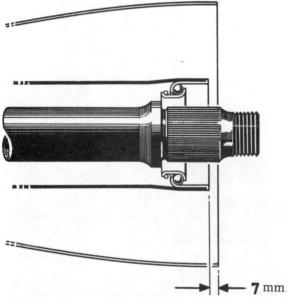

7 mm

FIG 9:8 Correct relative positions of steering post extension and top face of switch assembly

9:7 Servicing the steering gearbox

Removal:

Do operations 1, 2 and 3 in **Section 9:4**. Remove bolt securing lower universal joint to lower steering shaft and pull joint off shaft. Remove socket-head bolts from cap over bush (see **FIG 9:3**). Pull off bush and rubber boot. Unlock and remove coupling bolts (see **FIG 9:12**).

Working underneath car, remove undershield which covers crossmember. Release outer ball joints from steering levers. Tie rods are part 6 in **FIG 8:1** in preceding chapter. Do not hammer taper pins of joints out of steering levers but use an extracting tool like VW.266h.

Unscrew bolts holding steering gearbox to crossmember 12 in **FIG 8:1**. Remove the righthand crossmember brace (see **FIG 8:7**). Pulling it out to the right, remove the steering gearbox assembly.

Dismantling:

1 Release tie rods from eyebolts at ends of rack and remove damper (see **FIG 9:14**). Unlock and slacken the eyebolt locknuts, holding rack housing in a vice between soft jaws. **Do not overtighten.** Unscrew eyebolts and remove the stop plates and bellows.

2 Refer to **FIGS 9:15** and **9:16** for details of the construction of the rack and pinion steering gearbox. Rack 1 is carried in housing 2 in bushes 8 (see **FIG 9:15**). Engaging with it is pinion 5 which is connected by shafts and couplings to the steering wheel. The pinion bearings are mounted in a floating carrier so that a spring-loaded pressure block 4 can maintain the rack and pinion teeth in close contact to give freedom from backlash. The amount of pressure is adjustable through nut 3.

3 To dismantle, remove base plate 14 (see **FIG 9:16**). Unscrew adjusting nut 13, using the base plate as a spanner. Remove pressure block 6 and spring 7.

4 Unlock and remove the pinion shaft nut and use a puller to withdraw the flange 8. Prise out oil seal 9 with a screwdriver. Remove circlip 12 and possible spacers.

5 Using a puller such as P.282 which has an extracting bolt that screws on the pinion shaft thread, extract the pinion and ballbearing. Remove key 10 and press off the bearing.

6 Mark rack 5 for correct reassembly and then withdraw it from the housing. Pull out pinion carrier 2 and press out the second ballbearing.

7 To extract bushes 8, prise out the spring rings from the housing (see **FIG 9:15**). Push a thin punch into the small hole in the bevelled end of the housing to lift the ring. Remove supporting ring and then drive out the bush with a drift and supporting tube. Do not remove bushes unless worn.

Inspection:

Clean all the parts and check the rack and pinion for wear and damaged teeth. Check the ballbearings when

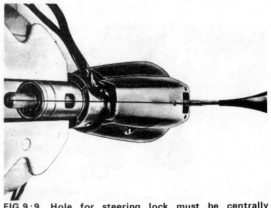

FIG 9:9 Hole for steering lock must be centrally aligned with switch assembly

clean and dry and discard if rough in action or if slack. Check housing bushes and renew if worn. Renew oil seal.

Reassembling:

1 To fit new bushes in the housing, insert the wide supporting rings first. Grease the outer surface of each bush and press into place with recessed face outwards. Fit the narrow ring and spring ring so that the gap in the latter is at right angles to the carrier bore.

2 Coat pinion carrier and inner bearing with multipurpose molybdenum disulphide grease such as Liqui-Moly LM-KFZ3 or LM-47L. Insert into housing. 40 g (1.3 oz) of this grease will be needed during reassembly.

3 Coat the rack with grease and fit into housing, checking the assembly marks made during dismantling. Press the remaining grease into the housing and insert the pinion with ballbearing and key. Press pinion right home, fit spacers and circlip and check axial play of pinion. There must be no play and correction is made by using spacers which are available in thicknesses of .10, .12, .15 and .30 mm (.004, .005, .006 and .012 inch).

4 Fit oil seal with sealing lip outwards. Fit pinion flange, checking that key is properly seated. Coat washer with jointing compound and tighten nut to 2.5 mkg (18 lb ft). Secure with a new splitpin.

5 Fit pressure block, spring and adjusting nut. Adjust gear as follows:

6 Adjustment varies with the type of pressure block. If the block is steel with a plastic contact face, the steering housing will have a large flange to accept the dust boot as in **FIG 9:17**. Adjust this type by tightening the nut until it is fully seated. The base plate may be used as a spanner to do this. Back the nut off three teeth. Use torque meter P:261 on the pinion nut to check the drag of the assembly over the full working length of the rack (see **FIG 9:17**). The correct drag is 8 cmkg (7 lb in). If higher than this, slacken the nut a little and recheck. After the initial slackening by three teeth it is possible that the drag may be less than the required figure. If the drag is not less than 4 cmkg (3.5 lb in), do not retighten the nut.

7 If the pressure block is all plastic, there will be no large bevelled flange to take the lower end of the rubber dust boot. In this case simply tighten the adjusting nut until the torque meter registers the correct drag of 8 cmkg (7 lb in).

8 With drag correctly set, refit base plate and paper gasket, tightening the bolts to 2.2 mkg (16 lb ft). Move the adjusting nut slightly if the pins in the plate do not engage the teeth easily. Surplus grease may be injected in the bolt hole opposite the base plate. Coat bolt threads with jointing compound when refitting.

9 Check the eyebolts for faulty Silentbloc bushes and look for cracks and deterioration of the bellows. **FIG 9:14** shows the correct settings for the eyebolts, and although this may be done by measurement it is better to use the setting fixture P.285. The angles are important to ensure free movement of the tie rods.

10 Fit the bellows to the housing. Put gasket compound on the eyebolt threads, the end faces of the rack and on both faces of the stop plate and lockwasher. Fit eyebolts, set them correctly and tighten nuts to 6.5 ·

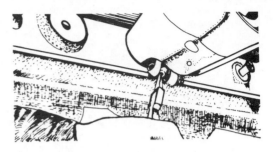

FIG 9:10 Removing or replacing locking pin between lugs of switch assembly clamp

FIG 9:11 Engaging dowel pin with slot when driving universal joint onto intermediate shaft

FIG 9:12 Releasing coupling from flange on pinion shaft

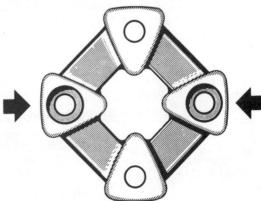

FIG 9:13 Recessed holes in coupling must engage flanges of pinion shaft and lower shaft

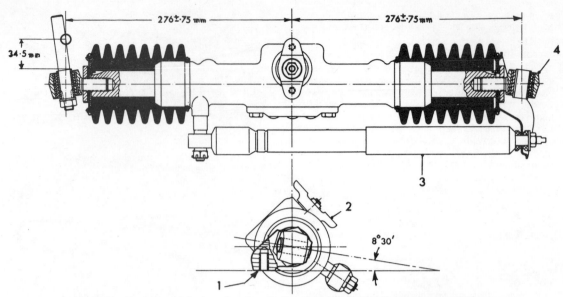

FIG 9:14   Correct positioning of rack eyebolts relative to centre line and mounting bosses

Key to Fig 9:14   1 Face of mounting boss   2 Pinion flange   3 Damper   4 Eyebolt with Silentbloc

mkg (47 lb ft), locking them when secure. Refit the damper, leaving one end disconnected.

Installing:

Reverse the order of dismantling but do not reconnect the tie rods to the steering levers. At this stage, check the drag at the steering wheel as shown in **FIG 9:18**. A drag of 10 cmkg (8¾ lb in) must be recorded with tie rods and damper disconnected. If check is satisfactory, connect damper and tie rods to complete the installation. If a major overhaul is in progress, check the tie rods and ball joints before fitting. Tie rods must not be bent and ball joints must have slight drag when the ballpin is articulated. Free movement or play calls for renewal of the joint. When connecting the inner ends of the rods, coat the bolts with molybdenum disulphide paste and tighten to 4.7 mkg (34 lb ft). Fit ball joint pins dry.

Fit the crossmember brace without strain and tighten nut to 6.5 mkg (47 lb ft) and bolt to 4.7 mkg (34 lb ft) as in **FIG 8:7**. Tighten steering gear mounting bolts on new lockwashers to 4.7 mkg (34 lb ft). Tighten ball joint castle nuts to 4.5 mkg (32½ lb ft) and fit new splitpins. Tighten socket-head screws for bush cap to 2.5 mkg (18 lb ft) as in **FIG 9:3**. Put new lockwashers on the coupling bolts and tighten to 2.5 mkg (18 lb ft) as in **FIG 9:12**.

9:8 Adjusting toe-in

Toe-in is shown in the top view of **FIG 9:19**. Note that the distance between the wheel rims at centre height is less at the front than the back. The front wheels are set parallel on 1968 models onwards.

When the wheels are on either lock at 20 deg. there may be an angle differential as shown in the lower view. 'A1' is parallel to 'A', and 'B' is the centre line of the wheel. The differential angle is thus 'C'. Before the 1968 models the deviation could be 40' to 1 deg. From 1968 models onwards it should lie between 0' and 30'. Excessive error

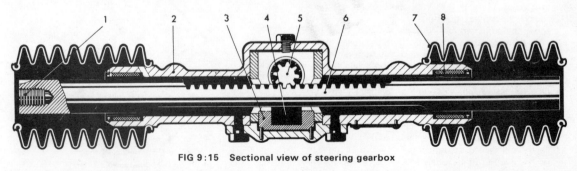

FIG 9:15   Sectional view of steering gearbox

Key to Fig 9:15   1 Thread for eyebolt   2 Housing   3 Adjusting nut   4 Pressure block   5 Steering pinion   6 Steering rack   7 Rubber bellows   8 Bush

may be due to bent steering arms, tie rods or the steering knuckle at the damper strut. **Corrections cannot be made at the steering tie rods.**

Adjustment:

Accurate equipment must be used for checking. Methods will vary, but the basic test is as follows:

Move steering wheel fully to the stop in one direction and note the angle of one particular spoke to any datum such as the instrument panel edge. Turn the wheel on the opposite lock and note the angle of the partner spoke on the other side. If the angles are not the same, the wheel must be removed and replaced in the correct position (see **Section 9:3**).

Now set the steering wheel in the mid-position and adjust the righthand and lefthand tie rods so that, on models prior to 1968, each road wheel has a toe-in of 20', while pressing the wheels together with a preload of

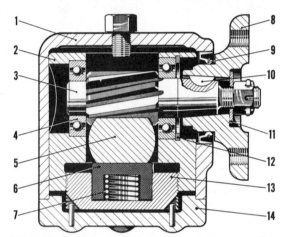

FIG 9:16 Section through steering pinion mounting and pressure block

Key to Fig 9:16 1 Housing 2 Pinion carrier 3 Pinion 4 Ballbearing 5 Rack 6 Pressure block 7 Spring 8 Flange 9 Oil seal 10 Key 11 Washer 12 Circlip 13 Adjusting nut 14 Base plate

FIG 9:17 Using torque meter on pinion flange nut to check steering drag

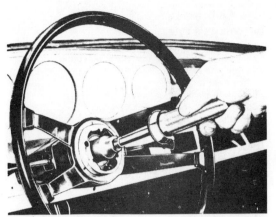

FIG 9:18 Checking steering drag at steering wheel nut, using a torque meter

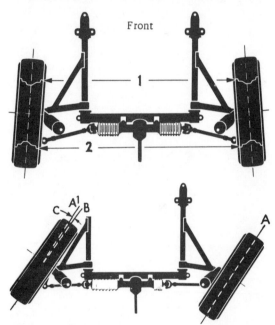

FIG 9:19 When front wheels toe-in, dimension 1 is less than 2 (top). Lower view shows 'A' parallel to 'A1', 'B' the wheel centre line and 'C' the angle differential with wheels locked over at 20 deg.

15 kg (33 lb). The yoke and ball joint are screwed into the tie rod and secured by clamps. Make sure the ends are set in the correct plane before tightening the clamps.

9:9 Steering and wheel alignment

It must be appreciated that incorrect wheel alignment will have an effect on steering. The correct settings of camber and castor angles for the front wheels are given in **Section 8:11** of the preceding chapter. It is also possible for errors in rear wheel alignment to affect steering qualities, so that it is always advisable to make a complete check of all height adjustment, suspension and steering angles on precision equipment.

9:10 Fault diagnosis

(a) Wheel wobble

1 Unbalanced wheels and tyres, uneven pressures
2 Free play in steering gear and connections
3 Front end damaged, incorrect steering angles
4 Incorrect toe-in adjustment
5 Worn or slack hub bearings
6 Faulty damper strut
7 Insufficient drag in steering gear

(b) Steering wander

1 Check 2, 3, 5 and 7 in (a) and 6 in (c)
2 Smooth front tyres, pressures too high or too low

(c) Heavy steering

1 Check 3 in (a)
2 Low or uneven tyre pressures
3 Too much drag in steering gear

4 Insufficient lubricant
5 Steering gearbox mountings out of line
6 Faulty steering damper
7 Weak or broken torsion bars
8 Faulty steering shafts and joints
9 Defective bearing assembly in post extension

(d) Lost motion

1 Check 2 in (a)
2 Loose steering wheel
3 Worn ball joints
4 Steering gearbox loose on mountings
5 Worn steering gearbox, ineffective pressure block
6 Universal joints loose on steering shafts

(e) Steering pulls to one side

1 Check 3 in (a) and 2 in (c)
2 One front brake binding
3 Broken or sagging front or rear suspension

CHAPTER 10

THE BRAKING SYSTEM

10:1 General description

Every model has front and rear disc brakes which are hydraulically operated, but the handbrake is cable-operated and expands shoes inside a drum which is integral with each rear disc. A diagrammatic layout of the system is given in **FIG 10:1**, early models having the single master cylinder 2. 1968 models onwards have the dual master cylinder shown in **FIG 10:18.** This has the advantage that failure in one set of brakes, either front or rear, leaves the remaining set in full working order.

Fluid reservoir 3 ensures that the system is always full. When pedal 1 is depressed it pushes on a piston in master cylinder 2, forcing fluid along metal pipes 4 and flexible pipes 5 to the brake cylinders in calipers 6 and 8. The pressure on the pistons in these cylinders forces them to press pads lined with friction material into braking contact with the discs 7 and 9 secured to the hubs. Because each disc is nipped between a pair of pads, the resultant braking is both smooth and powerful. The rubber seals round the pistons are slightly deformed when the brakes are applied. Releasing the brakes causes these seals to resume their original shape and this action slightly retracts the pistons, leaving the discs free to revolve. In consequence the footbrakes are self-adjusting.

Although early discs were solid and were the type always fitted to 911T models with manual gearboxes, ventilated discs were fitted to 911S cars, to 911T models with Sportomatic transmission, to later 911, to 911L and 911E models. These reduced operating temperatures to give improved braking. Later models with self-levelling suspension were also fitted with light alloy wheels. The handbrake housing was modified to incorporate the heater and hand throttle controls.

10:2 Routine maintenance

Every 6000 miles the whole system must be checked for fluid leakage, for damaged hoses and pipes and for condition and thickness of braking pads.

Cars in America that have dual-circuit brakes must have the warning device checked every 6000 miles.

Fluid level:

At regular intervals the fluid level in the reservoir must be checked and fluid added if required. The reservoir is below the luggage compartment (see **FIG 10:2**). Correct fluid level is approximately 2 cm (.80 inch) below the top ridge of the reservoir. If topping up is needed, use only genuine ATE Blue Fluid. **Be careful not to let the fluid drip on the body paintwork as it is a solvent.**

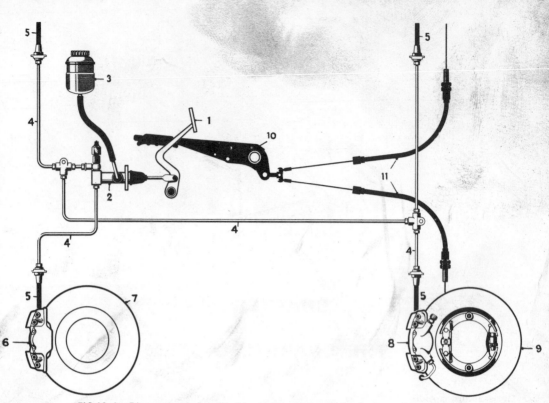

FIG 10:1   Diagrammatic layout of braking system using a single master cylinder

Key to Fig 10:1   1 Brake pedal   2 Master cylinder   3 Fluid reservoir   4 Metal pipes   5 Flexible hoses   6 Front caliper
7 Disc   8 Rear caliper   9 Disc   10 Handbrake lever   11 Handbrake cables

Handbrake adjustment:

When lever movement is excessive, adjust the handbrake as follows:

1 Raise car and remove rear wheels. Release handbrake. Push back the pads of the rear disc brakes so that the discs rotate freely.
2 Behind shrouds, loosen cable adjusting nuts to relieve cable tension (see lefthand view, **FIG 10:3**).

FIG 10:2   Location of fluid reservoir in luggage compartment

Insert screwdriver as in righthand view and turn adjusting sprocket until shoes lock inside drum and disc is immovable. Sprocket can be seen in **FIG 10:11.** Repeat adjustment on opposite wheel.

3 Remove cable slack at adjusting nuts (see **FIG 10:3**, left). Pull back cover round handbrake lever mounting and note two holes in flange near rear bolt. Looking vertically downwards, the ends of the cable crossbeam should be visible. The beam should be at right angles to the car centre line. If not, adjust at nuts behind shrouds. Tighten adjusting nut locknuts.
4 Now back off the two sprockets by about 4 or 5 teeth so that the discs can be turned freely. Check that handbrake is applied when pulled up about 4 teeth but is quite free when lever is released. Finally, depress brake pedal several times to set the pads and then check fluid level in reservoir.

10:3 Renewing brake pads

Check the thickness of pad linings at regular intervals. Wear limit is reached when plate touches cross-spring or when pad lining is worn down to 2 mm (.08 inch) thickness. Arrows in **FIG 10:4** show minimum desirable thickness.

When new, total thickness of lining and plate is approximately 15 mm (.60 inch). Touring and competition pads are available, the latter being marked TE.10. Front pads differ in size from rear ones, so pads are not interchangeable. Mark used pads before removal to ensure correct replacement. It is not permissible to change their positions. Front pads and rear pads must always be complete sets of one particular type. Although it is possible to renew one pad only, it is best to renew all the pads of an axle pair, either front or rear.

Changing pads:

1 Jack up car and remove wheels. Extract pins 7 and push out retaining pins 8 (see **FIG 10 : 5**), pressing down on the cross-spring 6 and pushing pins inwards.

2 If pads are still usable, mark their positions. Withdraw pads.

3 The next operation may cause overflowing of the fluid reservoir (see **FIG 10 : 2**) so drain it. Press both pistons into their bores, either with tool P.83 (see **FIG 10 : 9**) or with a strip of hardwood. Do not use steel tools which may damage disc or pistons.

4 Clean out the pad cavities with methylated spirits and a soft-edged tool. **Do not use other solvents.** Check condition of dust cover and clamping ring. Renew hardened or cracked covers.

FIG 10 : 3   Slackening handbrake cable adjuster behind rear brake (left). Using screwdriver to turn brake shoe adjuster for handbrake (right)

FIG 10 : 4   Arrows indicate minimum pad thickness, showing ample clearance from cross-spring

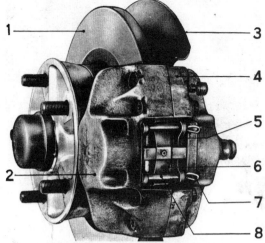

FIG 10 : 5   Details of front disc brake

Key to Fig 10 : 5   1 Disc   2 Caliper cover   3 Disc shroud
4 Caliper base housing   5 Pad segment   6 Cross-spring
7 Spring pin   8 Retaining pin

FIG 10 : 6   Arrow indicates metal fluid pipe to caliper on front brake

5 Polish the brake discs with fine emerycloth and smooth out any inner and outer ridges on each face.

6 Fit pads and check that they are free to move in the cavities. Reassemble in the reverse order, fitting new spring pins in the retaining pins if the original pins are distorted or worn. Put clean fluid in the reservoir and depress the brake pedal several times to set the pistons in the correct positions. Recheck the fluid level in the reservoir.

Do not use the brakes heavily during the first 200 km (125 miles) if new pads are fitted. Condition the pads by moderate pedal pressure, with intervals for cooling, unless an emergency occurs. The pads, with careful bedding-in, will then give effective braking without fade.

10 : 4 Servicing front brakes

Removal:

1 Remove pads (operations 1 and 2 in preceding instructions). Block brake pedal in slightly depressed

FIG 10:7 Removing bolts that secure brake carrier to front axle

FIG 10:8 Prising out spring ring that secures caliper piston dust cover

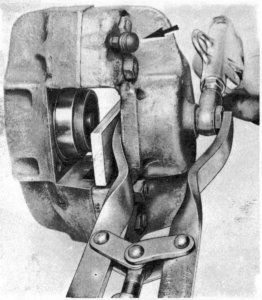

FIG 10:9 Using clamp to press piston back into cylinder. Arrow points to bleed screw

position, then detach fluid pipe at banjo connection behind caliper (see **FIG 10:6**).

2 Remove bolts to release caliper and shroud. Prise off hub cap

3 Slacken socket-head screw in clamping nut on end of axle, unscrew nut and remove thrust washer. Parts are shown in **FIG 8:3** in 'Front Suspension' chapter. Pull off disc and hub. If tight, do not hammer on disc but use a puller.

4 From behind axle, remove disc shroud. Unlock and remove bolts and lift off brake carrier (see **FIG 10:7**).

Dismantling:

1 If necessary, separate disc from hub after marking for correct reassembly.

2 Do not part the caliper halves unless there has been leakage. Loosen bleed screw arrowed in **FIG 10:9** and use gentle air pressure (1 atm or 14 lb/sq in) to eject any fluid in the caliper.

3 Remove clamping ring and dust cover (see **FIG 10:8**). Depress one piston with tool P.83 (see **FIG 10:9**) or use a clamp. Place a block of wood in the slot as shown and blow out the opposite piston with air pressure of 2 atm or 29 lb/sq in, raising pressure if necessary. **Serious injury may result if fingers are not kept out of slot during this operation.**

4 Remove piston seal from inside cylinder bore with a plastic or wooden tool so that the groove and bore are not damaged. Restore removed piston and seal and clamp in order to remove opposite piston. Clean all the parts in methylated spirit (industrial alcohol). **Do not use any other type of solvent or the rubber seals will be damaged.** Check cylinder bores and pistons for wear, scoring or pitting and renew faulty parts. Renew all seals as a matter of course. It is dangerous to refit any doubtful parts. The components of the automatic pad adjustment cannot be renewed. Always fit a new piston if the automatic device is defective.

Reassembling caliper:

1 Use ATE brake cylinder paste to coat the cylinder and piston parts. Insert seals in cylinder grooves.

2 Note cutaway step on piston pressure face. Use aligning tool P.84 or make up a thin sheet-metal gauge with an included angle of 20 deg. as shown in **FIG 10:10** to set piston correctly. Insert piston carefully so that it does not tilt or jam and align it so that the stepped-down part faces the disc rotation as shown. Use clamp to press piston into place. The aligning tool must rest against the upper edge of the brake pad slot. If caliper is installed, a piston may be turned by clamping the opposite piston and ejecting the required piston until it may be turned by hand.

3 Wipe off assembly grease and fit dust covers dry.

4 If caliper was separated into halves because of O-ring leakage, clean faces with methylated spirit (industrial alcohol), fit new rings and assemble with new bolts, nuts and spring washers, using genuine Porsche spares. Tighten to half the required torque and then fully tighten. Torque for front calipers is 3.4 mkg (24½ lb ft). Do not forget packing plate 7.3 mm (.287 inch) thick between halves when ventilated discs are fitted.

5 Fit disc to hub with marks aligned and tighten nuts to 2.3 mkg (16½ lb ft). Refit hub as described in **Chapter 8** and adjust bearings. Use a dial gauge to check the lateral runout of the disc faces as described in **Section 10:7**.

6 Fit caliper using new spring washers and tighten bolts to 7 mkg (50½ lb ft). Fit brake pads in original positions (see **Section 10:3**). Bleed the hydraulic system (see **Section 10:10**).

10:5 Servicing rear brakes

Removing:

1 Jack up car and remove rear wheels after chocking front wheels and releasing handbrake.

2 Remove brake pads (see **Section 10:3**). From behind, remove disc shrouds. Block brake pedal in slightly depressed position and detach fluid pipe from caliper, then detach caliper.

3 Remove two countersunk screws adjacent to wheel studs and pull off disc.

4 Refer to **FIG 10:11** and remove castle nut 1 and washer. From behind, pull out handbrake cable. Remove expander 2 and spring.

5 Turn retainer 3 to release it from pin, remove spring and pull out pin from rear. Lift upper shoe with screwdriver, withdraw adjuster 4 and unhook spring between shoes.

6 Release retainer from lower shoe. Remove both shoes in forward direction and unhook second return spring.

Servicing caliper:

For this operation, follow the instructions for front brake calipers in **Section 10:4**. There is a packing plate 10.6 mm (.417 inch) thick between the caliper halves when ventilated discs are fitted to car. Bolt torque for caliper halves is 1.8 mkg (13 lb ft).

Checking parts:

Clean and examine mechanical parts for wear. Renew broken or distorted springs and check that adjuster works freely. Discard oily brake linings as it is not possible to clean them satisfactorily. Worn linings must be replaced by Porsche-approved makes.

Reassembling:

1 Insert handbrake cable and fit washer against spacer tube. Fit inner expander struts. Fit special return spring 5 to both shoes with coils pointing inwards (see **FIG 10:11**).

2 Slide shoes rearwards onto brake carrier plate and fit the retaining pins, springs and retainers 3. Fit inner expander of handbrake into seats in shoes.

3 Lift upper shoe with screwdriver and fit adjuster 4. Sprocket faces down in righthand brake and up in lefthand brake. Fit return spring at adjuster end of shoes.

4 Slacken adjusting nut on handbrake cable right back. Fit expander spring, second half of expander 2 and tighten castle nut until one of its slots clears the splitpin hole. Fit a new splitpin. Make sure expander struts are correctly seated in shoes.

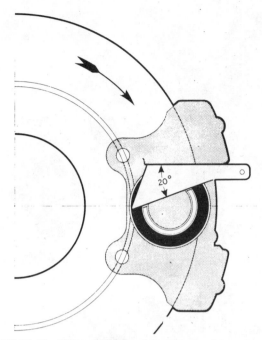

FIG 10:10 Using 20 deg. plate to set piston step correctly in relation to caliper and to disc rotation

FIG 10:11 Handbrake assembly with drum removed. Dotted lines show correct alignment of coils of right-hand spring

Key to Fig 10:11   1 Nut for cable   2 Brake shoe expander   3 Shoe retainer   4 Shoe adjuster   5 Interrupted return spring

5 Refit disc and check for runout (see **Section 10:7**). With ventilated discs, fit intermediate plate between caliper and rear axle control arm. Fit caliper and tighten bolts to 6 mkg (43½ lb ft). Fit pads in original positions. Bleed hydraulic system (see **Section 10:10**) and adjust handbrake (see **Section 10:2**).

FIG 10:12   A ventilated disc brake, showing disc 1 and packing or intermediate plate 2 (between caliper halves)

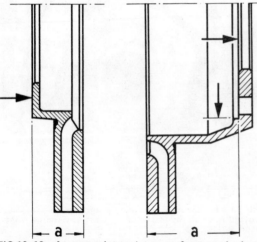

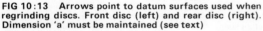

FIG 10:13   Arrows point to datum surfaces used when regrinding discs. Front disc (left) and rear disc (right). Dimension 'a' must be maintained (see text)

10:6   The handbrake carrier plate

This is part 6 in **FIG 7:6** in the 'Rear Suspension' chapter and the early instructions in **Section 7:4** cover the removal of the carrier plate and the correct procedure for reassembly.

10:7   Servicing brake discs

Solid type:

Front discs are 12.5 to 12.7 mm (.492 to .500 inch) thick when new and rear discs are 9.8 to 10.0 mm (.386 to .394 inch) thick, or alternatively, rear ones may be 10.3 to 10.5 mm (.406 to .413 inch). Wear limit, if symmetrical, is 11 mm (.43 inch) front, and 8.5 mm (.33 inch) rear.

Concentric scoring of discs is normal, but if it is excessive, with possible pitting or cracking, the disc must be reground or renewed. Remove up to .50 mm (.02 inch) equally from each side, the surface finish being within .006 mm (.00024 inch). Thickness must not vary more than .03 mm (.0012 inch). Reground discs must not runout more than .05 mm (.002 inch).

To check front disc runout when installed, remove the brake pads (see **Section 10:3**) and adjust the front wheel bearings. Set up a dial gauge so that its plunger bears on the disc face about 10 to 15 mm (.40 to .60 inch) below the outer edge. It is advisable to check both faces. Maximum permissible runout when mounted is .20 mm (.008 inch), and discs with excessive runout must be reground or renewed.

To check rear discs, remove pads and set up dial gauge as before. Brake disc must be fully tightened onto hub by refitting the wheel nuts on steel spacers so that the nuts may be tightened to 10 mkg ($72\frac{1}{4}$ lb ft). To avoid warping, tighten evenly and diagonally. Runout must not exceed figure given for front discs.

Ventilated discs:

A brake with ventilated disc is shown in **FIG 10:12**. Note plate 2 between caliper halves. Disc thickness is 19.8 to 20 mm (.780 to .787 inch) both front and rear.

Smooth, rounded concentric scoring is normal, but sharp ridges, cracking and pitting call for disc renewal or regrinding. This is also the remedy for excessive runout or variation in thickness.

When regrinding, remove no more than .70 mm (.028 inch) equally from each side, the minimum disc thickness being 18.6 mm (.732 inch). Surface finish must be within .006 mm (.0002 inch). Deviation in thickness .03 mm (.001 inch) maximum. Runout up to .05 mm (.002 inch) measured on faces 10 mm (.4 inch) inside the outer edge.

Wear limit off disc thickness is 1 mm (.04 inch) from each face. If worn symmetrically, lowest limit of disc thickness is 18 mm (.71 inch).

Check runout of mounted discs as described for solid discs, noting the extra tolerance allowed when discs are fitted to hubs.

Mounting of solid discs:

When regrinding discs it is most important to preserve the original symmetry, which is the reason for taking an equal amount off each side. To ensure that this may be checked by the operator, the following dimensions are given. Measurement 'a' in **FIG 10:13** is tabled together with the original disc thickness, and a simple calculation will enable the check to be made.

When thickness of new front disc is 12.5 to 12.7 mm (.492 to .500 inch), dimension 'a' is 35±.10 mm (1.378 ±.004 inch).

When thickness of new rear disc is 9.8 to 10.0 mm (.386 to .394 inch), dimension 'a' is 62 ± .10 mm (2.441 ± .004 inch).

When thickness of new rear disc is 10.3 to 10.5 mm (.406 to .413 inch), dimension 'a' is 62.25 ± .10 mm (2.451 ± .004 inch).

Mounting of ventilated discs:

The same symmetry must be maintained as stated for solid discs. Check against the following specification when regrinding.

When thickness of new front disc is 19.8 to 20.0 mm (.780 to .787 inch), dimension 'a' is 35 ± .10 mm (1.378 ± .004 inch).

With same thickness of new rear disc, dimension 'a' is 65 ± .10 mm (2.559 ± .004 inch).

Pad thickness:

All the preceding limits for wear and regrinding apply only if the pad thickness is not allowed to fall below 2.0 mm (.08 inch). **This is important if the brakes are to function correctly.**

Disc balance:

Ventilated discs are balanced at the factory by inserting spring clips into the ventilating slots. Do not remove these clips.

Ventilated disc cleanliness:

Using the car on dirty roads may lead to clogging of the ventilating slots. When washing the car, use a hose to clear the slots to ensure adequate cooling.

FIG 10:14 View under car showing pipes being detached from master cylinder

10:8 Servicing single master cylinder

Removing:

1 Jack up car. Detach accelerator pedal from rod by pulling pedal back. Remove mat and floorboard. From behind brake pedal, pull rubber boot off master cylinder (see part 11 in **FIG 10:15**).
2 Drain brake fluid reservoir (see **FIG 10:2**). Underneath car, remove shield from suspension crossmember. Detach pipes and switch wires from cylinder (see **FIG 10:14**).
3 Loosen clamp and withdraw hose connecting reservoir to cylinder. Release cylinder flange from body (2 nuts) and withdraw cylinder.

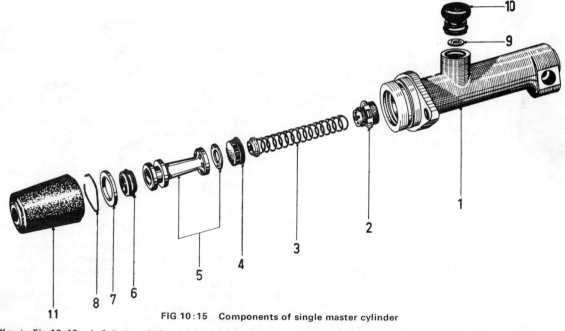

FIG 10:15   Components of single master cylinder

Key to Fig 10:15   1 Cylinder   2 Special check valve   3 Spring   4 Primary piston cup   5 Piston with washer   6 Secondary piston cup   7 Piston stop plate   8 Lock ring   9 Washer   10 Rubber grommet   11 Rubber boot

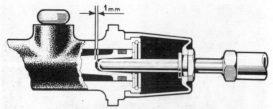

FIG 10:16 Correct clearance between master cylinder piston and pedal pushrod is 1 mm (.04 inch)

FIG 10:17 Adjusting length of brake pedal pushrod

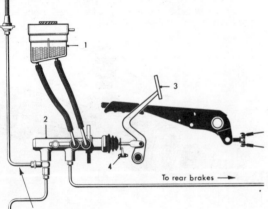

FIG 10:18 Diagram showing layout of dual master cylinder braking system

Key to Fig 10:18   1 Fluid reservoir   2 Dual master cylinder   3 Brake pedal   4 Mechanical stoplight switch

Dismantling:

Refer to **FIG 10:15.** Hold cylinder lightly between soft jaws in a vice.

1 Prise out ring 8. Withdraw stop plate 7.

2 Tap out piston and washer 5 with secondary cup 6.

3 With gentle air pressure of 1 atm (15 lb/sq in) at outlet port, blow out primary cup 4 and remove spring 3 and valve 2.

Cleaning and inspection:

Clean all parts in methylated spirit (industrial alcohol). **Use no other solvents as they may cause rapid deterioration of the rubber seals.** Always renew the seals or cups, which are available in kit form. Check the cylinder bore and piston surfaces for wear, scoring or corrosion, and discard if not smooth and polished. Check all ports and valve passages for obstruction. When clean and dry, the piston must produce suction drag when moved either way in the cylinder.

Reassembling:

Observe absolute cleanliness: Lightly coat cylinder bore, piston and cups with ATE brake cylinder paste. Do not allow mineral oil or grease to contact any internal parts. Reassemble in reverse order of dismantling, making sure that cups are carefully inserted in bore so that lips are not turned back. Remember to install the washer 5 in correct position. Make sure that the lock ring is firmly seated.

Installation:

Apply sealer to cylinder mounting flange and check that pushrod enters cylinder, then attach flange to body, using new spring washers. Tighten nuts to 2.5 mkg (18 lb ft). Inside car, check pushrod clearance shown in **FIG 10:16.** To adjust to 1 mm (.04 inch), loosen locknut and turn pushrod as shown in **FIG 10:17.** Connect pipes and wires.

Check that vent hole in reservoir cap is clear. Fill reservoir (see **Section 10:2**). Bleed brake system (see **Section 10:10**). Check operation of brakes, check for leaks with pedal depressed firmly and check stoplights. Refit undershield, tightening nuts to 6.5 mkg (47 lb ft) and bolts to 4.7 mkg (34 lb ft).

10:9 Servicing the dual master cylinder

Starting with the 1968 models, 911(USA), 911T and 911S cars are fitted with dual-circuit braking systems. The difference can be seen by comparing **FIG 10:18** with **FIG 10:1**. Note the twin-tank reservoir 1 and dual outlets from the master cylinder 2. Failure of one circuit still leaves the other circuit in operative condition. USA cars have an additional brake failure indicator actuated by the master cylinder. A mechanical stoplight switch 4 is operated by a disc on the pushrod.

Removing:

Refer to **Section 10:8,** the sequence being the same apart from the need to detach the additional pipelines.

Dismantling:

Refer to **FIG 10:19.** Hold cylinder lightly in a vice fitted with soft jaws.

1 Prise out ring 14. Remove stop plate 13 and piston 11 complete with all cups, washers, spring and stop 9.

2 Remove stroke limiting bolt 24 of secondary piston 7 and use gentle air pressure of 1 atm (15 lb/sq in) to blow out piston and cups. Cover any holes in cylinder which allow air to escape. Remove spring 2 and washers.

3 Hold neck of primary piston 11 between soft jaws in a vice and unscrew stroke limiting bolt 8, keeping the

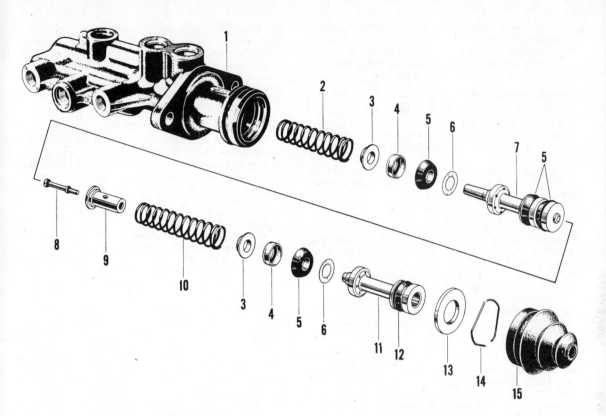

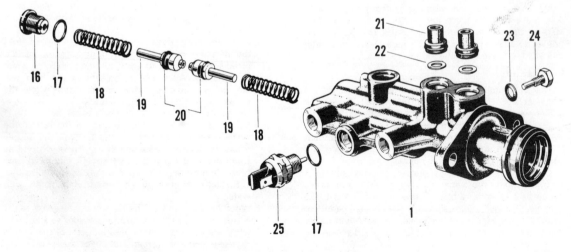

FIG 10:19   Components of dual master cylinder

Key to Fig 10:19   1 Cylinder   2 Secondary piston return spring   3 Spring seat   4 Supporting washer   5 Primary cup
6 Filler disc   7 Secondary piston   8 Stroke limiting bolt   9 Sleeve   10 Primary piston return spring   11 Primary piston
12 Secondary cup   13 Stop plate   14 Lock ring   15 Dust boot   16 Cap screw   17 O-ring   18 Spring   19 Piston   20 Piston
cup   21 Grommet   22 Washer   23 Gasket   24 Stop bolt   25 Circuit failure sender (for USA)

spring compressed to reduce the load on the threads. Separate the parts.

4 On USA cars, remove warning sender 25 and cap screw 16 and blow out parts 19 and 20 with gentle air pressure, blocking any escape holes for air.

Cleaning and inspection:

Wash all parts in methylated spirit (industrial alcohol). **Use no other solvents as they may lead to rapid deterioration of the rubber parts.** Dry the housing and clear all ports with compressed air. Renew all rubber parts at every overhaul. They are available in kit form.

Check piston and cylinder bore surfaces for wear, scoring or corrosion. Renew if not smooth and highly polished.

Reassembling:

Do not let mineral oil contact any internal parts. Observe absolute cleanliness at all times. Reassemble in the reverse order, lightly coating the bore, the piston and the cups with ATE brake cylinder paste. When inserting the cups, take care not to turn back the sealing lips. Make sure cups face correctly with lips entering first.

Insert secondary piston with filler disc, primary cup, supporting washer, spring seat and spring, with large coil of spring entering first. Using a piece of clean plastic rod, push the piston down the bore until it clears the hole for the stop bolt. Fit the bolt and washer, tightening to 1 to 1.2 mkg (7.2 to 8.7 lb ft). Check that bolt is properly seated ahead of the piston and that the piston moves freely to the bottom of the bore.

Fit filler disc, primary cup and supporting washer to primary piston. Use stroke limiting bolt to secure spring, spring seat and stop sleeve to piston. Insert in bore and fit lock ring, making sure it is well-seated.

On USA models, coat warning system plungers with ATE brake cylinder paste and install as shown in **FIG 10:19.** Use a new O-ring under the cap screw and tighten to 1.5 mkg (11 lb ft). Fit new O-ring to sender unit and tighten to the same torque.

Installation:

This operation is similar to the one described for the single master cylinder (see **Section 10:8**). Check the failure warning system on USA cars as follows:

Test the warning system every 6000 miles and whenever the hydraulic system has been under repair. Switch on the ignition. Apply handbrake and check that control lamp lights up. This will test the bulb.

Depress brake pedal to brake actuation point. A second operator must now simulate failure of one brake circuit by slackening a bleed screw on one of the brake calipers. Further depression of the brake pedal to actuation point for the other brake circuit should cause the control lamp to light up. Tighten the bleed screw and release pedal.

Repeat the operation but select a bleed screw in the second circuit. If the lamp does not light up during one of the tests, check the sender unit on the master cylinder and renew if necessary.

Stoplight switch:

This is mounted on a bracket to one side of the brake pedal and pushrod. Remove the two screws and detach the wires to release the switch.

To adjust the switch, place a packing piece 4 mm (.157 inch) thick under the pedal stop. This will be equivalent to a pedal pad travel of 21 mm (.827 inch). Adjacent to the cable connections on the switch is a screw and locknut. Slacken the nut and turn the screw to the point where the stoplights just go on. Tighten the locknut and check action.

10:10 Bleeding the brake system

Air being compressible, it follows that any air which is present in the fluid of the hydraulic brake system will lead to excessive pedal travel and a 'spongy' feel. The object of bleeding the system is to get rid of this air. With the exception of the pipe connecting the reservoir to the master cylinder, any other disconnection of pipes will allow air to enter and make bleeding necessary.

When the piston in the master cylinder is fully retracted, it uncovers a port which allows fluid from the reservoir to top up the system if any fluid has been lost by leakage. If any pipe is disconnected it means that this action will lead to complete draining of the reservoir. To prevent this, block the brake pedal in a slightly depressed position so that the supply port is covered.

Two operators are needed for the operation. For cars with lefthand drive, start at the outer bleed screw of the lefthand rear wheel, follow with the inner bleed screw, repeat on the other rear wheel, then do the righthand front wheel followed by the left. **At all times during the operation, make sure that there is plenty of fluid in the reservoir.** If the supply becomes exhausted, air will enter the master cylinder and the procedure must then be restarted. Proceed as follows:

1 Remove dust cover from bleed screw and fit bleed hose as shown in **FIG 10:20.** Immerse the free end of the tube in some clean brake fluid in a clean glass container. Top up the supply reservoir with ATE Blue brake fluid.

2 Pump the brake pedal until pressure can be felt, hold the pressure while the second operator opens the bleed screw about $\frac{1}{2}$ to $\frac{3}{4}$ of a turn and press the pedal to the floor. Air which is present in the fluid will emerge as bubbles from the immersed tube. Close the screw and let the pedal return slowly.

3 Repeat this until no more air bubbles can be seen.

4 Follow the correct sequence and do the rest of the system, keeping an eye on the level in the supply reservoir. **Do not make use of any fluid which has been drained from the system.** Be careful to keep brake fluid off the paintwork of the car as it will attack it. Spilled fluid must be washed off immediately with water.

5 When finished, top up the fluid in the reservoir to the correct level and apply strong pressure to the pedal while another operator checks all parts of the system for leaks. Test car on road and check that pedal travel does not increase after use. If pedal feels 'spongy' or if brakes pull to one side, repeat the operation of bleeding. It is always advisable to repeat operation when the whole system has been drained during a complete overhaul.

For competition work it may be necessary to use a fluid with a higher boiling point, and Castrol Girling Brake Fluid Amber is recommended. For best results, use fresh fluid throughout the system before each event.

Bleeding dual-circuit brakes:

The procedure is the same as that just outlined, the rear brakes being bled first, followed by the front.

10:11 Servicing handbrake

Adjusting the handbrake cables has been covered in **Section 10:2**. Note that there are two types of handbrake installation, the second and later type having the heater and hand throttle control levers mounted on the support housing as shown in **FIG 10:21**. The following instructions will deal with this type, but such details as removing and refitting the brake cables will do for both types.

Removing handbrake:

1 Remove tunnel cover and lever dust boot. Unscrew knob off heater control lever 1. Release support housing from tunnel (3 bolts).
2 Remove nut 5 and withdraw cup spring 4, pressure disc 3, friction disc 8 and heater control lever 1. Note that numbered parts are actually at the opposite end, so work on the end adjacent to the heater lever.
3 Lift the housing a little. The cables and equalizer beam can be seen attached to a clevis, the clevis pin being secured by a spring clip. Release the clip and pull out the pin.
4 Remove wire from control lamp switch and lift away handbrake assembly.

Dismantling:

1 Remove locking ring and withdraw drag link and washer from lower end of hand throttle lever. Remove nut from pivot shaft 6 and lift off hand throttle lever and friction assembly. Pull out pivot shaft.
2 Remove screw to rear of pivot and withdraw control switch. Push handbrake lever slightly to rear and out of the housing to remove the ratchet plate.

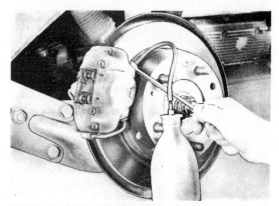

FIG 10:20 When bleeding brakes, tube is attached to bleed screw and free end is immersed in fluid in glass jar

3 Grind the rivet head off the ratchet pawl stud, drive out the stud and remove the pawl. If it is necessary to remove the handbrake lever, pull off the hand grip, which is glued on. This will release the button and rod, the ring and the spring.

Reassembling:

1 After fitting the handbrake control button, glue the grip in place, making sure that no surplus glue interferes with the action of the button.
2 Grease the ratchet plate pawl and pivot shaft with multipurpose lithium grease and insert into place.
3 Fit hand throttle friction discs dry. All friction assembly surfaces must be free from grease. Tighten self-locking nut until flush with end of pivot shaft.

Installation:

Do this in the reverse order of dismantling. Do not forget to attach the wire to the control lamp switch. Fit the heater control lever in the housing. Install the cable

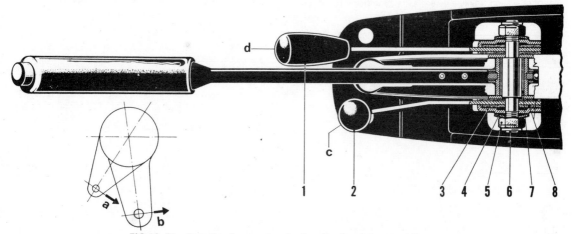

FIG 10:21 Details of mounting for handbrake and control levers

Key to Fig 10:21 1 Heater control lever   2 Hand throttle lever   3 Pressure disc   4 Cup spring   5 Self-locking nut   6 Pivot   7 Spacer sleeve   8 Friction disc   **a** Friction limit of heater lever is 10 kg (22 lb)   **b** Friction limit of hand throttle lever is 6 kg (13 lb)   **c** Hand throttle lever knob is pressed on   **d** Heater lever knob is screwed on

beam and check that the cables are correctly seated. Fit the housing to the tunnel and tighten the bolts to 2.5 mkg (18 lb ft). Reassemble the friction parts for the heater lever in the manner described for the hand throttle lever. Tighten the self-locking nut until the lever does not feel too stiff to move but does not slip back when heater is fully on. Check adjustment of heater flaps as in **Chapter 4.** Check adjustment of hand throttle control as in **Chapter 2.** Check handbrake adjustment (see **Section 10:2**).

Adjusting control lamp switch:

On some models the contact block for the switch is secured to the handbrake housing by a screw to the rear of the handbrake lever pivot. There is a slot for adjustment. Pull on the handbrake by one notch, loosen the screw and move the contact block by means of the screw until the control lamp lights up. Tighten the screw and check action again.

Servicing handbrake cables:

Removing:

1 Chock front wheels, release handbrake and raise rear of car. Remove rear wheels.
2 Remove handbrake housing from tunnel (3 bolts). Detach cables from equalizer beam (see 'Removing handbrake').
3 Block brake pedal in slightly depressed position to prevent draining of fluid from system and remove pipe-line from rear caliper. Detach caliper from mounting.
4 Remove countersunk screws and pull off brake disc and spacer. Release cable from expander (see **Section 10:5**). Pull cable out from rear of brake. Pull other end out of conduit tube in tunnel.

Refitting:

1 Feed cable into conduit tube while coating it with multipurpose lithium grease. Refit cable end to brake expander as described in **Section 10:5**.
2 Refit caliper, tightening bolts to 6 mkg (43 lb ft) on new spring washers. Refit handbrake housing to tunnel. Bleed brake system (see **Section 10:10**). Adjust handbrake (see **Section 10:2**).

10:12 Fault diagnosis

(a) 'Spongy' pedal action

1 Leak in hydraulic system
2 Worn master cylinder
3 Leaking caliper cylinders
4 Air in the fluid
5 Insufficient fluid in reservoir

(b) Excessive pedal movement

1 Check 1, 4 and 5 in (a)
2 Excessive pad wear
3 Too much free movement in pedal pushrod
4 Defective cups and valve in master cylinder
5 Wheel bearings slack
6 Disc or caliper mountings loose
7 Excessive runout or thickness variation of discs

(c) Brakes grab or pull to one side

1 Check 5, 6 and 7 in (b)
2 Oily pads or mixed grades
3 Worn suspension or steering connections
4 Uneven tyre pressures
5 Dirt in pad slots, dust covers defective
6 20 deg. piston step wrongly set
7 Seized piston in caliper cylinder

(d) Pedal must be pumped to get braking

1 Check 2, 4 and 5 in (a) and 4 in (b)

(e) Brakes get hot when not used

1 Check 4 and 5 in (b); 5 and 7 in (c)
2 Reservoir supply port in master cylinder blocked by piston cup
3 Insufficient free play in pedal pushrod
4 Rubber cups swollen due to wrong fluid
5 Handbrake adjusted too tightly, cables seized (rear)
6 Handbrake shoe return springs weak or broken (rear)

(f) Frequent topping up of fluid required

1 Check pipes, connections and cylinders for leaks

CHAPTER 11

THE ELECTRICAL SYSTEM

11 : 1 General description

The 12-volt system has the negative battery terminal earthed. A belt-driven alternator provides alternating current which is rectified to give DC current for battery charging. The single-unit regulator controls alternator voltage to 14V. There is no current control as output does not rise after reaching the rated figure. There is no cut-out unit and the rectifier output is connected directly to the battery. Some owners will be unfamiliar with the alternator so that it is strongly recommended that they read the recommendations at the start of **Section 11 : 4** and **11 : 5** before carrying out tests. A Bosch alternator is fitted to all models except 911T which has a Motorola.

The starter motor is mounted on the transmission casing. The sliding pinion is meshed with the flywheel ring gear by a solenoid which is actuated when the ignition is switched on. When the pinion is engaged, contacts in the solenoid complete the circuit and the starter motor turns the engine. When the engine fires, an overrunning clutch prevents the pinion from being driven, and it is disengaged by a spring.

Headlamps may have renewable bulbs or sealed-beam units. Flasher and reversing lights are fitted. Instrument lights may be dimmed by turning the switch knob. The revolution indicator is transistorized and is driven by electrical impulses from the ignition system. Electrical sender units operate the fuel, oil temperature and, in the case of 911S cars, the oil pressure gauges.

Electrical tests entail the use of accurate meters, but many mechanical faults may be cured by a reasonably skilled owner. It is recommended that serious wear and major electrical faults are best cured by using the Exchange service of the manufacturers. Wiring diagrams will be found at the end of this manual. **Always use wire for repairs which is the same cross-section as the original.**

11 : 2 Routine maintenance

Every 6000 miles, check the tension of the driving belt (see **Section 4 : 2** in the Cooling chapter). At the same mileage check the whole electrical system for correct functioning and check the condition of the battery. Once a year, check the alternator and starter brushes (see **Sections 11 : 4, 11 : 5** and **11 : 6**) and grease the alternator bearings.

General lubrication of the alternator and starter may be left until the engine is due for a major overhaul.

At regular intervals, check the electrolyte level in the battery and top up as described in **Section 11 : 3**.

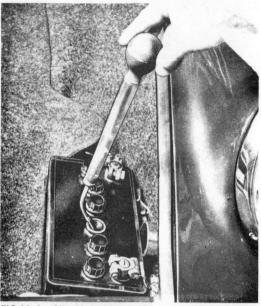

FIG 11:1 Checking the specific gravity of the battery electrolyte with a hydrometer

FIG 11:2 Blower housing released from strap and pulled rearwards for access to the alternator cables

FIG 11:3 Removing brush plate and brushes (Bosch alternator)

11:3 Battery maintenance

The battery is mounted in the luggage compartment. See that the mountings are secure and if the terminals are coated with white powder, brush this off, using a solution of baking soda to neutralize it. Check that the terminal connections are clean and bright and coat them with vaseline or grease. **Difficult starting is often due to dirty or loose connections.**

Check the electrolyte level at regular intervals. Correct level is about 10 mm ($\frac{1}{2}$ inch) above the plates. **Top up with distilled water only. Do not use rain water or tap water.** The electrolyte is a solution of sulphuric acid in distilled water made to a particular specific gravity. **If the electrolyte is being prepared, do not add water to the acid as this is highly dangerous.** Add the acid very slowly to the water.

The specific gravity of the electrolyte is a guide to the state of charge of the battery. Use a hydrometer as shown in **FIG 11:1**, sucking up enough electrolyte to float the graduated indicator. In a fully-charged battery the specific gravity will be 1.285 (32 deg. Beaume). In a half-charged battery it will be 1.230 (27 deg. Beaume). When battery is discharged it will be 1.142 (18 deg. Beaume).

Any electrical test of a battery must be made with a voltmeter which permits a high-discharge rate. During a test of 10 to 15 seconds the voltage of each cell must not drop below 1.6. If it does, the cell is faulty. Normal voltage without load is 2. Voltage of individual cells must not vary by more than .20.

Do not leave the battery in a discharged state or it will be ruined. If it is to be left unused for long periods, give it a freshening charge every month.

11:4 Servicing Bosch alternator

Before carrying out alternator tests it is important to understand that it must not be run without connection to the battery, neither must the cables be removed during a running test. Be careful not to reverse the battery connections. Entrust major repairs to a Bosch service station.

Testing system:

Control lamp should light up with ignition switched on. If it does not, bulb may be broken or wire disconnected. If lamp stays on with ignition switched off it indicates a defective rectifier. Disconnect battery at once to prevent damage to alternator and battery.

Start the engine. If control lamp does not go out with increasing engine speed or lights up at certain speeds, the rectifier is defective.

For a quick test with the alternator installed, run the engine at a steady 3000 rev/min. Switch on lamps and accessories to bring the load to 28 to 30 amp. Voltage between terminals B+ and D— should lie between 13.5 and 14.5 volts.

Removing alternator:

Remove the air cleaner. Release the fuel pipe clips from the upper shroud as in **FIG 11:2**. Remove alternator pulley nut and take off belt (see **Chapter 4, Section 4:2**). Release blower housing strap, pull assembly to rear and detach wires.

Dismantling:

Remove pulley, pulley hub and key. Mark location of alternator in blower housing and remove.

Brushes:

Removing the brush plate is shown in **FIG 11 : 3**, but first check the brushes for freedom in their housings. Hook up the springs and check brush length if no further dismantling is required. Minimum length is 14 mm (.55 inch). Unsolder brush leads to renew brushes. Check that brushes slide freely, rubbing sides on a smooth file if necessary. Resolder leads with resin-cored solder, taking taking care not to let solder run up the stranded flexible connector.

Rotor:

To continue dismantling, remove brush plate complete. Remove the six long screws and part the rotor from the stator housing (see **FIG 11 : 4**). The rotor may be pressed out of the end frame for attention to the bearings and slip rings. It is not advisable to attempt repairs to the rectifier diodes which are mounted on plates at the same end as the brushes.

If the stationary windings are removed from the housing the coils may be tested as shown in **FIG 11 : 5**. Use 40V AC and a pair of probes and check for continuity and earthing. Also check for resistance using an ohmmeter. Correct resistance is .26 ohm + 10 per cent.

Using the same test voltage, check the rotor coils for earthing, putting one probe on a slip ring and the other on the polepiece. Connect an ohmmeter across the slip rings to check rotor coil resistance. It must be 4 ohm + 10 per cent. If the slip rings are worn and pitted, skim them in a lathe, taking off the minimum amount of metal. When finished, check that runout does not exceed .03 mm (.001

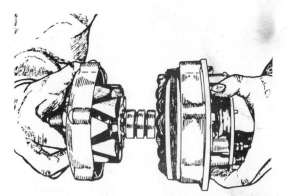

FIG 11 : 4   Separating rotor and end frame from stator housing (Bosch alternator)

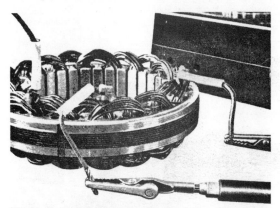

FIG 11 : 5   Using test probes to check the stator windings for shorts (Bosch alternator)

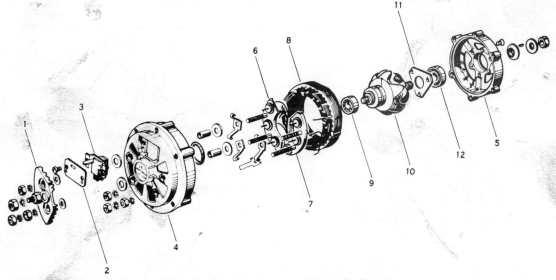

FIG 11 : 6   Component parts of Motorola alternator

Key to Fig 11 : 6   1 Isolation diode heat sink   2 Brush coverplate   3 Brush holder   4 Rear housing, supporting bearing and rotor   5 Front housing, supporting bearing and rotor   6 Positive diode heat sink   7 Negative diode heat sink   8 Stator   9 Ballbearing   10 Rotor   11 Bearing coverplate   12 Ballbearing

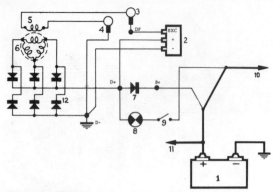

FIG 11:7 Circuit diagram of Motorola alternator, regulator and battery

Key to Fig 11:7 1 Battery 2 Regulator 3 Slip rings
4 Brushes 5 Rotor 6 Stator 7 Isolation diode
8 Generator control lamp 9 Ignition/starter switch 10 To
accessories 11 To starter 12 Diodes

FIG 11:8 Removing brush holder on Motorola alternator

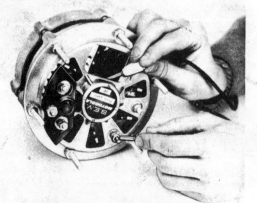

FIG 11:9 Checking rotor for shorts to D—by connecting one ohmmeter probe to a slip ring and the other to the D— terminal (Motorola alternator)

inch). Minimum slip ring diameter is 31.5 mm (1.24 inch) and maximum vertical runout of the rotor is .05 mm (.002 inch).

Bearings:

Renew bearings which are rough when spun without lubricant. In any case, renew bearings which have seen 60,000 miles of service. Adequately support end frame and rotor when pressing bearings into place. Coat one side of bearing with Bosche FT1v33 grease and fit to end frame with closed side entering first. Fit retaining plate.

Cleaning:

Parts must not be soaked in solvents. Momentary exposure to solvents is permissible for cleaning purposes. Always relubricate bearings after cleaning.

Reassembling:

Do this in the reverse order of dismantling. Check that the rotor turns freely after fitting the brushes.

Installation:

Fit alternator to blower housing with marks aligned. Seat blower housing on dowel in crankcase after connecting wires correctly. The red/white lead goes to terminal 1 (B+), the black lead goes to terminal 2 (DF), the brown lead goes to terminal 3 (D—) and the red lead goes to terminal 4 (D+). After fitting the pulley and belt, tighten the nut to 4 mkg (29 lb ft).

11:5 Servicing the Motorola alternator

The component parts are shown in **FIG 11:6**. An alternator is not self-exciting so that the necessary field current has to reach the unit by way of the generator control lamp 8 (see **FIG 11:7**) and the voltage regulator. For this reason it is important that the lamp is not burned out or of the wrong wattage. The field current is only about 2 amp and is conducted to the field coils by brushes 4 and slip rings 3. An isolation diode 7 protects the alternator against overloading and also allows current to flow to the control lamp. The rectifier consists of three positive and three negative diodes 12. These pass current from the alternator to the battery or load but not in the reverse direction, so that there is no need for a cut-out.

Precautions:

Observe the following:
1 Do not earth the field exciter terminals DF of the alternator, regulator or the connecting wire.
2 Do not wrongly connect the voltage regulator and not disconnect the regulator or the battery when the alternator is running.
3 Disconnect the battery before removing the alternator.
4 The voltage regulator must always be connected to alternator earth.
5 For alternator tests the battery must be in good condition and fully charged. When running alternator in car, battery must always be connected.
6 Disconnect battery before arc welding on car.
7 Heat damages diodes. Use pliers as heat sink when unsoldering or soldering. Wrong connections will cause damage to diodes.
8 Detach battery leads when charging battery in car.

Maintenance:

Apart from checking belt tension (see **Chapter 4, Section 4 : 2**) there is no need for routine maintenance of the alternator or the voltage regulator. Bearings are lubricated for life.

Testing alternator:

Make sure alternator connections are as given in 'Installation' for the Bosch alternator. Connect voltage regulator leads so that blue and red go to D+, black goes to DF and brown goes to D—. The regulator is mounted on a bracket near the ignition coil (see **FIG 11 : 16**).

For a quick test with alternator installed, run the engine at 2500 ± 150 rev/min with lamps and accessories switched on to give a load of 28 to 30 amp. Voltage between terminals B+ and D— must lie between 13.4 and 14.6 volts.

Removing alternator:

Do this according to the instructions under the same head in **Section 11 : 4**.

Checking brushgear:

Remove brush holder (2 bolts, see **FIG 11 : 8**). Use ohmmeter and probes to check brushes for continuity, the insulated brush with the DF terminal and the earthed brush with the holder. Resistance should be nil. Resistance should be infinitely high when probes are touching brushes only.

Checking rotor:

Test for shorting to D— by connecting one ohmmeter probe to D— and the other to one of the slip rings as in **FIG 11 : 9**. Resistance should be infinite.

Test rotor coil for continuity by connecting one ohmmeter probe to each slip ring. The circuit resistance should be 4.5 to 6.5 ohm. Renew rotor if faulty.

Testing isolation diode:

First test the heat sink for earthing by connecting one ohmmeter probe to D+61 and the other to D— on the alternator and then in reverse. Resistance should be infinite in one direction and less than 50 ohm in the other. If readings differ from these, check heat sink insulation behind housing.

Test the diode by connecting one ohmmeter probe to terminal B+ and the other to D+61 and then reversing them. Resistance should be infinite in one direction and less than 50 ohm in the other.

Testing rectifier diodes:

Positive diodes are marked red and negative black. Test negative diodes by connecting ohmmeter as shown in **FIG 11 : 10**. Reverse connections and note result, which should be the same as described for the isolation diode. For positive diodes connect ohmmeter to D+61 and diode and then reverse connections to get same results as for the isolation diode.

Testing stator coil:

This is done as in **FIG 11 : 11**, the stator dismantling sequence being given later. Visually, a shortcircuit may be seen as burnt insulation at one spot. To test electrically,

FIG 11 : 10 Using ohmmeter probes to test diodes. Illustration shows negative diode being checked by connecting one probe to D— and the other to the diode terminal (Motorola alternator)

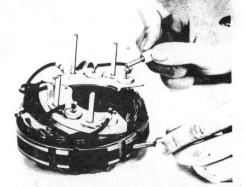

FIG 11 : 11 Connect one ohmmeter probe to a coil end and the other to the stator. Resistance must be infinite. Repeat on all coil ends (Motorola alternator)

FIG 11 : 12 Soldering stator leads to diodes, using pliers as heat sink to avoid damage (Motorola alternator)

connect one ohmmeter probe to one end of coil and the other to the stator frame. Resistance must be infinite. Check all coil ends and renew stator if any test shows lower resistance.

Dismantling alternator:

1 Remove brush assembly (see **FIG 11 : 8**). Remove isolation diode assembly 1 in **FIG 11 : 6** (2 outer nuts).

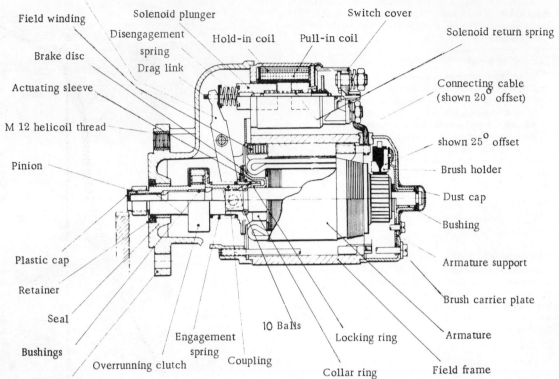

Actuating lever

Field winding

Brake disc

Actuating sleeve

M 12 helicoil thread

Pinion

Plastic cap

Retainer

Seal

Bushings

Drive housing

Solenoid plunger

Disengagement spring

Drag link

Hold-in coil

Pull-in coil

Switch cover

Solenoid return spring

Connecting cable (shown 20° offset)

shown 25° offset

Brush holder

Dust cap

Bushing

Armature support

Brush carrier plate

Armature

Field frame

Collar ring

Locking ring

10 Balls

Engagement spring

Overrunning clutch

Coupling

FIG 11:13 Section through starter motor showing solenoid and actuating lever for engaging pinion with flywheel gear

2 Remove through-bolts and separate front housing 5 and rotor 10 from stator and rear housing 4.

3 Rotor may be pressed out of front housing and the ballbearing pulled off the rear end. To remove the bearing in the front cover, remove the bearing cover (3 screws) and press out the bearing.

4 Release diode assembly 6 and 7 from the rear housing and withdraw together with the stator 8. Mark the negative and positive diode leads if the diodes are to be removed. It would be best to leave servicing the diodes to a service station but the method is as follows:

5 Hold each lead with a pair of pliers on the diode side so that heat cannot travel into diode, and quickly unsolder the connections.

Reassembling:

1 If stator leads were unsoldered from diodes, pull them through the clips so that they lie correctly and will not need bending after soldering. Make sure connections are correct, noting that positive diodes are marked red and negative black.

2 Hold diode leads with pliers as in **FIG 11:12. Use a hot iron and solder lead as quickly as possible.**

3 Fit stator and diode assemblies into housing after placing an insulating washer and sleeve on each fixing stud of the positive diode assembly.

4 After fitting stator and diode assemblies, put insulating washers on the two positive diode studs and secure both assemblies with nuts. Make sure the stator leads are properly arranged.

5 Press rotor into front bearing in housing. Press other ballbearing into place up to the stop on the rear end of rotor shaft.

6 Make sure that the bore in the rear housing is clear and that the O-ring is in good condition. Joint the two housings together and tighten the six bolts evenly and diagonally.

7 Secure the isolation diode assembly in position and then attach the brush assembly. Install the alternator as described in **Section 11:4.**

11:6 Servicing starter motor

Details of the starter motor are shown in **FIG 11:13.** When the ignition and starter key is turned for starting, the solenoid is energized, the plunger is drawn in and the actuating lever starts to move the actuating sleeve to the left. When the associated locking ring has moved about 2 or 3 mm ($\frac{1}{8}$ inch) the balls round a groove in the shaft are freed and allow the pinion to move into engagement with the flywheel ring gear. The solenoid plunger has simultaneously closed a switch which passes current to the motor. If the engine fires, it may run up to a speed which would drive the motor by way of the pinion. To prevent this, a one-way or overrunning clutch is provided which allows the pinion to drive the ring gear but stops it being driven. When the switch is released the solenoid return spring starts to retract the pinion and pressure from the engagement spring pushes the locking ring over the balls and a braking disc comes into action to slow down the armature. The overrunning clutch consists of five spring-loaded rollers confined by cam-shaped recesses which allow rotation in one direction and jam in the other.

Removal:

1 Disconnect battery earth cable. Detach cables from terminal 30 on starter solenoid.
2 Detach ignition switch control wire from starter terminal 50.
3 Remove flange bolts and lift starter away.

Removing and refitting solenoid:

1 Remove wire connector from terminal next to motor body. Release solenoid from drive housing.
2 Pull pinion out a little and withdraw the solenoid while disconnecting the plunger from the actuating lever.

Solenoids are not adjustable and a defective one must be renewed. It is a good plan to renew the solenoid at major engine overhauls.

Install solenoid in the reverse order. Hold the cable terminals when tightening the nuts so that the studs cannot turn and possibly cause internal twisting. Tighten nuts moderately. If solenoid is new, adjust the plunger so that distance from the centre of the hole in the clevis to the mounting flange is $32.4 \pm .10$ mm ($1.276 \pm .004$ inch) when the plunger is in position.

When the solenoid is energized the travel of the plunger must be $10 \pm .20$ mm ($.394 \pm .008$ inch), of which 3 mm ($.118$ inch) is engagement reserve.

Checking brushes and commutator:

1 Remove cover from end of starter opposite to pinion.
2 Lift brush springs and pull brushes out of holders by flexible leads. If length of brush allows lead to touch holder then it is too worn for further use and must be renewed.
3 Clean commutator with a stick wrapped in petrol-soaked cloth. Keep dirt and excess petrol out of the end bearing.

Check brush springs for tension. Renew brushes if worn, oil-soaked or if leads are loose or frayed. Always renew brushes in sets.

If commutator is badly scored or burned, remove the armature and skim the commutator in a lathe. Use fine sandpaper for polishing. Do not use emerycloth. Under-cut as explained in 'Inspection and Testing'.

When refitting the brushes make sure that they are free in their holders and check that the flexible leads are out of the way.

Dismantling starter:

1 Remove dust cap from end opposite to the pinion. Remove the O-rings, the lock ring on the shaft and the spacers.
2 Detach cable from inner terminal of solenoid. Remove solenoid mounting screws and withdraw solenoid while unhooking plunger from actuating lever (see **FIG 11:13**).

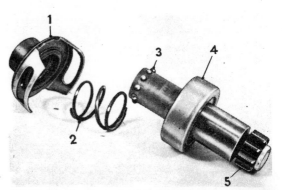

FIG 11:14 Components of the starter pinion assembly

Key to Fig 11:14   1 Actuating sleeve   2 Spring
3 Locking balls   4 Overrunning clutch   5 Pinion

FIG 11:15 Starter motor with brush carrier plate removed, showing commutator and metal and insulating washers on shaft

FIG 11:16 Location of the voltage regulator is indicated by arrow

3 Remove the two long through-bolts and the end cover or armature support. Withdraw brushes, making a note of their locations. Positive brushes have leads which are soldered to the field windings, negative brush leads go to the brush holders.
4 Remove the brush carrier plate and the metal and insulating washers from the armature shaft (see **FIG 11:15**). Pull complete field frame off the drive housing, taking care of the rubber seal and the metal plate.

FIG 11:17   To set headlamp beam vertically, turn screw 'a' to right to lower and to left to raise it. Turn screw 'b' for horizontal setting, turning to right sets beam to left, turning to left sets beam to right. Screw 'c' secures rim

5 Remove the actuating lever pivot bolt and withdraw the armature and lever. Hold armature in a vice with soft jaws. Refer to **FIG 11:14** and press actuating sleeve 1 towards the overrunning clutch 4 and catch the locking balls 3 as they fall out. Release the sleeve and spring.

6 When cleaning the parts, do not put the armature or the overrunning clutch in solvent and keep solvent away from the self-lubricating bearing bushes. Normally, during a major overhaul it is advisable to renew these bushes. Clean off all carbon dust from the armature and from the brush carrier.

Inspecting and testing:

Check action of actuating lever, sleeve and overrunning clutch. Renew parts if sleeve and lever do not move freely, or if lever is bent. If necessary renew the brake disc. Renew pinion and shaft if teeth are worn.

Check the field windings for signs of excessive heat or melted solder. They must not protrude beyond the pole-pieces. Check coil for continuity and shorting to earth, using a 40V AC test lamp.

Test armature and brush carrier plate for short to earth in the same way. The insulated brush holders must not be shorting to earth. Apply test prods to cylindrical body of armature and to each commutator segment in turn. The test lamp should not light.

Check condition of commutator. Minimum diameter is 33.5 mm (1.319 inch) and maximum runout should not exceed .05 mm (.002 inch). Clean out excessive wear and pitting by skimming the commutator in a lathe, providing the diameter is not reduced below the stipulated figure. The mica insulation between the commutator segments must be removed to a depth of about .80 mm (.03 inch) using a piece of fine hacksaw blade ground on the sides to the correct width. Take care not to damage the segments or the soldered joints.

Brushes which are worn, broken or which have defective leads must be renewed. Always fit a complete

set. Unsolder the leads one at a time to avoid confusion, and when soldering the new leads into place do not let the solder run too far up the flexible part.

Armature shaft bushes are of the self-lubricating type, so make sure that new bushes are well-impregnated with oil. At the pinion end, drill out the rivets to release the seal and press out the bush. Press a new bush into place with a shouldered mandrel having a pilot the same diameter as the shaft until it is flush on the inside. Do not reamer this type of bush after fitting. Centre a new seal with a suitable mandrel and secure the retainer with small screws, nuts and spring washers, peening the screw ends to prevent loss of the nuts.

Reassembling:

Hold armature in vice and stick balls into locking ring with grease such as Bosch Ft2v3. Fit actuating sleeve, brake disc and spring to overrunning clutch and locking ring and push assembly onto shaft until balls engage the groove in the shaft. Check that pinion and clutch are properly seated and that the mechanical engagement parts move freely when released. Grease all parts.

Fit actuating lever to sleeve and push armature and lever into drive housing. Grease and fit lever pivot stud. Fit rubber seal between solenoid and field recesses so that its tab seats correctly in the cutout provided. Push field frame over armature. Fit greased metal and insulating washers to shaft as shown in **FIG 11:15.** Fit brush carrier plate, aligning the notch which prevents turning, in the correct position. When the brushes and springs are fitted the spring pressure can be checked with a sensitive spring balance. Hook balance under end of spring and check moment of lifting. Recorded pressure should be 1150 to 1350 g (40.6 to 47.6 oz).

Seat rubber grommet for field lead correctly and refit end cover. Earthing points between brush carrier plate and cover and between cover and field housing must be clean and bright. Secure the two through-bolts. Fit spacer washers and locking ring to end of shaft and check that end float lies between .10 and .15 mm (.004 to .006 inch). Secure flange of end cap. Fit solenoid and connect field lead to inner terminal.

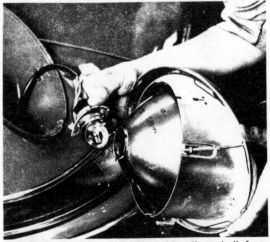

FIG 11:18   Removing retainer and headlamp bulb from back of reflector

11:7 The voltage regulator

The voltage regulator is mounted in the position shown in **FIG 11:16**. It is a single unit controlling the field circuit of the alternator and there is no current regulator or cut-out. As there is no provision for servicing, it is important to consult a Service Station if the regulator gives trouble. Renewal is the best cure for a defective unit.

Great care must be taken to ensure that the connections to the regulator are correctly fitted. The blue and red leads go to D+, the black lead to DF and the brown lead to D—.

Symptoms of regulator trouble may be no charge, or too low or too high an output from the alternator.

11:8 Servicing the lights

Bulb-type headlamps:

When working on the headlamps avoid touching the reflecting surface or the bulb with the fingers. To renew a bulb, remove screw 'c' in **FIG 11:17** and withdraw lamp assembly. Pull cable connector off tabs. Press retaining ring inwards and turn to the left to release the bayonet catch. Withdraw bulb (see **FIG 11:18**). Insert a new bulb, holding it with clean cloth or soft paper to avoid touching with the fingers. Aligning tab in base of bulb must fit into cut-out. Press retainer in and turn to right and then fit the connector. Refit lamp unit and check beam setting.

Sealed-beam headlamps:

Remove unit as just described and pull connector off tabs. Remove spring clips from lamp rim by pressing down and in with a thumb. Do not try to prise out with a screwdriver or the springs will fly. Pull out inner retaining ring and sealed-beam unit. Refit in the reverse order and check beam setting.

Beam setting:

This is best done on proper equipment and in accordance with the regulations of the country concerned. If it must be done by the owner, select a piece of level ground and mount a board as shown in **FIG 11:19**, distance 'd' being about 5 m (16½ feet). Tyres must be properly

FIG 11:20 Fuses are mounted under luggage compartment mat. Numbers indicate circuits protected (see wiring diagrams)

inflated and car bounced to normalize suspension. Board must be central on car axis.

Mark height of headlamp centres on board as at 'b'. Mark line 'c' on board at 1 per cent of distance 'd'. If 5 m or 16½ feet, 'c' will be 50 mm or 2 inches. Mark width between headlamp centres (value 'a') on line 'c' centrally about axis. Make a cross at the intersection. From now on, remember that the example is for a lefthand drive car, so reverse the setting for a righthand drive one.

Cover one headlamp while setting the other. First adjust horizontally to bring the point of the angle between the dark and light areas onto the cross on the board. Make adjustments by turning screw 'a' in **FIG 11:17**.

Adjust vertically by turning screw 'b' until the horizontal plane of the dark and bright areas lies on the line marked at 'c' (see **FIG 11:19**). After setting vertically, check the horizontal setting again.

Dim headlamps:

Connect a voltmeter to terminals yellow and brown or white and brown behind the light unit. Switch on lights and run engine at 2000 rev/min. Meter reading should be 12 to 12.5V. If below this, check battery terminals for dirty contact or loose fixing, check regulator and lighting switch terminals, fuse contacts and connections to light unit. If no improvement, try a new bulb. If reading remains low the fault probably lies with the battery, the alternator or the regulator.

Renewing bulbs in other lights:

Access to fog lamp bulbs is by removing retaining ring, withdrawing lamp unit and pulling snap-fit socket out of unit. Bulb is of bayonet fixing type. After removing other light units, use a screwdriver to lift the plastic holder at the cut-off corner and withdraw holder and bayonet fixing bulb. Holder will snap into place when refitting. To reach the festoon bulb in the interior light, gently prise out the lamp base with a screwdriver, working along the rear edge. Make sure bulb contacts hold bulb firmly. Luggage compartment and number plate lamps also have festoon bulbs.

Control and instrument lamps are accessible after pulling luggage compartment mat forward. The lamp sockets are a push fit.

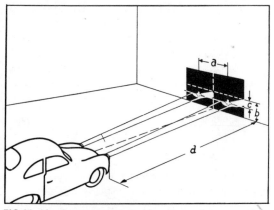

FIG 11:19 Arrangement for headlamp beam setting. 'a' is width of headlamp centres, 'b' is height of centres from ground, 'c' is 1 per cent of distance 'd' from lamps to board or wall

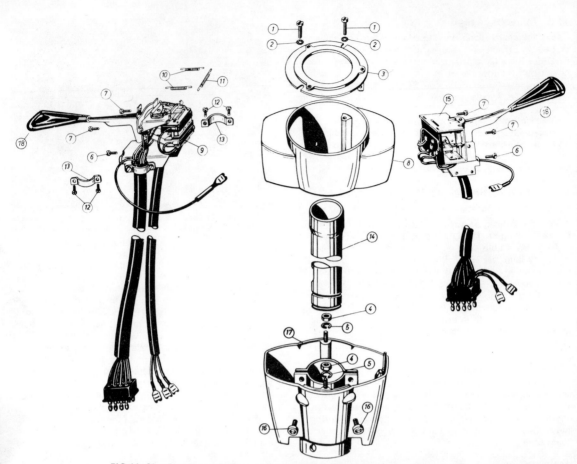

FIG 11:21 Components of combination switches fitted to steering column

Key to Fig 11:21   1 Screw   2 Serrated lockwasher   3 Contact ring   4 Nut   5 Lockwasher   6 Screw   7 Round head countersunk screw   8 Upper housing assembly   9 Combination switch   10 Spring   11 Spring   12 Screw   13 Clamp   14 Steering post extension   15 Wiper and washer switch   16 Allen bolt   17 Lower housing assembly   18 Lever knob

11:9 Fuses

These will be found under the luggage compartment mat as shown in **FIG 11:20**. Note that the circuits protected by individual fuses may be identified by referring the numbers to those listed in the wiring diagrams in the Appendix to this manual. If a fuse blows it is essential to find the reason why before fitting a new one. Spare 8/15 and 25/40 amp fuses should be carried in the car.

11:10 Steering column switches

The combination switch assembly is shown in **FIG 11:21**. To remove it, first remove the steering wheel (see **Chapter 9**). Separate all wiring connections. Remove horn contact ring 3. Remove nuts and pull upper housing assembly 8 upwards, pushing the leads and connectors through the holes provided. Remove combination switch 9 (3 screws).

Faulty switch units are best renewed as an assembly, but a broken flasher return spring may be renewed separately. Check all electrical contacts for firm seating

and cleanliness. Refit the parts in the reverse order, making sure the connections are correctly made. There is a relay for the headlamp flasher switch under the left floorboard.

11:11 Flasher unit

This is located under the luggage compartment mat adjacent to the steering column. It is a push fit in a three-pronged connector. There is an indicator lamp to show when a flasher bulb has failed, a magnetic switch breaking the earth connection to the lamp. The flasher unit cannot be repaired and it must be renewed in the event of failure.

11:12 The wiper and washer units

Removing wiper motor and linkage:

Pull luggage compartment mat forward and remove the front ventilating case after releasing the clip and air duct. These are located just below the grille in front of the wiper blades. Pull off the five cables from the wiper motor.

Remove the wiper arms and the rubber grommets, unscrew the large nuts to release the spindles and withdraw the motor and linkage downwards. The linkage joints are service-free.

When refitting the assembly, make sure the wire connections are correctly made. Check that the linkage moves freely. Fit the wiper blades so that they wipe a symmetrical arc.

Windscreen washer:

Up to chassis No. 302.695 the washer reservoir fitted into a recess along the side of the luggage compartment floor. To service this type, pump reservoir completely dry, remove cap and hose and turn reservoir to remove it. To remove the pump, detach the cables and suction and pressure hoses. Loosen plastic straps and lift out pump.

To service the later type, remove the two screws securing the reservoir and remove it. Remove the pump as just described.

11:13 The reversing light switch

This is screwed into the side of the transmission housing and is actuated by a pushrod when reverse gear is engaged. It may be removed by pulling off the rubber cap, detaching the cable connectors and unscrewing it. Make sure the pushrod is properly installed with the rounded end entering first.

11:14 Fault diagnosis

(a) Battery discharged

1 Terminals loose or dirty
2 Battery internally faulty
3 Shortcircuits in system
4 Alternator not charging
5 Regulator defective

(b) Insufficient charging current

1 Check 1, 4 and 5 in (a)
2 Driving belt slipping

(c) Battery will not hold charge

1 Low level of electrolyte
2 Battery plates sulphated
3 Electrolyte leakage from cracked case or top seal
4 Plate separators ineffective

(d) Battery overcharged

1 Check 5 in (a)
2 Poor connections between regulator and alternator

(e) Alternator output low or nil

1 Check 3 and 5 in (a) and 2 in (b)
2 Faulty brushes, rotor coil or isolation diode

(f) Noisy alternator

1 Worn belt, loose pulley
2 Defective bearings

(g) Control lamp not lighting with ignition on

1 Defective bulb or broken connection

(h) Control lamp stays on with ignition switched off

1 Defective diodes in alternator (disconnect battery at once)

(i) Control lamp stays on

1 Check 1 in (h)

(j) Starter motor lacks power or will not operate

1 Battery discharged, loose connections
2 Solenoid switch contacts worn or dirty
3 Brushes worn or sticking, springs weak or broken
4 Commutator, armature or field coils defective
5 Engine abnormally stiff

(k) Starter motor runs but does not turn engine

1 Pinion or flywheel gear defective

(l) Starter pinion stays in mesh

1 Bent armature shaft, dirty or defective pinion
2 Solenoid switch faulty

(m) Lamps inoperative or erratic

1 Battery low, bulbs burned out
2 Switch faulty, poor earthing, loose connections, broken wires

CHAPTER 12

THE BODYWORK

12:1 Paintwork

Porsche body finish is of the oven-baked synthetic enamel type and major re-finishing must be entrusted to experts with the necessary facilities. Small areas which need re-painting may be done with air-drying synthetic enamel. It is not recommended to use cellulose lacquers for this purpose because there will be a change in colour, baked enamels lightening and cellulose enamels darkening with age. In the case of metallic finishes, small areas cannot be successfully retouched and a complete part such as a wing or door must be resprayed.

Before spraying, the existing damage must be rectified and any finish that is to take new paint must be prepared by careful cleaning, particularly if it has been protected with wax polish or polish containing silicones. Wash with a detergent solution and use a silicone remover. Do not remove grease with petrol and do not wipe clean with a dry cloth. A pad wetted with white spirit is the best way of removing lint or dust.

Prime all bare patches and use body putty for deep blemishes. Rub smooth with grade 320 Wet-or-Dry paper, using plenty of water. Finish with 400 grade paper and abrade all glossy surfaces which are to be re-painted. Give a light spray with a pre-matching colour and again get the highest degree of surface finish with the 400 paper and water. Dry thoroughly and give at least two coats of thinned enamel, letting each coat dry before applying the next. Give an extra coat of metallic paint, holding the gun farther away to prevent flotation of the metallic particles. Leave to dry several days and then polish.

12:2 Servicing doors

Removing:

If this is to be done by extracting the hinge pins, use an impact tool such as P.290 which is hooked under each pin and the pin driven out upwards.

Refitting:

Check the hinges for alignment as shown in **FIG 12:1**. Grease pins well to prevent squeaks and fit door. Check gap all round. If door must be raised so that gap between lower edge and sill is 3.5 to 4.5 mm ($\frac{9}{64}$ to $\frac{11}{64}$ inch), slacken bolts fixing hinges to pillar and lift and re-tighten. Now check door gap down edge. To increase gap set hinges with hammer as shown in **FIG 12:2**. The door may be set outward with the hand-made tool shown on the left in **FIG 12:3**, the operation being shown in **FIG 12:4**.

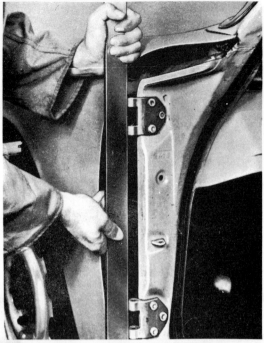

FIG 12:1 Using a straightedge to check the alignment of the door hinges

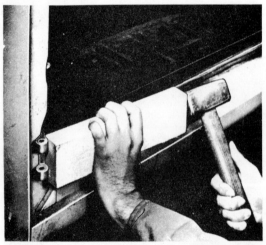

FIG 12:2 Setting hinge with a block of wood and a hammer

The distance between the door and the flange should be 9 mm (.35 inch) and the simple gauge shown in the centre of **FIG 12:3** will enable the gap to be checked as shown in **FIG 12:5**. The righthand gauge is used to check the gap between the door and the body aperture.

Note that a new door shell is not welded at one point so that it may be twisted to make it fit the body. When satisfactory, the door is made rigid by welding and end pieces cut and fitted to the front and rear upper door edges.

Dismantling door:

1 Remove window winder and ring. Remove safety lock button. Remove ornamental strip from window frame (screw at front, screw and snap nut at rear).
2 Press remote control push button at armrest out of nipple. Remove handgrip from passenger's side (2 bolts under ornamental strip). Remove two socket-head bolts from armrest and pivot it upwards about the single bolt. Remove bolt and armrest.
3 Release door panel by removing self-tapping screws and prising the clips out of the rubber grommets. Note the two screws, one at each end of the pocket.
4 Remove waterproofing from access holes in door. Remove window well covering rail (clips) and rubber strip. Remove door travel limiter.
5 Remove outside door handle. Remove window frame, which is secured by bolts at the places marked in **FIG 12:7**. Pull frame out in an upwards direction. Remove window winding mechanism and extract from window elevating rail. Remove door lock.

Door lock variations:

New and old versions are shown in **FIG 12:6**. Note the long through-pin on the left compared with the two short pins on the right. The early two-pin lock could jam if an attempt was made to open the door from the inside and the outside simultaneously. It is therefore advisable to fit the later version. This, however, entails a change in the outside handle door button. The door button actuating lever must be replaced by one with a longer pin, the new part being No. 901.531.919.20 for the left side (Lefthand drive) and 901.531.920.20 for the righthand side. When fitting the new parts make sure that the longer pin does not rest on the lock or the door may burst open on very rough roads.

Reassembling door:

Grease all moving parts of lock and winder mechanisms. Note that there are two types of winder, one with rollers and the other with plastic sliders. These are not readily interchangeable.

1 Fit winder and lightly tighten bolts, using washers and lockwashers. Turn mechanism into the up position and push the window glass and caulked elevating rail into the mechanism forward from the rear. The new type of winder will eliminate rattles on older installations.
2 Crank window to half-open and push window frame into place. Adjust frame and tighten bolts in sequence shown in **FIG 12:7**, noting that the short bolt is used in the upper position at the rear of the door. Gap for weatherstrip depends on age of car. Early 911 models had a hollow type of strip which may be replaced by a thicker type needing a gap of 12 mm (.47 inch). New-type strips need a gap of 9 mm (.35 inch). Use cement to secure the strip.
3 Fit outside handle and door travel limiter. Fit rubber strip in window well covering rail and cut to size. Fasten rail with clips.
4 Put a strip of pliable rubber putty under the edges of the chrome trim in the upper edge of the door and fix trim. Putty prevents wind roar.
5 Wind window fully up and tighten mechanism. Cement into place the travel stops for the cranking mechanism. On early types of cranking mechanism,

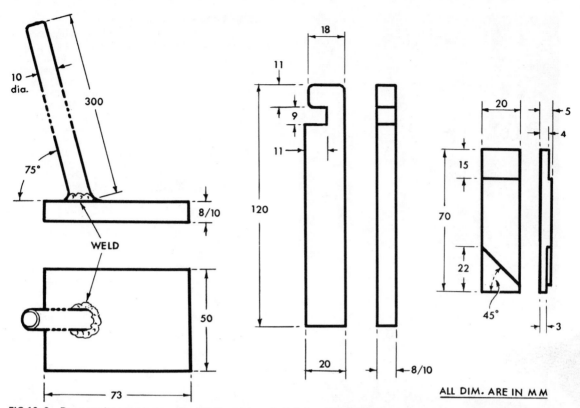

ALL DIM. ARE IN MM

FIG 12:3 Door can be reset outwards with the tool on the left (see FIG 12:4). Check gap between door and door flange with central gauge (see FIG 12:5). Use gauge on right to check gap round door edge. All items are made from mild steel

cement a 50 mm (2 inch) square piece of foam rubber 8 mm (.3 inch) thick between the glass-elevating rail and the cranking mechanism to prevent friction.

6 Cement felt liners 6 mm (.24 inch) thick to the sheet metal under the remote control rods for the lock. Cement waterproof material over the access holes inside the door. Fasten door panel by sliding clips into rubber grommets. Insert self-tapping screws, putting one in each corner of door pocket.

7 Set armrest vertically and fit single bolt at rear end. Turn rest horizontally and fit remaining two bolts. Fix handgrip with two bolts under ornamental strip.

8 Guide pushbutton of remote control at armrest forward from the rear and press it into the centre of the nipple. If the button binds, enlarge the hole with a file. Secure the ornamental strip and velvet liner. There is a nut and self-tapping screw at the rear and one screw at the front. Fit the safety lock button.

9 Fit the window winder handle and ring with the handle down when the window is up. Close all apertures in the door with rubber caps. When door is refitted and correctly aligned, check action of lock and lockplate.

12:3 Luggage compartment lid

A gas-cushioned prop keeps the lid steady at any raised position. For opening the lid there is a control knob in the passenger's compartmentl There is also a safety

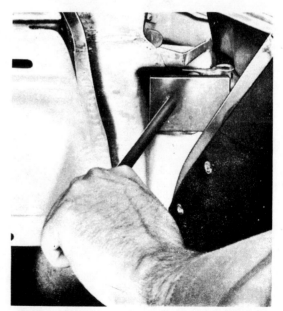

FIG 12:4 Using tool on left in FIG 12:3 to reset door outwards

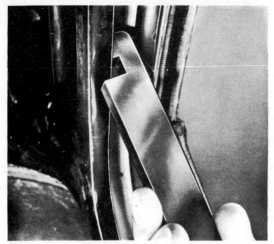

FIG 12:5 Using central gauge in FIG 12:3 to check gap between door and door flange

FIG 12:6 Latest door lock with long through-pin on left. Lock on right is earlier version with two short pins

latch. If the control cable breaks the lid opens automatically but the latch prevents it rising too far.

When removing a lid, scribe round the hinge brackets where they are bolted so that the lid may be refitted in the same place. If a new lid is being fitted, attach the hinge brackets and the gas prop. The piston of the prop must face down. Install the lock and roughly adjust it. Tension the lock spring with a piece of wire. Check fit of lid in body aperture.

Gap between top edge of lid and centre piece of windscreen should be 4 to 5 mm (.16 to .20 inch). Check that there is a gap of 1 to 1.5 mm (.04 to .06 inch) round the edges. Adjust lid height by inserting washers where the hinge brackets are bolted to the lid. Washers placed at the front end will lower the lid, and when placed at the rear will raise it.

12:4 The rear lid

This is also controlled by a knob inside the car and is also fitted with a gas prop. Mark the hinge positions before removing them if the same lid is to be refitted. When installing the lid, fit the hinges and the gas prop so that the piston of the prop is attached to the lid frame.

Check the gap round the lid when it is closed. Gap at top edge should be 3.5 to 4.5 mm (.14 to .18 inch). At sides gap should be 2.5 to 3.5 mm (.10 to .14 inch). Bottom gap depends on height of wings. Lower edge must be flush with wing edges.

Fit lid lock and control cable and check that lock bolt catches properly when slammed.

12:5 Fitting bumpers

Front:

Straighten surface below front edge of lid to get an even gap between bumper and lid. Fit bumper without rubber strip and check distance to flasher housing and adjust if necessary. Fit flasher lens.

Adjust the bumper brackets so that there will be considerable tension during reassembly. Bend rear bracket forward for this purpose. Fit bumper reinforcement to models 911 and 911S by coating thickly with epoxy resin cement and sliding into place in the bumper.

Secure bumper braces so that there will be as much preload tension on the bumpers as possible. Cement the sealing rubber to the body and install the bumper.

Rear:

Fit bumper side pieces and straighten the attaching tabs. Fit the bumper centre piece, insert the bumper horns and adjust to equal height. File gap between bumper and horn if necessary. Remove the fitted parts.

Cement sealing rubber strip and cut off edges. Fit bumper parts and horns and cover holes with plastic caps.

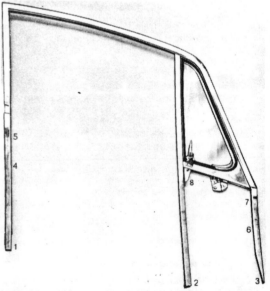

FIG 12:7 Sequence for tightening bolts which secure the window frame

12:6 Fitting front wings

Before fitting the lefthand wing, install the fuel filler cover. Apply body sealer strip to the mounting flange of the wing and then fit the snap nuts. Fit wing, and screw in bolts finger tight. While guiding the wing into place make sure the cable conduit for the filler cover release is correctly positioned. Do not, at this stage, install the sealing strip as it may be necessary to apply body solder in places. As a result, the gap between the wing and the door may be wider at the top edge by 1 mm (.04 inch).

Tighten the second bolt in from the rear end first and lightly tighten one at the front. Do the rearmost top bolt followed by the lowest one by the door sill, then tighten the remaining bolts on the vertical flange starting at the top. Finally, work along the top flange, starting at the rear.

When satisfied with the fit, drill two 4 mm (.16 inch) holes through the attaching flanges at front and rear locations, insert steel rivets in the holes and weld the heads to the body panel. These will act as dowels so that when the wing is removed for painting and then refitted it can be restored to its correct position and be properly aligned.

12:7 Fitting side panel windows

Fit the cover strip at the bottom, enlarging the holes with a file if necessary. Put body sealing strip under the cover strip and secure cover with Quicklock nuts. Put sealing strip under the vertical mounts for the window. Insert the window and tighten securely.

APPENDIX

TECHNICAL DATA

WIRING DIAGRAMS

HINTS ON MAINTENANCE AND OVERHAUL

GLOSSARY OF TERMS

INDEX

911T   — 110 bhp

911/911L — 130 bhp

911S — 160 bhp

TECHNICAL DATA

Metric sizes are given first, followed by inch sizes in brackets. The word 'limit' indicates the maximum permissible wear or clearance

ENGINE

Capacity	1991 cc (121.5 cu in)
Bore and stroke	80 x 66 (3.15 x 2.60)
Compression ratio:	
911T	8.6:1 *110 bhp*
911, 911L	9:1 *130 bhp*
911E	9.1:1
911S	9.8:1 *160 bhp*
Firing order	1-6-2-4-3-5

Crankshaft:

Main bearings 1 to 7	Split inserts, tri-metal
Main bearing 8	Sleeve, hard lead
Thrust taken	Main bearing 1
Main journal diameters:	
Bearings 1 to 7 (Standard)	56.990 to 56.971 (2.2437 to 2.2429)
Bearing 8 (standard)	30.993 to 30.980 (1.2202 to 1.2197)
Undersizes	—.25, —.50 and —.75 (—.01, —.02 and —.03)
Main bearing running clearance:	
Bearings 1 to 7	.030 to .088 (.0012 to .0034)
Bearing 8	.048 to .104 (.0019 to .004)
End float	.110 to .195 (.0043 to .0076, limit .30 (.011)
Interference fits:	
To timing and distributor gears	—.002 to —.038 (—.0001 to —.0014)
To flywheel	.000 to .049 (.000 to .0019)
To pulley	+.007 to +.073 (+.0003 to +.0028)
Runout (on V-blocks)	Maximum .03 (.0012)
Big-end journal diameters	As main bearings 1 to 7
Big-end undersizes	As main bearings

Connecting rods:

Big-end running clearance	As main bearings 1 to 7
Gudgeon pin running clearance	.020 to .039 (.0008 to .0015), limit .055 (.002)
Small-end bush interference fit in rod	—.014 to —.055 (—.0005 to —.002)

Pistons:

Type (except 911S)	Cast light alloy
Type, 911S	Forged light alloy
Clearance in cylinder:	
Up to and including 1967 models	.055 to .075 (.0022 to .0029) limit .180 (.007)
1968 models on (except 911S)	.035 to .055 (.0014 to .002)
1968 models on (911S)	.045 to .065 (.0018 to .0026)

Piston rings:

Types	2 compression, 1 oil control
Gap	.30 to .45 (.012 to .018), limit 1.00 (.039)
Side clearance in groove:	
Top ring	.075 to .107 (.003 to .004)
Second ring	.060 to .072 (.0023 to .0028)
Oil control ring	.025 to .052 (.001 to .002)
Limit	.20 (.008)

Gudgeon (piston) pin:

Colour code white ... ... Tolerance 0 to .003 (0 to .0001) on diameter of 22 (.866)

Colour code black ... ... Tolerance of —.003 to —.006 (—.0001 to —.0002) on diameter of 22 (.866)

Cylinders:

Type 911T ... ... Grey cast iron
Type (all other models) ... ... Grey cast iron bores with light alloy cooling fins (Biral)
Bore sizes ... ... See Chapter 1
Height (group 5) ... ... 82.200 to 82.225 (3.236 to 3.237)
Height (group 6) ... ... 82.225 to 82.250 (3.237 to 3.238)

Camshafts:

Bearings:
    Type ... ... 3 plain, direct in housing
    Diameter ... ... 46.926 to 46.942 (1.8474 to 1.8481)
    Running clearance ... ... .025 to .066 (.001 to .0025), limit .10 (.004)
Runout (at centre bearing) ... ... Maximum .02 (.0008)
End float ... ... .15 to .20 (.006 to .008)
Sprocket mounting diameter ... ... 29.979 to 30.000 (1.179 to 1.181)
Sprocket fit on shaft ... ... 0 to .034 (.0013) clearance

Camshaft housings:

Bores for camshaft ... ... 46.967 to 46.992 (1.849 to 1.850)
Bores for rocker shafts ... ... 18.000 to 18.018 (.7086 to .7093)
Rocker shaft diameter ... ... 17.992 to 18.000 (.7083 to .7086)
Rocker clearance ... ... .016 to .035 (.0006 to .0013), limit .080 (.003)
Rocker end float ... ... .100 to .350 (.004 to .014), limit .500 (.020)

Clearances (timing case):
    Carrier shaft to tensioner housing ... ... .010 to .045 (.0006 to .0018)
    Carrier shaft to sprocket carrier ... ... .016 to .045 (.0006 to .0018)
    Sprocket carrier to sprocket shaft ... ... .000 to .029 (.000 to .0011)
    Sprocket to shaft ... ... .032 to .061 (.0012 to .0024)
    Shaft to chain guide rail ... ... .105 to .129 (.004 to .005)
    Shaft to chain housing ... ... —.014 to —.038 (—.0005 to —.0014)
Sprocket alignment ... ... Maximum deviation .25 (.01)

Intermediate shaft:

Bearing 1 diameter ... ... 29.767 to 29.780 (1.1719 to 1.1724)
Bearing 2 diameter ... ... 23.967 to 23.980 (.9435 to .9440)
Running clearance ... ... .020 to .054 (.0007 to .0021), limit .10 (.004)
End float ... ... .080 to .150 (.003 to .006)
Sprocket mounting diameter ... ... 36.026 to 36.037 (1.4183 to 1.4187)
Sprocket interference fit ... ... —.010 to —.037 (—.0003 to —.0014)

Valves:

Head diameter, inlet:
    Except 911S and 1968 911T onwards ... $39 \pm .10$ ($1.535 \pm .004$)
    911S and 1968 911T onwards ... $42 \pm .10$ ($1.654 \pm .004$)
Head diameter, exhaust:
    Except 911S and 1968 911T onwards ... $35 \pm .10$ ($1.378 \pm .004$)
    911S and 1968 911T onwards ... $38 \pm .10$ ($1.496 \pm .004$)
Stem diameter:
    Inlet ... ... 8.97 —.012 (.353 —.0005)
    Exhaust ... ... 8.95 —.012 (.352 —.0005)

Valve stem clearance:
Inlet	.03 to .057 (.001 to .002), limit .15 (.006)
Exhaust	.05 to .077 (.002 to .003), limit .20 (.008)

Overall length:
Inlet (except 911S)	111.15 ± .05 (4.376 ± .002)
911S	114.0 ± .05 (4.488 ± .002)
Exhaust (except 911S)	111.75 ± .05 (4.40 ± .002)
911S	113.5 ± .05 (4.47 ± .002)
Seat angle	45 deg.

Valve springs:

Installed length (inlet):
Except 911S and 911T	36.0 ± .30 (1.42 ± .01) up to Engine No. 911.000
Except 911S and 911T	35.0 ± .30 (1.38 ± .01) from Engine No. 911.001
911S	35.5 + .50 (1.40 + .02)
911T (dual springs)	35.0 ± .30 (1.38 ± .01)
911T (single spring)	41.0 — .50 (1.61 — .02)

Installed length (exhaust):
911 up to Engine No. 911.000	36.0 ± .30 (1.42 ± .01)
911 From Engine No. 911.001	35.0 ± .30 (1.38 ± .01)
911S and 911T (dual springs)	35.0 ± .30 (1.38 ± .01)
911T (single spring)	41.0 — .50 (1.61 — .02)

Spring-load at installed length with both end collars:
911 and 911S	20 kg (44 lb) at 42 to 42.5 (1.65 to 1.67)
911T	26 kg (57 lb) at 44.5 to 45 (1.75 to 1.77)
Load variation	± 5 per cent on used springs

Valve lift (inlet):
911S and 911 up to Engine No. 911.000 ...	11.5 (.453)
911 from Engine No. 911.001	10.5 (.413)
911T	9.7 (.382)

Valve lift (exhaust):
Except 911T	10.5 (.413)
911T	8.9 (.35)

Valve clearance:
Inlet and exhaust (cold)	.10 (.004)

Valve timing (clearance .10 or .004 inch):
Inlet opens BTDC	29 deg. (911), 15 deg. (911T), 38 deg. (911S) and 20 deg. (911L)
Inlet closes ABDC	39 deg. (911), 29 deg. (911T), 50 deg. (911S) and 34 deg. (911L)
Exhaust opens BBDC	39 deg. (911), 41 deg. (911T), 40 deg. (911S) and 40 deg. (911L)
Exhaust closes BTDC	5 deg. (911T)
Exhaust closes ATDC	19 deg. (911), 20 deg. (911S) and 6 deg. (911L)
For timing of 911 from Engine No. 911.001 ...	See 911L

Inlet valve lift at TDC with clearance of .10 (.004):
911 up to Engine No. 909.927	4.2 to 4.6 (.165 to .181), desired value 4.3 (.169)
911T	2.3 to 2.7 (.091 to .106), desired value 2.5 (.098)
911S	5.0 to 5.4 (.197 to .213), desired value 5.2 (.205)

911L ... ... 3.0 to 3.3 (.118 to .130), desired value 3.15 (.124)

Valve guides:

Diameter (standard)	13.06 to 13.049 (.514 to .5137)
Diameter (first oversize)	13.260 to 13.249 (.522 to .5216)
Diameter (second oversize)	13.460 to 13.449 (.530 to .5294)
Bore in head (standard)	13.00 to 13.018 (.5118 to .5125)
Bore in head (first oversize)	13.20 to 13.218 (.5196 to .5203)
Bore in head (second oversize)	13.40 to 13.418 (.5275 to .5282)

Valve seats:

Diameter (standard inlet)	42.180 to 42.164 (1.6606 to 1.6599)
Diameter (standard exhaust)	38.20 to 38.184 (1.5039 to 1.5033)
Diameter (oversize inlet)	42.50 to 42.484 (1.6732 to 1.6724)
Diameter (oversize exhaust)	38.76 to 38.744 (1.5259 to 1.5253)
Bore in head (standard inlet)	42.00 to 42.025 (1.6535 to 1.6545)
Bore in head (standard exhaust)	38.00 to 38.025 (1.4960 to 1.4970)
Bore in head (oversize inlet)	42.320 to 42.345 (1.6661 to 1.6670)
Bore in head (oversize exhaust)	38.560 to 38.585 (1.5180 to 1.5190)

Flywheel:

Bore for crankshaft	65.00 to 65.030 (2.559 to 2.560)
Clearance in bore	Up to .049 (.0019)
Lateral runout at clutch mounting	Maximum .040 (.0015)
Lateral runout at clutch face	Maximum .040 (.0015)
Vertical runout...	Maximum .200 (.0078)
Bronze bush for rear end of transmission shaft ...	Running clearance .075 to .229 (.003 to .009). Interference fit in steel bush —.001 to —.035 (—.000 to —.013)
Steel bush	Interference fit —.001 to —.035 (—.000 to —.0013)

Oil pump:

Spring (pressure release and safety valve):

Free length	70 (2.75)
Compressed length	33.3 (1.31)
Pressure at length of 52 (2.04)	10.6 kg (76.7 lb ft)
Pressure at length of 46 (1.81)	14.1 kg (102 lb ft)

Crankcase:

Bore for main bearings	62.00 to 62.019 (2.4409 to 2.4416)

Bore for intermediate shaft:

Bearing 1	29.80 to 29.821 (1.732 to 1.1740)
Bearing 2	24.00 to 24.021 (.9448 to .9457)

FUEL SYSTEM

Solex carburetter 40.PI:

Venturi	30
Main jet	117.5 to Engine No. 900.323, 130 to Engine No. 903.359 and 125 to Engine No. 903.910
Air correction jet	150 to Engine No. 900.323, 160 to Engine No. 903.359 and 180 .to Engine No. 903.910
Emulsion tube	25 to Engine No. 900.323, 8 (open bottom) to Engine No. 903.359 and 8 (open bottom) to Engine No. 903.910
Idle jet	60 to Engine No. 903.359, 55 to Engine No. 903.910

Idle air bleed	1.0
Pump injector nozzle	.5 dia. to Engine No. 903.359 and .8 dia. to Engine No. 903.910
Pump jet	.5 dia.
Float needle valve	2.0
Float weight	7 g
Injection quantity	.45 to .50 cc (2 strokes, warm) and .55 to .60 cc (2 strokes, cold)

Weber carburetter:

Types	40.IDS.3C and 3C1 (911S), 40.IDAP.3C and 3C1 (911L with emission control), 40.IDAP.3C and 3C1 (911 with emission control), 40.IDA.3C and 3C1 (911L) and 40.IDT.3C and 3C1 (911T)
Venturi	32 (911S and 911T), 30 (all others)
Main jet	110 (911T), 125 (all others)
Air correction jet	185 (911S and 911T), 180 (all others)
Idle jet	50 (911T), 52 (911 and 911L with EEC), 55 (911L Sportomatic)
Idle air bleed	110 (all)
Pump jet	50 (all)
Emulsion tube	F2 (911T), F3 (911S), F26 (all others)
Float weight	25.5 g
Float needle valve	1.75
Enrichment jet	70 (911S)
Pump injection quantity	$.8 \pm .2$ cc per stroke (911S and 911L with Sportomatic), $.5 \pm .1$ per stroke (all others)
Float chamber vent	4.5 dia. (911S), 6.0 dia. (all others)

Fuel pump:

Mechanical:

Fuel delivery (each pump)	800 cc in 1 minute at 3000 rev/min
Fuel pressure	.18 to .22 atm ($2\frac{1}{2}$ to $3\frac{1}{4}$ lb/sq in)

Electric (Bendix):

Minimum delivery	900 cc per minute
Pressure with closed float needle valve ...	.28 to .33 atm (4 to 5 lb/sq in)
Maximum current	.65 amp

Electric (Hardi):

Minimum delivery	900 cc per minute
Pump pressure	.28 to .30 atm (4 to 4.4 lb/sq in)
Contact point gap	1.2 (.048)

IGNITION SYSTEM

Sparking plug type:

911	Bosch W.250.P21 or WG.265.T2SP, Beru 260/14/3S and Champion N6Y
911T	Bosch W.230.T30, Beru 240/14/3
911S	Bosch W.265.P21 or WG.265.T2SP, Beru 260/14/3S
Sparking plug gap	Bosch W (.35 or .012), Bosch WG (40 or .014), Beru (50 or .018), Champion (.55 or .019)
Firing order	1-6-2-4-3-5

Ignition timing (see **Chapter 3**):

911	TDC basic, 30 deg. BTDC at 6000 rev/min (no load)

Engines with EECS	...	...	...	...	3 deg. ATDC (idling), 30 ± 2 deg. BTDC at 6000 rev/min
911T	...	...	...	...	...	TDC (basic), 35 deg. BTDC at 6000 rev/min (with or without load)
911S	...	...	...	...	...	5 deg. BTDC (basic), 30 deg. BTDC at 6000 rev/min (with or without load)

Distributor type:

911	...	...	...	...	...	...	Bosch JFR.6
911L and 911S	...	...	...	...	...	Bosch JFDR.6 (yellow label for 911S)
911T	...	...	...	...	...	Marelli S.112.AX

CLUTCH

| **Type** | ... | ... | ... | ... | ... | ... | Single dry plate with diaphragm spring |
| **Pedal clearance** | ... | ... | ... | ... | ... | 20 to 25 ($\frac{3}{4}$ to 1) |

Driven plate:

| Thickness uncompressed | ... | ... | ... | ... | 10.1 —.40 (.397 —.015) |
| Runout of linings | ... | ... | ... | ... | Maximum .60 (.023) |

TRANSMISSION

| **Type, manual gearchange** | ... | Four or five forward speeds and one reverse. All synchromesh, all-indirect. Integral with final drive in one casing |
| **Type, Sportomatic** | ... | ... | Four forward speeds and one reverse. Hydrodynamic torque converter and vacuum-controlled single dry plate clutch |

Pinion to ring gear (crownwheel):

Ratio:

| Manual gearbox | ... | ... | ... | ... | ... | ... | 7:31 |
| Sportomatic | ... | ... | ... | ... | ... | ... | 7:27 |

Gear ratios (standard):

911 (5-speed):

1st	...	...	...	...	...	...	...	12:34
2nd	...	...	...	...	...	...	...	18:32
3rd	...	...	...	...	...	...	...	23:28
4th	...	...	...	...	...	...	...	26:25
5th	...	...	...	...	...	...	...	28:23

911 (5-speed from transmission No. 221.722):

1st	...	...	...	...	...	...	...	11:34
2nd	...	...	...	...	...	...	...	18:34
3rd	...	...	...	...	...	...	...	22:29
4th	...	...	...	...	...	...	...	25:26
5th	...	...	...	...	...	...	...	28:24

911 (4-speed):

1st	...	...	...	...	...	...	...	11:34
2nd	...	...	...	...	...	...	...	19:32
3rd	...	...	...	...	...	...	...	24:27
4th	...	...	...	...	...	...	...	28:24

911S and 911T (4-speed):

1st	...	...	...	...	...	...	...	11:34
2nd	...	...	...	...	...	...	...	19:31
3rd	...	...	...	...	...	...	...	25:26
4th	...	...	...	...	...	...	...	29:23

911S (5-speed transmission type 901/02):

1st	...	...	...	...	...	...	...	11:34
2nd	...	...	...	...	...	...	...	18:34
3rd	...	...	...	...	...	...	...	22:29
4th	...	...	...	...	...	...	...	25:26
5th	...	...	...	...	...	...	...	29:23

911T from 1968 models (except USA):

1st	...	...	...	...	...	...	...	14:37
2nd	...	...	...	...	...	...	...	18:32
3rd	...	...	...	...	...	...	...	22:29
4th	...	...	...	...	...	...	...	26:26
5th	...	...	...	...	...	...	...	28:23

911 (1966-67 models), 911S (1967 model), 911S (from 1968 model except USA), 911L (from 1968 model) and 911 (from 1968 model, USA) ... ... See preceding figures

911 (from 1968 model, USA) and 911L with Sportomatic:

1st	...	...	...	...	...	...	...	15:36
2nd	...	...	...	...	...	...	...	19:31
3rd	...	...	...	...	...	...	...	23:28
4th	...	...	...	...	...	...	...	26:25

911S and 911T (from 1968 model except USA) with Sportomatic:

1st	...	...	...	...	...	...	...	15:36
2nd	...	...	...	...	...	...	...	19:31
3rd	...	...	...	...	...	...	...	23:28
4th	...	...	...	...	...	...	...	27:25

911 (from 1968 model, USA) 911L, 911S, and 911T (from 1968 model except USA)   Any four or five-speed ratios on request

Tolerances:

Backlash between gears ... ... .06 to .12 (.0023 to .0047) new, limit .22 (.0086)

End float of free gears on either shaft:

1st speed ... ... .30 to .40 (.011 to .015) new, limit .50 (.019)

2nd, 3rd and 4th ... ... .20 to .30 (.007 to .011) new, limit .40 (.015)

Selector shaft clearance ... ... .095 to .156 (.004 to .006) new, limit .40 (.015)

Selector shaft runout ... ... .10 (.004) maximum

Shift fork end float ... ... .10 to .30 (.004 to .011), limit .50 (.019)

Synchronizing ring outside diameter, installed ... ... 76.12 to 76.48 (2.996 to 3.011), renew when any of molybdenum coating has worn off

Pilot journal at rear of input shaft:

Runout ... ... .10 (.004) maximum

Clearance in flywheel bush ... ... .145 to .231 (.006 to .009), limit .30 (.011)

STEERING

Type	ZF rack and pinion
Steering ratio	1:16.5 in centre
Steering turns (stop to stop)	2.8 (approx.)
Turning circle	10.3 m($33\frac{3}{4}$ ft)

Track:

Original	...	1337 (52.6)
After Chassis No. 305.101 ...	...	1353 (53.3)
1968 models onwards	...	1367 (53.8)

Cars with self-levelling suspension:

With steel wheels $5\frac{1}{2}$J x 15 ...	...	1362 (53.6)
With light alloy wheels 6J x 15 ...	...	1374 (54.1)
With light alloy wheels $5\frac{1}{2}$J x 14 ...	...	1364 (53.7)

Wheel alignment:

Toe-in (total before 1968 models) ...	40' (wheels pressed with load of 15 kg (33 lb)
Toe-in (total) 1968 models on	0' (wheels pressed with load of 15 kg (33 lb)
Angle differential in 20 deg. turn (before 1968 models)	40' to 1 deg. 10'
Angle differential in 20 deg. turn (1968 models on)	0' to 30'
Camber angle (wheels straight-ahead) ...	0' ± 20' (max. deviation left to right 20')
Castor angle	6 deg. 45' ± 45' (max. deviation left to right 30')

FRONT SUSPENSION

Type (not self-levelling)	Independent torsion bar springing with control arms and damper struts
Type, self-levelling (911E and optional on 911T and 911S)	Control arms and hydropneumatic suspension struts without springs

Dampers:

BOGE	911T, 911L, Targa (standard)
KONI	911S (standard), optional for all except Targa

Stabilizers (anti-roll bars): Not fitted to 911 or cars with self-levelling suspension)

Diameter before 1968 models:

911L	13 (.512) standard
911S	14 (.55) standard
Optional	11, 14 and 15 (.43, .55 and .59)

Diameter from 1968 models on:

911L (except USA)	11 (.43) standard
911L (USA) and 911S	15 (.59) standard
Optional	13, 14 and 15 (.512, .55 and .59)

Height adjustment:

Difference between wheel centre height and rear centre of torsion bar	108 ± 5 (4.25 ± .20). Max. deviation left and right 5 (.20)

REAR SUSPENSION

Type	Independent, with torsion bar springing. Triangulated control arm, telescopic dampers

Stabilizer (anti-roll bar):

911S before 1968 models	16 (.63) diameter
911S, 1968 models on	15 (.59) diameter
Optional for all cars before 1968 models ...	15 (.59)
Optional for all cars from 1968 models on	15 and 16 (.59 and .63)

Dampers:

BOGE	911T, 911L and Targa (standard)
KONI	911S (standard). Optional for all others except Targa

From 1968 models on, internal rubber buffers have 9 rings instead of original 8

Track:

Original	1317 (51.8)
After Chassis No. 305.101	1321 (52.0)
From 1968 models on with solid brake discs ...	1335 (52.5)
Cars with ventilated brake discs	1339 (52.7)

Torsion bar diameter:

Before 1968 models	23 (.905)
1968 models on	22 (.866)

Torsion bar adjustment:

All cars before 1968 models	...	...	...	36 deg. radius arm angle
All cars from 1968 models on	...	...	...	39 deg. radius arm angle

Wheel alignment:

Toe-in (per wheel)	...	$0' \pm 10'$
Camber angle (before 1968 models)	... ...	$-55'$ to -1 deg. $35'$
Camber angle (1968 models on)...	...	$-30'$ to -1 deg. $10'$

Latest adjustment angles may be applied to earlier models)

Height adjustment:

Centre of torsion bar carrier above wheel centre height ... ... 12 ± 5 (.47 $\pm$ .2). Maximum deviation between left and right 8 (.32)

BRAKES

Type ... ... Footbrake, disc front and rear, hydraulically operated. Handbrake, mechanical in rear drums. Dual-circuit hydraulic system from 1968 models on

Disc diameter:
- Solid ... ... 282 (11.1) front, 285 (11.22) rear
- Vented ... ... 282.5 (11.12) front, 286 (11.26) rear

Handbrake:
- Drum diameter 180 (7.09)
- Lining width 32 (1.26)

Disc thickness (new):
- Solid ... ... 12.7—.2 (.50—.008) front, 10.0—.2 (.394—.008) or 10.5—.20 (.413—.008) rear
- Vented ... ... 20.0—.20 (.787—.008) front and rear

Disc thickness (minimum when evenly worn):
- Solid ... ... 11.0 (.43) front and 8.5 (.33) rear
- Vented ... ... 18.0 (.71)
- Maximum deviation in thickness ... ... .03 (.001) solid and vented

Disc runout ... ... .05 (.002) solid and vented

Minimum pad thickness ... ... 2.0 (.08)

Master cylinder bore:
- Single and dual-circuit systems ... ... 19.05 (.75)

Wheel brake cylinder bores:
- 911T (not Sportomatic) ... ... 48 (1.89) front, 35 (1.38) rear
- 911T Sportomatic, 911L and 911S ... 48 (1.89) front, 38 (1.49) rear

ELECTRICAL EQUIPMENT

System	12-volt, negative earth (ground)
Battery	45 amp/hr
Generator (alternator)	12-volt, 500 watt, 35 to 40A at 14 volts, Bosch or Motorola (911T)

Alternator data (Bosch):
- Minimum brush length ... ... 14 (.55)
- Brush spring pressure ... ... 300 to 400 g ($10\frac{1}{2}$ to 14 oz)
- Resistance:
  - Stationary windings ... ... .26 ohm + 10 per cent
  - Rotor windings ... ... 4 ohm + 10 per cent (originally 3.5 ohm)

- Slip rings:
  - Runout ... ... .03 (.001) maximum
  - Minimum diameter 31.5 (1.24)
- Rotor runout ... ... .05 (.002) maximum

Alternator data (Motorola):
Rotor coil resistance ... ... 4.5 to 6.5 ohm
Alternator test:
Bosch ... ... Load current 28 to 30A. Voltage should be 13.5 to 14.5 at 3000 rev/min
Motorola ... ... Load current 28 to 30A. Voltage should be 13.4 to 14.6 at 2500 ± 150 rev/min
Starter:
Type ... ... Bosch EB 12-volt, .80 hp (0001.212.002)
Speed test (free) ... ... 11.5V, 33 to 50A at 6400 to 7900 rev/min
Starter data:
Brush spring pressure ... ... 1200 + 150—50 g (42.3 + 5.3—1.76 oz)
Armature end float ... ... .10 to .15 (.004 to .006)
Commutator runout ... ... Maximum .05 (.002)
Commutator minimum diameter 33.5 (1.32)
Bulbs (all 12V):
Twin filament headlamp ... ... 45/40 watt
Sealed-beam headlamp ... ... 50/40 watt
Parking and number plate ... ... 4 watt
Flashers (except USA) ... ... 18 watt
Flashers and reversing lights (USA) ... ... 32 cp or 25 watt
Stop and tail (except USA) ... ... 18/5 watt
Stop and tail (USA) ... ... 32/4 cp or 25/3.2 watt
Reversing lights ... ... 25 watt
Interior lights ... ... 10 watt
Luggage compartment light ... ... 5 watt
Instrument and control lamps ... ... 2 watt
Parking lights (USA) ... ... 2 cp or 2 watt
Fuses:
Wipers and auxiliary heater ... ... 25/40 amp
All others... ... ... 8/15 amp

CAPACITIES

Fuel tank ... ... 62 litres (including 6 litre reserve) (16.4 US gallons or 13.6 Imp. gallons)
Engine (not Sportomatic) ... ... 9 litres (9.5 US qts. or 2 Imp. gallons)
Engine and Sportomatic unit ... ... 11.5 litres (12.1 US qts., 2.55 Imp. gallons)
Transmission ... ... 2.5 litres (2.6 US qts., 4.4 Imp. pints)
Brake fluid reservoir ... ... .20 litre (.16 US qt., .35 Imp. pint)
Windscreen washer reservoir ... ... 2 litres (1.6 US qts., 3.5 Imp. pints)

TORQUE WRENCH SETTINGS
Settings in mkg (lb ft in brackets)

Engine:

Crankcase bolts	2.2 to 2.5 (16 to 18)
Camshaft housing to cylinder head	2.2 (16)
Crankcase through-bolts and nuts	3.5 (25.3)
Flywheel bolts	15 (108.5)
Connecting rod bolts	5 (36.2)
Cylinder head nuts	3 to 3.3 (21.7 to 23.9)
Camshaft sprocket nut	10 (72.3)
Rocker arm shafts	1.8 (13)
Pulley to crankshaft	8 (58)
Pulley to generator	4 (29)

Transmission:

Housing nuts	2.5 (18)
Guide tube nuts	1.0 (7.2)
Withdrawal fork screw	1.0 (7.2)
Bolt for elbow drive	2.5 (18.1)
Detent plug	2.5 (18.1)
Filler and drain plugs	2.0 to 2.5 (14.5 to 18.1)
Bolts for clamping plate (intermediate plate) ...	2.5 (18.1)
Input shaft nut	10 to 12 (72.3 to 86.8)
Castle nut on input shaft	6.0 to 6.5 (43.4 to 47)
Reinforced castle nut on input shaft	9 to 11 (65.1 to 79.6)
Pinion shaft bolt	11 to 12 (79.6 to 86.8)
Selector fork bolts	2.5 (18.1)
Crownwheel (ring gear) bolts	9.5 to 10 (68.7 to 72.3)
Bolts for universal joint flanges	4.5 to 5 (32.5 to 36.2)
Ballpin for clutch withdrawal fork	2.1 to 2.3 (15.2 to 16.6)

Extra for Sportomatic transmission:

Housing nuts	2.1 to 2.3 (15.2 to 16.6)
Screw for elbow drive	1.5 (10.8)
Torque converter and servo unit nuts	2.1 to 2.3 (15 to 17)
Torque converter and starter nuts	3.5 to 4 (25 to 29)
Parking lock cap in front cover	3.5 to 4 (25 to 29)
Clutch pressure plate bolts	1.4 (10)
Freewheeling support bolts	1.4 (10)
Torque converter to coupling plate bolts	2.4 to 2.6 (17.4 to 18.8)
Bypass switch	4.5 to 5 (32.5 to 36.2)
Reversing light switch	4.5 to 5 (32.5 to 36.2)

Rear axle:

Control arm bolts	12 (86.8)
Radius arm bolts	9 (65.1)
Radius arm camber bolts	6 (43.4)
Radius arm tracking bolts	5 (36.2)
Damper bolt	7.5 (54.2)
Castle nut for halfshaft	30 to 35 (217 to 253)
Bolts for halfshaft flange (NADELLA)	4.7 (34)
Bolts for halfshaft flange (LOBRO)	4.3 (31.1)
Radius arm cover bolts	4.7 (34)
Wheel nuts	13 (94)

Steering and front axle:

Castle nut for ball joint	4.5 (32.5)
Steering lever bolts	4.7 (34)
Damper nut	8 (57.9)
Castle nut for control arm	7.5 (54.2)
Castle nut for tie rod ball stud	4.5 (34)

Bolt for clamping nut (axle)	...	...	...	...	2.5 (18.1)
Bolt for Flanblock mounting	...	...	...	...	4.7 (34)
Bolts for bearing carrier	...	...	...	...	4.7 (34)
Crossmember bolt	...	...	...	...	9 (65.1)
Bolt for crossmember brace	...	...	...	...	4.7 (34)
Nut for crossmember brace	...	...	...	...	6.5 (47)
Bolts for bush support (stabilizer)	...	...	...	...	2.5 (18.1)
Bolts for stabilizer lever	...	...	...	...	2.5 (18.1)
Bolt for tie rod yoke	...	...	...	...	4.7 (34)
Bolts for steering housing	...	...	...	...	4.7 (34)
Lower shaft bearing cap bolts	...	...	...	...	2.5 (18.1)
Steering coupling bolts	...	...	...	...	2.5 (18.1)
Eyebolt locknut	...	...	...	...	6.5 (47)
Castle nut for pinion flange	...	...	...	...	2.5 (18.1)
Steering housing base plate bolts	...	...	...	...	2.2 (15.9)
Steering wheel nut	...	...	...	...	8 (57.9)
Bolts for switch assembly clamp	...	...	...	...	2.5 (18.1)
Bolts for steering post	...	...	...	...	2.5 (18.1)
Bolts for universal joint	...	...	...	...	3.5 (25.3)
Bolts for post extension	...	...	...	...	2.5 (18.1)
Wheel nuts	...	...	...	...	13 (94)
Bolts for splined universal joints	...	...	...	...	2.5 (18.1)

Brakes:

Master cylinder flange nut	...	...	...	...	2.5 (18.1)
Nut, bottom shield	...	...	...	...	6.5 (47)
Bolt, bottom shield	...	...	...	...	4.7 (34)
Nut, disc to hub	...	...	...	...	2.3 (16.6)
Brake carrier bolts	...	...	...	...	4.7 (34)
Disc shroud bolts	...	...	...	...	2.5 (18)
Bolt, front caliper	...	...	...	...	7 (50.6)
Bolt, rear caliper	...	...	...	...	6 (43.4)
Bolt, brake carrier plate	...	...	...	...	2.5 (18.1)
Castle nut, half-axle	...	...	...	...	30 to 35 (217 to 253)
Half-axle flange bolt	...	...	...	...	4.7 (34)
Socket-head bolt, front caliper	...	...	...	...	3.4 (24.6)
Socket-head bolt, rear caliper	...	...	...	...	1.8 (13)
Hollow bolt, hydraulic banjo	...	...	...	...	2 (14.5)

Key to Fig 13:1 1 Starter motor 2 Alternator 3 Control box 4 Ignition distributor 5 Ignition coil 6 Spark plugs 7 Fuel pump 8 Resistor 9 Battery 11 Headlamps 12 Fog lamps 13 Flasher/parking lights 14 Tail/stop/flasher/reversing lights 15 Number plate light 19 Interior light 20 Trunk light 24 Small combination instrument 25 Large combination instrument 26 Transistorized tachometer 27 Speedometer 28 Clock 32 Flasher/dimmer/signal/wiper/washer switch with signal knob on steering wheel 33 Starter/ignition switch 34 Light switch 36 Fog lamp switch with control light 37 Handbrake control light switch 38 Door post contact switch 39 Brake light switch 40 Trunk light switch 41 Reversing light switch 42 Horn relay 43 Relay for light signal 44 Flasher light unit 45 Control light unit 46 Control light relay 47 Oil temperature transmitter 48 Fuel tank unit 49 Oil pressure transmitter 50 Oil level transmitter 51 Resistor relay 52 Windscreen wiper motor 53 Windscreen washer pump 54 Horn 55 Cigarette lighter 56 Control light switch 57 Control light fuse 61 Fuse box

Fuses: 1 Stoplight, flashers/reversing lights 2 Interior light, cigarette lighter, clock 3 Auxiliary heater 4 Windscreen wipers and washer 5 Fog lamps 6 Number plate light, trunk light 7 Parking light, righthand 8 Parking light, lefthand 9 Low beam, righthand 10 Low beam, lefthand 11 High beam, righthand, high beam control light 12 High beam, lefthand
Disconnecting battery with running engine results in immediate destruction of alternator

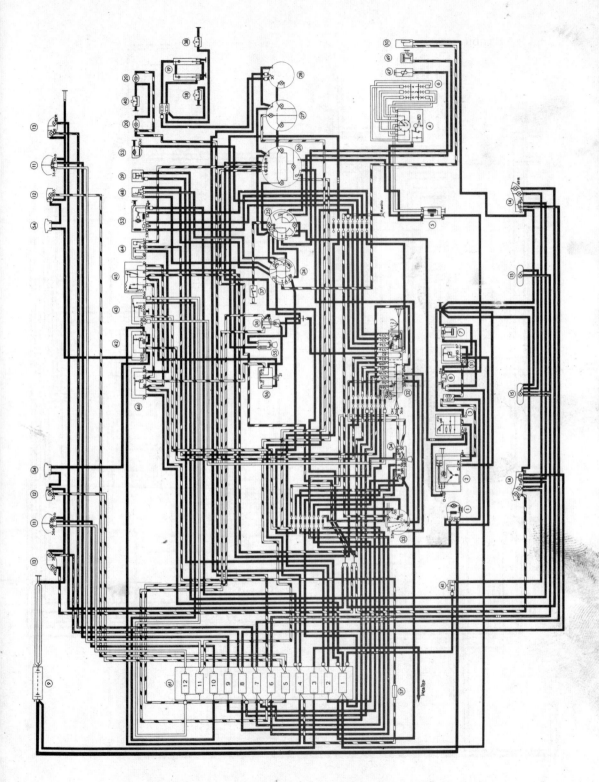

FIG 13:1   Wiring diagram for all 911 models except 911S

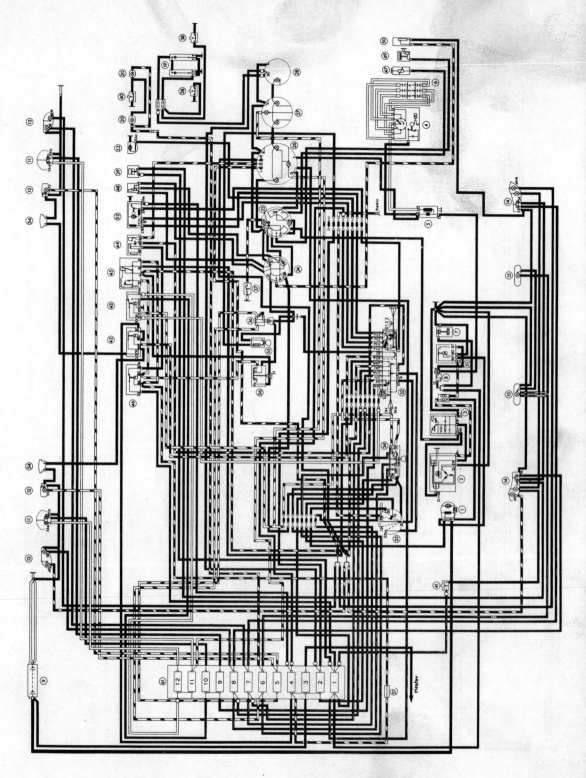

FIG 13:2 Wiring diagram for 911S cars

Key to Fig 13:2 1 Starter motor 2 Alternator 3 Control box 4 Ignition distributor 5 Ignition coil 6 Spark plugs 7 Fuel pump 8 Resistor 9 Battery 11 Headlamps 12 Fog lamps 13 Flasher/parking lights 14 Tail/stop/flasher/reversing lights 15 Number plate light 19 Interior light 20 Trunk light 24 Small combination instrument 25 Large combination instrument 26 Transistorized tachometer 27 Speedometer 28 Clock 32 Flasher/dimmer/signal/wiper/washer switch with signal knob on steering wheel 33 Starter/ignition switch 34 Light switch 36 Fog lamp switch with control light 37 Handbrake control light switch 38 Door post contact switch 39 Brake light switch 40 Trunk light switch 41 Reversing light switch 42 Horn relay 43 Relay for light signal 44 Flasher light unit 45 Control light unit 46 Control light relay 47 Oil temperature transmitter 48 Fuel tank unit 49 Oil pressure transmitter 50 Oil level transmitter 51 Resistor relay 52 Windscreen wiper motor 53 Windscreen washer pump 54 Horn 55 Cigarette lighter 56 Control light switch 57 Control light fuse 61 Fuse box

Fuses: 1 Stoplight/flashers/reversing lights 2 Interior light, cigarette lighter, clock 3 Auxiliary heater 4 Windscreen wipers and washer 5 Fog lamps 6 Number plate light, trunk light 7 Parking light, righthand 8 Parking light, lefthand 9 Low beam, righthand 10 Low beam, lefthand 11 High beam, righthand, high beam control light 12 High beam, lefthand
Disconnecting battery with running engine results in immediate destruction of alternator

Inches		Decimals	Millimetres	Inches to Millimetres		Millimetres to Inches	
				Inches	mm	mm	Inches
	1/64	.015625	.3969	.001	.0254	.01	.00039
1/32		.03125	.7937	.002	.0508	.02	.00079
	3/64	.046875	1.1906	.003	.0762	.03	.00118
1/16		.0625	1.5875	.004	.1016	.04	.00157
	5/64	.078125	1.9844	.005	.1270	.05	.00197
3/32		.09375	2.3812	.006	.1524	.06	.00236
	7/64	.109375	2.7781	.007	.1778	.07	.00276
1/8		.125	3.1750	.008	.2032	.08	.00315
	9/64	.140625	3.5719	.009	.2286	.09	.00354
5/32		.15625	3.9687	.01	.254	.1	.00394
	11/64	.171875	4.3656	.02	.508	.2	.00787
3/16		.1875	4.7625	.03	.762	.3	.01181
	13/64	.203125	5·1594	.04	1.016	.4	.01575
7/32		.21875	5.5562	.05	1.270	.5	.01969
	15/64	.234375	5.9531	.06	1.524	.6	.02362
1/4		.25	6.3500	.07	1.778	.7	.02756
	17/64	.265625	6.7469	.08	2.032	.8	.03150
9/32		.28125	7.1437	.09	2.286	.9	.03543
	19/64	.296875	7.5406	.1	2.54	1	.03937
5/16		.3125	7.9375	.2	5.08	2	.07874
	21/64	.328125	8.3344	.3	7.62	3	.11811
11/32		.34375	8.7312	.4	10.16	4	.15748
	23/64	.359375	9.1281	.5	12.70	5	.19685
3/8		.375	9.5250	.6	15.24	6	.23622
	25/64	.390625	9.9219	.7	17.78	7	.27559
13/32		.40625	10.3187	.8	20.32	8	.31496
	27/64	.421875	10.7156	.9	22.86	9	.35433
7/16		.4375	11.1125	1	25.4	10	.39370
	29/64	.453125	11.5094	2	50.8	11	.43307
15/32		.46875	11.9062	3	76.2	12	.47244
	31/64	.484375	12.3031	4	101.6	13	.51181
1/2		.5	12.7000	5	127.0	14	.55118
	33/64	.515625	13.0969	6	152.4	15	.59055
17/32		.53125	13.4937	7	177.8	16	.62992
	35/64	.546875	13.8906	8	203.2	17	.66929
9/16		.5625	14.2875	9	228.6	18	.70866
	37/64	.578125	14.6844	10	254.0	19	.74803
19/32		.59375	15.0812	11	279.4	20	.78740
	39/64	.609375	15.4781	12	304.8	21	.82677
5/8		.625	15.8750	13	330.2	22	.86614
	41/64	.640625	16.2719	14	355.6	23	.90551
21/32		.65625	16.6687	15	381.0	24	.94488
	43/64	.671875	17.0656	16	406.4	25	.98425
11/16		.6875	17.4625	17	431.8	26	1.02362
	45/64	.703125	17.8594	18	457.2	27	1.06299
23/32		.71875	18.2562	19	482.6	28	1.10236
	47/64	.734375	18.6531	20	508.0	29	1.14173
3/4		.75	19.0500	21	533.4	30	1.18110
	49/64	.765625	19.4469	22	558.8	31	1.22047
25/32		.78125	19.8437	23	584.2	32	1.25984
	51/64	.796875	20.2406	24	609.6	33	1.29921
13/16		.8125	20.6375	25	635.0	34	1.33858
	53/64	.828125	21.0344	26	660.4	35	1.37795
27/32		.84375	21.4312	27	685.8	36	1.41732
	55/64	.859375	21.8281	28	711.2	37	1.4567
7/8		.875	22.2250	29	736.6	38	1.4961
	57/64	.890625	22.6219	30	762.0	39	1.5354
29/32		.90625	23.0187	31	787.4	40	1.5748
	59/64	.921875	23.4156	32	812.8	41	1.6142
15/16		.9375	23.8125	33	838.2	42	1.6535
	61/64	.953125	24.2094	34	863.6	43	1.6929
31/32		.96875	24.6062	35	889.0	44	1.7323
	63/64	.984375	25.0031	36	914.4	45	1.7717

UNITS	Pints to Litres	Gallons to Litres	Litres to Pints	Litres to Gallons	Miles to Kilometres	Kilometres to Miles	Lbs. per sq. In. to Kg. per sq. Cm.	Kg. per sq. Cm. to Lbs. per sq. In.
1	.57	4.55	1.76	.22	1.61	.62	.07	14.22
2	1.14	9.09	3.52	.44	3.22	1.24	.14	28.50
3	1.70	13.64	5.28	.66	4.83	1.86	.21	42.67
4	2.27	18.18	7.04	.88	6.44	2.49	.28	56.89
5	2.84	22.73	8.80	1.10	8.05	3.11	.35	71.12
6	3.41	27.28	10.56	1.32	9.66	3.73	.42	85.34
7	3.98	31.82	12.32	1.54	11.27	4.35	.49	99.56
8	4.55	36.37	14.08	1.76	12.88	4.97	.56	113.79
9		40.91	15.84	1.98	14.48	5.59	.63	128.00
10		45.46	17.60	2.20	16.09	6.21	.70	142.23
20				4.40	32.19	12.43	1.41	284.47
30				6.60	48.28	18.64	2.11	426.70
40				8.80	64.37	24.85		
50					80.47	31.07		
60					96.56	37.28		
70					112.65	43.50		
80					128.75	49.71		
90					144.84	55.92		
100					160.93	62.14		

UNITS	Lb ft to kgm	Kgm to lb ft	UNITS	Lb ft to kgm	Kgm to lb ft
1	.138	7.233	7	.967	50.631
2	.276	14.466	8	1.106	57.864
3	.414	21.699	9	1.244	65.097
4	.553	28.932	10	1.382	72.330
5	.691	36.165	20	2.765	144.660
6	.829	43.398	30	4.147	216.990

HINTS ON MAINTENANCE AND OVERHAUL

There are few things more rewarding than the restoration of a vehicle's original peak of efficiency and smooth performance.

The following notes are intended to help the owner to reach that stage of perfection. Providing that he possesses the basic manual skills he should have no difficulty in performing most of the operations detailed in this manual. It must be stressed, however, that where recommended in the manual, highly-skilled operations ought to be entrusted to experts who have the necessary equipment to carry out the work satisfactorily.

Quality of workmanship

The hazardous driving conditions on the roads to-day demand that vehicles should be as nearly perfect, mechanically, as possible. It is therefore most important that amateur work is carried out with extra care, bearing in mind the often inadequate working conditions, and also the inferior tools which may have to be used. It is easy to counsel perfection in all things, and we recognise that it may be setting an impossibly high standard. **We do however, suggest that every care should be taken to ensure that a vehicle is as safe to take on the road as it is humanly possible to make it.**

Safe working conditions

Even though a vehicle may be stationary, it is still potentially dangerous if certain sensible precautions are not taken when working on it while it is supported on jacks or blocks. It is indeed preferable not to use jacks alone, but to supplement them with carefully placed blocks, so that there will be plenty of support if the car rolls off the jacks during a strenuous manoevre. Axle stands are an excellent way of providing a rigid base which is not readily disturbed. **Piles of bricks are a dangerous substitute.**

Be careful not to get under heavy loads on lifting tackle, as the load may fall. It is preferable not to work alone when lifting an engine, or when working underneath a vehicle which is supported well off the ground. To be trapped, particularly under the vehicle, may have unpleasant results if help is not quickly forthcoming.

Make some provision, however humble, to deal with fires. Always disconnect a battery if there is a likelihood of electrical shorts. These may start a fire if there is leaking fuel about. This applies particularly to leads which can carry a heavy current, like those in the starter circuit. While on the subject of electricity, we must also stress the danger of using equipment which is run off the mains and which has no earth or has faulty wiring connections. Many workshops have damp floors, and electrical shocks are of such a nature that it is sometimes impossible to let go of a live lead or piece of equipment due to the muscular spasms which take place.

Work demanding special care

This involves the servicing of braking, steering and suspension systems. **On the road, failure of the braking system may be disastrous.** Make quite sure that there can be no possibility of failure through the bursting of rusty brake pipes or rotten hoses, nor to a sudden loss of pressure due to defective seals or valves.

Problems

The chief problems which face an operator are:
1 External dirt.
2 Difficulty in undoing tight fixings.
3 Dismantling unfamiliar mechanisms.
4 Deciding in what respect parts are defective.
5 Confusion about the correct order for reassembly.
6 Adjusting running clearance.
7 Road testing.
8 Final tuning.

Practical suggestions to solve the problems

1 Preliminary cleaning of large parts—engines, transmissions, steering, suspensions, etc.—should be carried out before removal from the car. Where road dirt and mud alone are present, wash clean with a high pressure water jet, brushing to remove stubborn adhesions, and allow to drain and dry. Where oil or grease is also present, wash down with a proprietary compound (Gunk, Teepol etc.) applying with a stiff brush into all crevices. Cover the distributor and ignition coil with a polythene bag and then apply a strong water jet to clear the loosened deposits. Allow to drain and dry. The assemblies will then be sufficiently clean to remove and transfer to the bench for the next stage.

On the bench, further cleaning can be carried out, first wiping the parts as free as possible from grease with old newspaper. Avoid using rag or cotton waste which can leave clogging fibres behind. Any remaining grease can be removed with a brush dipped in paraffin. If necessary, traces of paraffin can be removed by carbon tetrachloride. Avoid using paraffin or petrol in large quantities for cleaning inside a garage because of the high rate of fire risk.

When all exteriors have been cleaned, dismantling can begin. This ensures that dirt will not enter into interiors and orifices revealed by dismantling. In the next phase, where components have to be cleaned, use carbon tetrachloride in preference to petrol and keep the containers covered except when in use. After the components have been cleaned, plug small holes with tapered hard wood plugs cut to size and blank off larger orifices with grease proof paper and masking tape. Do not use soft wood plugs or matchsticks as they may break.

2 It is not advisable to hammer on the end of a screw thread, but if it must be done, first screw on a nut to protect the thread, and use a lead hammer. This applies particularly to the removal of tapered cotters. Nuts and bolts seem to 'grow' together, especially in exhaust systems. If penetrating oil does not work, try the judicious application of heat, but be careful of starting a fire. Asbestos sheet or cloth is useful to isolate heat.

Tight bushes or pieces of tail-pipe rusted into a silencer can be removed by splitting them with an open-ended hacksaw. Tight screws can sometimes be started by a tap from a hammer on the end of a suitable screwdriver. Many tight fittings will yield to the judicious use of a hammer. but it must be a soft-faced hammer if damage is to be avoided. Use a heavy block on the opposite side to absorb shock. Any parts of the steering system which have been damaged should be renewed, as attempts to repair them may lead to cracking and subsequent failure. Steering ball joints should be disconnected using a recommended tool to prevent damage.

3 It often happens that an owner is baffled when trying to dismantle an unfamiliar piece of equipment. So many modern devices are pressed together or assembled by spinning-over flanges, that they must be sawn apart. The intention is that the whole assembly must be renewed. However, parts which appear to be in one piece to the naked eye, may reveal close-fitting joint lines when inspected with a magnifying glass, and this may provide the necessary clue to dismantling.

Lefthanded screw threads are used where rotational forces would tend to unscrew a righthanded screw thread.

Be very careful when dismantling mechanisms which may come apart suddenly. Work in an enclosed space where the parts will be contained, and drape a piece of cloth over the device if springs are likely to fly in all directions. Mark everything which might be reassembled in the wrong position. Scratched symbols may be used on unstressed parts, or a sequence of tiny dots from a centre punch can be useful. Stressed parts such as springs and torsion bars should never be scratched or centre-popped as this may lead to cracking under working conditions.

Store parts which look alike in the correct order for reassembly. Never rely upon memory to assist in the assembly of complicated mechanisms, especially when they will be dismantled for a long time, but make notes and drawings to supplement the diagrams in the manual, and put labels on detached wires.

Rust stains may indicate unlubricated wear. This can sometimes be seen round the outside edge of a bearing cup in a universal joint. Look for bright rubbing marks on parts which normally should not make heavy contact. These may prove that something is bent or running out of truth. For example, there may be bright marks on one side of a piston, at the top near the ring grooves, and others at the bottom of the skirt on the other side. This could well be the clue to a bent connecting rod.

Suspected cracks can be proved by heating the component in a light oil to approximately 100°C, removing, drying off, and dusting with french chalk. If a crack is present the oil retained in the crack will stain the french chalk.

4 In determining wear against the permissible limits set in the manual, accurate measurement can only be achieved by the use of a micrometer. In many cases the wear is given to the fourth place of decimals. This can be read by the vernier scale on the barrel of a good micrometer. Bore diameters are more difficult to determine. If, however, the matching shaft is accurately measured, the degree of play in the bore can be felt as a guide to its suitability. In other cases, the shank of a twist drill of known diameter is a handy check.

Many methods have been devised for determining the clearance between bearing surfaces. To-day the best and simplest is by the use of Plastigage, obtainable from most garages. A thin plastic thread is laid between the two surfaces and the bearing is tightened, flattening the thread. On removal, the width of the thread is compared with a scale supplied with the thread and the clearance is read off directly.

Sometimes joint faces leak persistently, even after gasket renewal. The fault will then be traceable to distortion, dirt or burrs. Studs which are screwed into soft metal frequently raise burrs at the point of entry. A quick cure for this is to chamfer the edge of the hole in the part which fits over the stud.

5 **Always check a replacement part with the original one before it is fitted.**

If parts are not marked, and the order for reassembly is not known, a little detective work will help. Look for marks which are due to wear to see if they can be mated. Joint faces may not be identical due to manufacturing errors, and parts which overlap may be stained, giving a clue to the correct position.

Most fixings leave identifying marks especially if they were painted over on assembly. It is then possible to decide whether a nut, for instance, has a plain, a spring, or a shakeproof washer under it. All running surfaces become 'bedded' together after long spells of work and tiny imperfections on one part will be found to have left corresponding marks on the other. This is particularly true of shafts and bearings and even a score on the cylinder wall will show on the piston.

6 Checking end float or rocker clearances by feeler gauge may not always give accurate results because of wear. For instance, the rocker tip which bears on a valve stem may be deeply pitted, in which case the feeler will be simply bridging a depression. Thrust washers may also wear depressions in opposing faces to make accurate measurement difficult. End float is then easier to check by using a dial gauge.

Steering assemblies often wear in the straight-ahead position. If any part is adjusted, make sure that it remains free when moved from lock to lock. Do not be suprised if an assembly like a steering gearbox, which is known to be carefully adjusted outside the car, becomes stiff when it is bolted in place. This will be due to distortion of the case by the pull of the mounting bolts, particularly if the mounting points are not all touching together. This problem may be met in other equipment and is cured by careful attention to the alignment of mounting points.

7 After a major overhaul, particularly if a great deal of work has been done on the braking, steering and suspension systems, it is advisable to approach the problem of testing with care.

If the braking system has been overhauled, apply heavy pressure to the brake pedal and get a second operator to check every possible source of leakage. The brakes may work extremely well, but a leak could cause complete failure after a few miles.

Do not fit the hub caps until every wheel nut has been checked for tightness, and make sure the tyre pressures are correct. Check the levels of lubricants and hydraulic fluids. Being satisfied that all is well, take the car on the road and test the brakes at once. Check the steering and the action of the handbrake.

Do all this at moderate speeds on quiet roads, and make sure there is no other vehicle behind you when you try a rapid stop.

Finally, remember that many parts settle down after a time, so check all fixings for tightness after the car has been on the road for a hundred miles or so.

8 It is useless to tune an engine which has not reached its normal running temperature. In the same way, the tune of an engine which is stiff after a rebore will be different when the engine is running free.

Trouble may not always be due to what seems the obvious cause. Ignition, carburation and mechanical condition are interdependent and spitting back through the carburetter, which might be attributed to a weak mixture, can be caused by a sticking inlet valve.

For one final hint on tuning, **never adjust more than one thing at a time or it will be impossible to tell which adjustment produced the desired result.**

GLOSSARY OF TERMS

Allen key   Cranked wrench of hexagonal section for use with socket head screws.

Alternator   Electrical generator producing alternating current. Rectified to direct current for battery charging.

Ambient temperature   Surrounding atmospheric temperature.

Annulus   Used in engineering to indicate the outer ring gear of an epicyclic gear train.

Armature   The shaft carrying the windings, which rotates in the magnetic field of a generator or starter motor. That part of a solenoid or relay which is activated by the magnetic field.

Axial   In line with, or pertaining to, an axis.

Backlash   Play in meshing gears.

Balance lever   A bar where force applied at the centre is equally divided between connections at the ends.

Banjo axle   Axle casing with large diameter housing for the crownwheel and differential.

Bendix pinion   A self-engaging and self-disengaging drive on a starter motor shaft.

Bevel pinion   A conical shaped gearwheel, designed to mesh with a similar gear with an axis usually at 90 deg. to its own.

bhp   Brake horse power, measured on a dynamometer.

bmep   Brake mean effective pressure. Average pressure on a piston during the working stroke.

Brake cylinder   Cylinder with hydraulically operated piston(s) acting on brake shoes or pad(s).

Brake regulator   Control valve fitted in hydraulic braking system which limits brake pressure to rear brakes during heavy braking to prevent rear wheel locking.

Camber   Angle at which a wheel is tilted from the vertical.

Capacitor   Modern term for an electrical condenser. Part of distributor assembly, connected across contact breaker points, acts as an interference suppressor.

Castellated   Top face of a nut, slotted across the flats, to take a locking splitpin.

Castor   Angle at which the kingpin or swivel pin is tilted when viewed from the side.

cc   Cubic centimetres. Engine capacity is arrived at by multiplying the area of the bore in sq cm by the stroke in cm by the number of cylinders.

Clevis   U-shaped forked connector used with a clevis pin, usually at handbrake connections.

Collet   A type of collar, usually split and located in a groove in a shaft, and held in place by a retainer. The arrangement used to retain the spring(s) on a valve stem in most cases.

Commutator   Rotating segmented current distributor between armature windings and brushes in generator or motor.

Compression   The ratio, or quantitative relation, of the total volume (piston at bottom of stroke) to the unswept volume (piston at top of stroke) in an engine cylinder.

Condenser   See capacitor.

Core plug   Plug for blanking off a manufacturing hole in a casting.

Crownwheel   Large bevel gear in rear axle, driven by a bevel pinion attached to the propeller shaft. Sometimes called a 'ring wheel'.

'C'-spanner   Like a 'C' with a handle. For use on screwed collars without flats, but with slots or holes.

Damper   Modern term for shock-absorber, used in vehicle suspension systems to damp out spring oscillations.

Depression   The lowering of atmospheric pressure as in the inlet manifold and carburetter.

Dowel   Close tolerance pin, peg, tube, or bolt, which accurately locates mating parts.

Drag link   Rod connecting steering box drop arm (pitman arm) to nearest front wheel steering arm in certain types of steering systems.

Dry liner   Thinwall tube pressed into cylinder bore

Dry sump   Lubrication system where all oil is scavenged from the sump, and returned to a separate tank.

Dynamo   See Generator.

Electrode   Terminal, part of an electrical component, such as the points or 'Electrodes' of a sparking plug.

Electrolyte   In lead-acid car batteries a solution of sulphuric acid and distilled water.

End float   The axial movement between associated parts, end play.

EP   Extreme pressure. In lubricants, special grades for heavily loaded bearing surfaces, such as gear teeth in a gearbox, or crownwheel and pinion in a rear axle.

Fade	Of brakes. Reduced efficiency due to overheating.
Field coils	Windings on the polepieces of motors and generators.
Fillets	Narrow finishing strips usually applied to interior bodywork.
First motion shaft	Input shaft from clutch to gearbox.
Fullflow filter	Filters in which all the oil is pumped to the engine. If the element becomes clogged, a bypass valve operates to pass unfiltered oil to the engine.
FWD	Front wheel drive.
Gear pump	Two meshing gears in a close fitting casing. Oil is carried from the inlet round the outside of both gears in the spaces between the gear teeth and casing to the outlet, the meshing gear teeth prevent oil passing back to the inlet, and the oil is forced through the outlet port.
Generator	Modern term for 'Dynamo'. When rotated produces electrical current.
Grommet	A ring of protective or sealing material. Can be used to protect pipes or leads passing through bulkheads.
Grubscrew	Fully threaded headless screw with screwdriver slot. Used for locking, or alignment purposes.
Gudgeon pin	Shaft which connects a piston to its connecting rod. Sometimes called 'wrist pin', or 'piston pin'.
Halfshaft	One of a pair transmitting drive from the differential.
Helical	In spiral form. The teeth of helical gears are cut at a spiral angle to the side faces of the gearwheel.
Hot spot	Hot area that assists vapourisation of fuel on its way to cylinders. Often provided by close contact between inlet and exhaust manifolds.
HT	High Tension. Applied to electrical current produced by the ignition coil for the sparking plugs.
Hydrometer	A device for checking specific gravity of liquids. Used to check specific gravity of electrolyte.
Hypoid bevel gears	A form of bevel gear used in the rear axle drive gears. The bevel pinion meshes below the centre line of the crownwheel, giving a lower propeller shaft line.
Idler	A device for passing on movement. A free running gear between driving and driven gears. A lever transmitting track rod movement to a side rod in steering gear.
Impeller	A centrifugal pumping element. Used in water pumps to stimulate flow.
Journals	Those parts of a shaft that are in contact with the bearings.
Kingpin	The main vertical pin which carries the front wheel spindle, and permits steering movement. May be called 'steering pin' or 'swivel pin'.
Layshaft	The shaft which carries the laygear in the gearbox. The laygear is driven by the first motion shaft and drives the third motion shaft according to the gear selected. Sometimes called the 'countershaft' or 'second motion shaft.'
lb ft	A measure of twist or torque. A pull of 10 lb at a radius of 1 ft is a torque of 10 lb ft.
lb/sq in	Pounds per square inch.
Little-end	The small, or piston end of a connecting rod. Sometimes called the 'small-end'.
LT	Low Tension. The current output from the battery.
Mandrel	Accurately manufactured bar or rod used for test or centring purposes.
Manifold	A pipe, duct, or chamber, with several branches.
Needle rollers	Bearing rollers with a length many times their diameter.
Oil bath	Reservoir which lubricates parts by immersion. In air filters, a separate oil supply for wetting a wire mesh element to hold the dust.
Oil wetted	In air filters, a wire mesh element lightly oiled to trap and hold airborne dust.
Overlap	Period during which inlet and exhaust valves are open together.
Panhard rod	Bar connected between fixed point on chassis and another on axle to control sideways movement.
Pawl	Pivoted catch which engages in the teeth of a ratchet to permit movement in one direction only.
Peg spanner	Tool with pegs, or pins, to engage in holes or slots in the part to be turned.
Pendant pedals	Pedals with levers that are pivoted at the top end.
Phillips screwdriver	A cross-point screwdriver for use with the cross-slotted heads of Phillips screws.
Pinion	A small gear, usually in relation to another gear.
Piston-type damper	Shock absorber in which damping is controlled by a piston working in a closed oil-filled cylinder.
Preloading	Preset static pressure on ball or roller bearings not due to working loads.
Radial	Radiating from a centre, like the spokes of a wheel.

Radius rod	Pivoted arm confining movement of a part to an arc of fixed radius.
Ratchet	Toothed wheel or rack which can move in one direction only, movement in the other being prevented by a pawl.
Ring gear	A gear tooth ring attached to outer periphery of flywheel. Starter pinion engages with it during starting.
Runout	Amount by which rotating part is out of true.
Semi-floating axle	Outer end of rear axle halfshaft is carried on bearing inside axle casing. Wheel hub is secured to end of shaft.
Servo	A hydraulic or pneumatic system for assisting, or, augmenting a physical effort. See 'Vacuum Servo'.
Setscrew	One which is threaded for the full length of the shank.
Shackle	A coupling link, used in the form of two parallel pins connected by side plates to secure the end of the master suspension spring and absorb the effects of deflection.
Shell bearing	Thinwalled steel shell lined with anti-friction metal. Usually semi-circular and used in pairs for main and big-end bearings.
Shock absorber	See 'Damper'.
Silentbloc	Rubber bush bonded to inner and outer metal sleeves.
Socket-head screw	Screw with hexagonal socket for an Allen key.
Solenoid	A coil of wire creating a magnetic field when electric current passes through it. Used with a soft iron core to operate contacts or a mechanical device.
Spur gear	A gear with teeth cut axially across the periphery.
Stub axle	Short axle fixed at one end only.
Tachometer	An instrument for accurate measurement of rotating speed. Usually indicates in revolutions per minute.

TDC	Top Dead Centre. The highest point reached by a piston in a cylinder, with the crank and connecting rod in line.
Thermostat	Automatic device for regulating temperature. Used in vehicle coolant systems to open a valve which restricts circulation at low temperature.
Third motion shaft	Output shaft of gearbox.
Threequarter floating axle	Outer end of rear axle halfshaft flanged and bolted to wheel hub, which runs bearing mounted on outside of axle casing. Vehicle weight is not carried by the axle shaft.
Thrust bearing or washer	Used to reduce friction in rotating parts subject to axial loads.
Torque	Turning or twisting effort. See 'lb ft'.
Track rod	The bar(s) across the vehicle which connect the steering arms and maintain the front wheels in their correct alignment.
UJ	Universal joint. A coupling between shafts which permits angular movement.
UNF	Unified National Fine screw thread.
Vacuum servo	Device used in brake system, using difference between atmospheric pressure and inlet manifold depression to operate a piston which acts to augment brake pressure as required. See 'Servo'.
Venturi	A restriction or 'choke' in a tube, as in a carburetter, used to increase velocity to obtain a reduction in pressure.
Vernier	A sliding scale for obtaining fractional readings of the graduations of an adjacent scale.
Welch plug	A domed thin metal disc which is partially flattened to lock in a recess. Used to plug core holes in castings.
Wet liner	Removeable cylinder barrel, sealed against coolant leakage, where the coolant is in direct contact with the outer surface.
Wet sump	A reservoir attached to the crankcase to hold the lubricating oil.

INDEX

Make				Author	Title
ALFA ROMEO					
1600 Giulia TI 1961–67	..	..	..	Ball	Alfa Romeo Giulia 1962–70 Autobook
1600 Giulia Sprint 1962–68	..	..	..	Ball	Alfa Romeo Giulia 1962–70 Autobook
1600 Giulia Spider 1962–68	..	..	..	Ball	Alfa Romeo Giulia 1962–70 Autobook
1600 Giulia Super 1965–70	..	..	..	Ball	Alfa Romeo Giulia 1962–70 Autobook
ASTON MARTIN					
All models 1921–58	..	..	..	Coram	Aston Martin 1921–58 Autobook
AUSTIN					
A30 1951–56	..	..	..	Ball	Austin A30, A35, A40 Autobook
A35 1956–62	..	..	..	Ball	Austin A30, A35, A40 Autobook
A40 Farina 1957–67	..	..	..	Ball	Austin A30, A35, A40 Autobook
A40 Cambridge 1954–57	..	..	..	Ball	BMC Autobook Three
A50 Cambridge 1954–57	..	..	..	Ball	BMC Autobook Three
A55 Cambridge Mk 1 1957–58	..	..	..	Ball	BMC Autobook Three
A55 Cambridge Mk 2 1958–61	..	..	..	Ball	Austin A55 Mk 2, A60 1958–69 Autobook
A60 Cambridge 1961–69	..	..	..	Ball	Austin A55 Mk 2, A60 1958–69 Autobook
A99 1959–61	..	..	..	Ball	BMC Autobook Four
A110 1961–68	..	..	..	Ball	BMC Autobook Four
Mini 1959–70	..	..	..	Ball	Mini 1959–70 Autobook
Mini Clubman 1969–70	..	..	..	Ball	Mini 1959–70 Autobook
Mini Cooper 1961–70	..	..	..	Ball	Mini Cooper 1961–70 Autobook
Mini Cooper S 1963–70	..	..	..	Ball	Mini Cooper 1961–70 Autobook
1100 Mk 1 1963–67	..	..	..	Ball	1100 Mk 1 1962–67 Autobook
1100 Mk 2 1968–70	..	..	..	Ball	1100 Mk 2, 1300 Mk 1, 2, America 1968–71 Autobook
1300 Mk 1, 2 1968–71	..	..	..	Ball	1100 Mk 2, 1300 Mk 1, 2, America 1968–71 Autobook
America 1968–71	..	..	..	Ball	1100 Mk 2, 1300 Mk 1, 2, America 1968–71 Autobook
1800 Mk 1, 2 1964–71	..	..	..	Ball	1800 1964–71 Autobook
1800 S 1969–71	..	..	..	Ball	1800 1964–71 Autobook
Maxi 1500 1969–71	..	..	..	Ball	Austin Maxi 1969–71 Autobook
Maxi 1750 1970–71	..	..	..	Ball	Austin Maxi 1969–71 Autobook
AUSTIN HEALEY					
100/6 1956–59	..	..	..	Ball	Austin Healey 100/6, 3000 1956–68 Autobook
Sprite 1958–70	..	..	..	Ball	Sprite, Midget 1958–70 Autobook
3000 Mk 1, 2, 3 1959–68	..	..	..	Ball	Austin Healey 100/6, 3000 1956–68 Autobook
BEDFORD					
CA Mk 1 and 2 1961–69	..	..	..	Ball	Vauxhall Victor 1, 2 FB 1957–64 Autobook
Beagle HA 1964–66	..	..	..	Ball	Vauxhall Viva HA 1964–66 Autobook
BMW					
1600 1966–70	..	..	..	Ball	BMW 1600 1966–70 Autobook
1600–2 1966–70	..	..	..	Ball	BMW 1600 1966–70 Autobook
1600TI 1966–70	..	..	..	Ball	BMW 1600 1966–70 Autobook
1800 1964–70	..	..	..	Ball	BMW 1800 1964–70 Autobook
1800TI 1964–67	..	..	..	Ball	BMW 1800 1964–70 Autobook
2000 1966–70	..	..	..	Ball	BMW 2000, 2002 1966–70 Autobook
2000A 1966–70	..	..	..	Ball	BMW 2000, 2002 1966–70 Autobook
2000TI 1966–70	..	..	..	Ball	BMW 2000, 2002 1966–70 Autobook
2000CS 1967–70	..	..	..	Ball	BMW 2000, 2002 1966–70 Autobook
2000CA 1967–70	..	..	..	Ball	BMW 2000, 2002 1966–70 Autobook
2002 1968–70	..	..	..	Ball	BMW 2000, 2002 1966–70 Autobook
CITROEN					
DS19 1955–65	..	..	..	Ball	Citroen DS19, ID19 1955–66 Autobook
ID19 1956–66	..	..	..	Ball	Citroen DS19, ID19 1955–66 Autobook

Make				Author	Title

COMMER

Cob Series 1, 2, 3 1960–65	..	..	..	Ball	Hillman Minx 1 to 5 1956–65 Autobook
Imp Vans 1963–68	..	..	..	Smith	Hillman Imp 1963–68 Autobook
Imp Vans 1969–71	..	..	..	Ball	Hillman Imp 1969–71 Autobook

DE DION BOUTON

One-cylinder 1899–1907	..	..	Mercredy	De Dion Bouton Autobook One
Two-cylinder 1903–1907	..	..	Mercredy	De Dion Bouton Autobook One
Four-cylinder 1905–1907	..	..	Mercredy	De Dion Bouton Autobook One

DATSUN

1300 1968–70	..	..	..	Ball	Datsun 1300, 1600 1968–70 Autobook
1600 1968–70	..	..	..	Ball	Datsun 1300, 1600 1968–70 Autobook

FIAT

500 1957–61	..	..	..	Ball	Fiat 500 1957–69 Autobook
500D 1960–65	..	..	..	Ball	Fiat 500 1957–69 Autobook
500F 1965–69	..	..	..	Ball	Fiat 500 1957–69 Autobook
500L 1968–69	..	..	..	Ball	Fiat 500 1957–69 Autobook
600 633cc 1955–61	..	..	..	Ball	Fiat 600, 600D 1955–69 Autobook
600D 767cc 1960–69	..	..	..	Ball	Fiat 600, 600D 1955–69 Autobook
850 Sedan 1964–70	..	..	..	Ball	Fiat 850 1964–70 Autobook
850 Coupé 1965–70	..	..	..	Ball	Fiat 850 1964–70 Autobook
850 Roadster 1965–70	..	..	..	Ball	Fiat 850 1964–70 Autobook
850 Family 1965–70	..	..	..	Ball	Fiat 850 1964–70 Autobook
850 Sport 1968–70	..	..	..	Ball	Fiat 850 1964–70 Autobook
124 Saloon 1966–70	..	..	..	Ball	Fiat 124 1966–70 Autobook
124S 1968–70	..	..	..	Ball	Fiat 124 1966–70 Autobook
124 Spyder 1966–70	..	..	..	Ball	Fiat 124 Sport 1966–70 Autobook
124 Coupé 1967–69	..	..	..	Ball	Fiat 124 Sport 1967–70 Autobook

FORD

Anglia 100E 1953–59	..	..	..	Ball	Ford Anglia Prefect 100E Autobook
Anglia 105E 1959–67	..	..	..	Smith	Ford Anglia 105E, Prefect 107E 1959–67 Autobook
Anglia Super 123E 1962–67	..	..	..	Smith	Ford Anglia 105E, Prefect 107E 1959–67 Autobook
Capri 109E 1962	..	..	..	Smith	Ford Classic, Capri 1961–64 Autobook
Capri 116E 1962–64	..	..	..	Smith	Ford Classic, Capri 1961–64 Autobook
Capri 1300, 1300GT 1968–71	..	..	Ball	Ford Capri 1300, 1600 1968–71 Autobook
Capri 1600, 1600GT 1968–71	..	..	Ball	Ford Capri 1300, 1600 1968–71 Autobook
Classic 109E 1961–62	..	..	..	Smith	Ford Classic, Capri 1961–64 Autobook
Classic 116E 1962–63	..	..	..	Smith	Ford Classic, Capri 1961–64 Autobook
Consul Mk 1 1950–56	..	..	..	Ball	Ford Consul, Zephyr, Zodiac 1, 2 1950–62 Autobook
Consul Mk 2 1956–62	..	..	..	Ball	Ford Consul, Zephyr, Zodiac 1, 2 1950–62 Autobook
Corsair Straight Four 1963–65	..	..	Ball	Ford Corsair Straight Four 1963–65 Autobook
Corsair Straight Four GT 1963–65	..	..	Ball	Ford Corsair Straight Four 1963–65 Autobook
Corsair V4 3004E 1965–68	..	..	..	Smith	Ford Corsair V4 1965–68 Autobook
Corsair V4 GT 1965–66	..	..	..	Smith	Ford Corsair V4 1965–68 Autobook
Corsair V4 1663cc 1969–70	..	..	..	Ball	Ford Corsair V4 1969–70 Autobook
Corsair 2000, 2000E 1966–68	..	..	Smith	Ford Corsair V4 1965–68 Autobook
Corsair 2000, 2000E 1969–70	..	..	Ball	Ford Corsair V4 1969–70 Autobook
Cortina 113E 1962–66	..	..	..	Smith	Ford Cortina 1962–66 Autobook
Cortina Super 118E 1963–66	..	..	..	Smith	Ford Cortina 1962–66 Autobook
Cortina Lotus 125E 1963–66	..	..	..	Smith	Ford Cortina 1962–66 Autobook
Cortina GT 118E 1963–66	..	..	..	Smith	Ford Cortina 1962–66 Autobook
Cortina 1300 1967–68	..	..	..	Smith	Ford Cortina 1967–68 Autobook
Cortina 1300 1969–70	..	..	..	Ball	Ford Cortina 1969–70 Autobook
Cortina 1500 1967–68	..	..	..	Smith	Ford Cortina 1967–68 Autobook
Cortina 1600 (including Lotus) 1967–68	..	Smith	Ford Cortina 1967–68 Autobook
Cortina 1600 1969–70	..	..	..	Ball	Ford Cortina 1969–70 Autobook
Escort 100E 1955–59	..	..	..	Ball	Ford Anglia Prefect 100E Autobook
Escort 1100 1967–71	..	..	..	Ball	Ford Escort 1967–71 Autobook

Make				Author	Title
Escort 1300 1967–71	..	..	..	Ball	Ford Escort 1967–71 Autobook
Prefect 100E 1954–59		..	..	Ball	Ford Anglia Prefect 100E Autobook
Prefect 107E 1959–61		..	..	Smith	Ford Anglia 105E, Prefect 107E 1959–67 Autobook
Popular 100E 1959–62		..	..	Ball	Ford Anglia Prefect 100E Autobook
Squire 100E 1955–59	..	..	:.	Ball	Ford Anglia Prefect 100E Autobook
Zephyr Mk 1 1950–56		..	..	Ball	Ford Consul, Zephyr, Zodiac 1, 2 1950–62 Autobook
Zephyr Mk 2 1956–62		..	..	Ball	Ford Consul, Zephyr, Zodiac 1, 2 1950–62 Autobook
Zephyr 4 Mk 3 1962–66		..	..	Ball	Ford Zephyr, Zodiac Mk 3 1962–66 Autobook
Zephyr 6 Mk 3 1962–66		..	..	Ball	Ford Zephyr, Zodiac Mk 3 1962–66 Autobook
Zodiac Mk 3 1962–66	..	..	..	Ball	Ford Zephyr, Zodiac Mk 3 1962–66 Autobook
Zodiac Mk 1 1953–56	..	..	..	Ball	Ford Consul Zephyr, Zodiac 1, 2 1950–62 Autobook
Zodiac Mk 2 1956–62	..	..	..	Ball	Ford Consul, Zephyr, Zodiac 1, 2 1950–62 Autobook
Zephyr V4 2 litre 1966–70	..	..	..	Ball	Ford Zephyr V4, V6, Zodiac 1966–70 Autobook
Zephyr V6 2.5 litre 1966–70	..	..	..	Ball	Ford Zephyr V4, V6, Zodiac 1966–70 Autobook
Zodiac V6 3 litre 1966–70	..	..	..	Ball	Ford Zephyr V4, V6, Zodiac 1966–70 Autobook

HILLMAN

Avenger 1970–71	..	..	..	Ball	Hillman Avenger 1970–71 Autobook
Avenger GT 1970–71	..	..	..	Ball	Hillman Avenger 1970–71 Autobook
Hunter GT 1966–70	..	..	..	Ball	Hillman Hunter 1966–70 Autobook
Minx series 1, 2, 3 1956–59	..	..	..	Ball	Hillman Minx 1 to 5 1956–65 Autobook
Minx series 3A, 3B, 3C 1959–63		..	..	Ball	Hillman Minx 1 to 5 1956–65 Autobook
Minx series 5 1963–65		..	..	Ball	Hillman Minx 1 to 5 1956–65 Autobook
Minx series 6 1965–67		..	..	Ball	Hillman Minx 1965–67 Autobook
New Minx 1500, 1725 1966–70		..	..	Ball	Hillman Minx 1966–70 Autobook
Imp 1963–68	..	..	..	Smith	Hillman Imp 1963–68 Autobook
Imp 1969–71	..	..	..	Ball	Hillman Imp 1969–71 Autobook
Husky series 1, 2, 3 1958–65	..	..	..	Ball	Hillman Minx 1 to 5 1956–65 Autobook
Husky Estate 1969–71		..	..	Ball	Hillman Imp 1969–71 Autobook
Super Minx Mk 1, 2, 3 1961–65		..	..	Ball	Hillman Super Minx 1961–65 Autobook
Super Minx Mk 4 1965–67	..	..	..	Ball	Hillman Minx 1965–67 Autobook

HUMBER

Sceptre Mk 1 1963–65		..	..	Ball	Hillman Super Minx 1961–65 Autobook
Sceptre Mk 2 1965–67		..	..	Ball	Hillman Minx 1965–67 Autobook
Sceptre 1967–70	..	..	..	Ball	Hillman Hunter 1966–70 Autobook

JAGUAR

XK 120 1948–54	..	..	..	Ball	Jaguar XK 120, 140, 150 Mk 7, 8, 9 1948–61 Autobook
XK 140 1954–57	..	..	..	Ball	Jaguar XK 120, 140, 150 Mk 7, 8, 9 1948–61 Autobook
XK 150 1957–61	..	..	..	Ball	Jaguar XK 120, 140, 150 Mk 7, 8, 9 1948–61 Autobook
XK 150S 1959–61	..	..	..	Ball	Jaguar XK 120, 140, 150 Mk 7, 8, 9 1948–61 Autobook
Mk 7, 7M, 8, 9 1950–61	..	..	..	Ball	Jaguar XK 120, 140, 150 Mk 7, 8, 9 1948–61 Autobook
2.4 Mk 1, 2 1955–67	..	..	..	Ball	Jaguar 2.4, 3.4, 3.8 Mk 1, 2 1955–69 Autobook
3.4 Mk 1, 2 1957–67	..	..	..	Ball	Jaguar 2.4, 3.4, 3.8 Mk 1, 2 1955–69 Autobook
3.8 Mk 2 1959–67	..	..	..	Ball	Jaguar 2.4, 3.4, 3.8 Mk 1, 2 1955–69 Autobook
240 1967–69	..	..	..	Ball	Jaguar 2.4, 3.4, 3.8 Mk 1, 2 1955–69 Autobook
340 1967–69	..	..	..	Ball	Jaguar 2.4, 3.4, 3.8 Mk 1, 2 1955–69 Autobook
E Type 3.8 1961–65	..	..	..	Ball	Jaguar E Type 1961–70 Autobook
E Type 4.2 1964–69	..	..	..	Ball	Jaguar E Type 1961–70 Autobook
E Type 4.2 2+2 1966–70	..	..	..	Ball	Jaguar E Type 1961–70 Autobook
E Type 4.2 Series 2 1969–70	..	..	..	Ball	Jagua E Type 1961–70 Autobook
S Type 3.4 1963–68	..	..	..	Ball	Jaguar S Type and 420 1963–68 Autobook
S Type 3.8 1963–68	..	..	..	Ball	Jaguar S Type and 420 1963–68 Autobook
420 1963–68	..	..	..	Ball	Jaguar S Type and 420 1963–68 Autobook
XJ6 2.8 litre 1968–70	..	..	..	Ball	Jaguar XJ6 1968–70 Autobook
XJ6 4.2 litre 1968–70	..	..	..	Ball	Jaguar XJ6 1968–70 Autobook

Make					Author	Title

JOWETT

Javelin PA 1947–49	..	..	..	..	Mitchell	Jowett Javelin Jupiter 1947–53 Autobook
Javelin PB 1949–50	..	..	..	..	Mitchell	Jowett Javelin Jupiter 1947–53 Autobook
Javelin PC 1950–51	..	..	..	..	Mitchell	Jowett Javelin Jupiter 1947–53 Autobook
Javelin PD 1951–52	..	..	..	..	Mitchell	Jowett Javelin Jupiter 1947–53 Autobook
Javelin PE 1952–53	..	..	..	..	Mitchell	Jowett Javelin Jupiter 1947–53 Autobook
Jupiter Mk 1 SA 1949–52					Mitchell	Jowett Javelin Jupiter 1947–53 Autobook
Jupiter Mk 1A SC 1952–53	..	..	..		Mitchell	Jowett Javelin Jupiter 1947–53 Autobook

LANDROVER

Series 1 1948–58	..		..	..	Ball	Landrover 1, 2 1948–61 Autobook
Series 2 1997 cc 1959–61		..	..	..	Ball	Landrover 1, 2 1948–61 Autobook
Series 2 2052 cc 1959–61		..	..	..	Ball	Landrover 1, 2 1948–61 Autobook
Series 2 2286 cc 1959–61		..	..	..	Ball	Landrover 2, 2A 1959–70 Autobook
Series 2A 2286 cc 1961–70	..	..	..		Ball	Landrover 2, 2A 1959–70 Autobook
Series 2A 2625 cc 1967–70	..	..	..		Ball	Landrover 2, 2A 1959–70 Autobook

MG

TA 1936–39	..	..	..	..	Ball	MG TA to TF 1936–55 Autobook
TB 1939	..	..	..	..	Ball	MG TA to TF 1936–55 Autobook
TC 1945–49	..	..	..	..	Ball	MG TA to TF 1936–55 Autobook
TD 1950–53	..	..	..	..	Ball	MG TA to TF 1936–55 Autobook
TF 1953–54	..	..	..	..	Ball	MG TA to TF 1936–55 Autobook
TF 1500 1954–55	..	..	..		Ball	MG TA to TF 1936–55 Autobook
Midget 1961–70					Ball	Sprite, Midget 1958–70 Autobook
Magnette ZA, ZB 1955–59					Ball	BMC Autobook Three
MGA 1500, 1600 1955–62	..				Ball	MGA, MGB 1955–68 Autobook
MGA Twin Cam 1958–60	..		..		Ball	MGA, MGB 1955–68 Autobook
MGB 1962–68	..		..		Ball	MGA, MGB 1955–68 Autobook
MGB 1969–71	..		..	..	Ball	MG MGB 1969–71 Autobook
1100 Mk 1 1962–67	..	..	..	..	Ball	1100 Mk 1 1962–67 Autobook
1100 Mk 2 1968	..				Ball	1100 Mk 2, 1300 Mk 1, 2, America 1968–71 Autobook
1300 Mk 1, 2 1968–71	..				Ball	1100 Mk 2, 1300 Mk 1, 2, America 1968–71 Autobook

MERCEDES-BENZ

190B 1959–61					Ball	Mercedes-Benz 190 B, C, 200 1959–68 Autobook
190C 1961–65	..	..	..	..	Ball	Mercedes-Benz 190 B, C, 200 1959–68 Autobook
200 1965–68	..	..	..	..	Ball	Mercedes-Benz 190 B, C, 200 1959–68 Autobook
220B 1959–65		..	..	..	Ball	Mercedes-Ben 220 1959–65 Autobook
220SB 1959–65		..	..	..	Ball	Mercedes-Benz 220 1959–65 Autobook
220SEB 1959–65	..		..	..	Ball	Mercedes-Benz 220 1959–65 Autobook
220SEBC 1961–65	..		..	..	Ball	Mercedes-Benz 220 1959–65 Autobook
230 1965–67	..	..	..	..	Ball	Mercedes-Benz 230 1963–68 Autobook
230 S 1965–68	..		..	..	Ball	Mercedes-Benz 230 1963–68 Autobook
230 SL 1963–67	..		..	..	Ball	Mercedes-Benz 230 1963–68 Autobook
250 S 1965–68	..		..	..	Ball	Mercedes-Benz 250 1965–67 Autobook
250 SE 1965–67	..		..	..	Ball	Mercedes-Benz 250 1965–67 Autobook
250 SE BC 1965–67	..		..	..	Ball	Mercedes-Benz 250 1965–67 Autobook
250 SL 1967	..	..	..	..	Ball	Mercedes-Benz 250 1965–67 Autobook

MORGAN

Four wheelers 1936–69	..		..	Clarke	Morgan 1936–69 Autobook

MORRIS

Oxford 2, 3 1954–59	..	..	..	..	Ball	BMC Autobook Three
Oxford 5, 6 1959–69	..	..	..	..	Ball	Morris Oxford 5, 6 1959–70 Autobook
Minor series 2 1952–56	..	..	..		Ball	Morris Minor 1952–71 Autobook
Minor 1000 1957–71	..		..	..	Ball	Morris Minor 1952–71 Autobook
Mini 1959–70	..		..	..	Ball	Mini 1959–70 Autobook
Mini Clubman 1969–70		..	..	..	Ball	Mini 1959–70 Autobook
Mini Cooper 1961–70	..		..	..	Ball	Mini Cooper 1961–70 Autobook

Make					Author	Title
Mini Cooper S 1963–70	..	..	..		Ball	Mini Cooper 1961–70 Autobook
1100 Mk 1 1962–67	..	..	..	..	Ball	1100 Mk 1 1962–67 Autobook
1100 Mk 2 1968–70	..	..	..	..	Ball	1100 Mk 2, 1300 Mk 1, 2, America 1968–71 Autobook
1300 Mk 1, 2 1968–71	..	..	..		Ball	1100 Mk 2, 1300 Mk 1, 2, America 1968–71 Autobook
1800 Mk 1, 2 1966–71	..	..	..		Ball	1800 1964–71 Autobook
1800 S 1968–71	..	..	..		Ball	1800 1964–71 Autobook

NSU

Prinz 1000 L, LS 1963–67	..	..	..		Ball	NSU 1000 1963–70 Autobook
Prinz TT, TTS 1965–70	..	..	..		Ball	NSU 1000 1963–70 Autobook
1000 C 1967–70	..	..	..		Ball	NSU 1000 1963–70 Autobook
TYP 110 1966–67	..	..	..		Ball	NSU 1000 1963–70 Autobook
110 SC 1967	..	..	..		Ball	NSU 1000 1963–70 Autobook
1200, C, TT 1967–70	..	..	..		Ball	NSU 1000 1963–70 Autobook

OPEL

Kadett 993 cc 1962–65	..	..	..	Ball	Opel Kadett, Olympia 993 cc, 1078 cc 1962–70 Autobook
Kadett 1078 cc 1965–70	..	..	..	Ball	Opel Kadett, Olympia 993 cc and 1078 cc 1962–70 Autobook
Kadett 1492 cc 1967–70	..	..	..	Ball	Opel Kadett, Olympia 1492 cc, 1698 cc and 1897 cc 1967–70 Autobook
Kadett 1698 cc 1967–70	..	..	..	Ball	Opel Kadett, Olympia 1492 cc, 1698 cc and 1897 cc 1967–70 Autobook
Kadett 1897 cc 1967–70	..	..	..	Ball	Opel Kadett, Olympia 1492 cc, 1698 cc and 1897 cc 1967–70 Autobook
Olympia 1078 cc 1967–70	..	..	..	Ball	Opel Kadett, Olympia 993 cc and 1078 cc 1962–70 Autobook
Olympia 1492 cc 1967–70	..	..	..	Ball	Opel Kadett, Olympia 1492 cc, 1698 cc and 1897 cc 1967–70 Autobook
Olympia 1698 cc 1967–70	..	..	..	Ball	Opel Kadett, Olympia 1492 cc, 1698 cc and 1897 cc 1967–70 Autobook
Olympia 1897 cc 1967–70	..	..	..	Ball	Opel Kadett, Olympia 1492 cc, 1698 cc and 1897 cc 1967–70 Autobook
Rekord C 1.5, 1.7, 1.9 1966–70	,	..		Ball	Opel Rekord C 1966–70 Autobook

PEUGEOT

404 1960–69	..	..	..	..	Ball	Peugeot 404 1960–69 Autobook

PLYMOUTH

Cricket 1971	..	..	..	..	Ball	Hillman Avenger 1970–71 Autobook

PORSCHE

356A 1957–59	..	..	..	..		Ball	Porsche 356A, 356B, 356C 1957–65 Autobook
356B 1959–63	..	..	..			Ball	Porsche 356A, 356B, 356C 1957–65 Autobook
356C 1963–65	..	..	..			Ball	Porsche 356A, 356B, 356C 1957–65 Autobook
911 1964–67	..	..	..			Ball	Porsche 911 1964–69 Autobook
911L 1967–68	..	..	..			Ball	Porsche 911 1964–69 Autobook
911S 1966–69	..	..	..			Ball	Porsche 911 1964–69 Autobook
911T 1967–69	..	..	..			Ball	Porsche 911 1964–69 Autobook
911E 1968–69	..	..	..			Ball	Porsche 911 1964–69 Autobook
912 1582 cc 1965–70	..	..	..			Ball	Porsche 912 1965–70 Autobook

RENAULT

R4L 748 cc 845 cc 1961–65	..	..	..	Ball	Renault R4, R4L, 4 1961–70 Autobook
R4 845 cc 1962–66	..	..	..	Ball	Renault R4, R4L, 4 1961–70 Autobook
4 845 cc 1966–70	..	..	..	Ball	Renault R4, R4L, 4 1961–70 Autobook
6 1968–70	..	..	..	Ball	Renault 6 1968–70 Autobook
R8 956 cc 1962–65	..	..	..	Ball	Renault 8, 10, 1100 1962–70 Autobook
8 956 cc 1108 cc 1965–70	..	..	..	Ball	Renault 8, 10, 1100 1962–70 Autobook
8S 1108 cc 1968–70	..	..	..	Ball	Renault 8, 10, 1100 1962–70 Autobook

Make				Author	Title
1100, 1108cc 1964–69	..	..	..	Ball	Renault 8, 10, 1100 1962–70 Autobook
R10 1108cc 1967–69 ..	..	..	..	Ball	Renault 8, 10, 1100 1962–70 Autobook
10 1289cc 1969–70 ..	..	..	..	Ball	Renault 8, 10, 1100 1962–70 Autobook
16 1470cc 1965–70 ..	..	..	..	Ball	Renault R16 1965–70 Autobook
16TS 1565cc 1968–70	..	..	..	Ball	Renault R16 1965–70 Autobook

RILEY

1.5 1957–65 ..	..	..	..	Ball	BMC Autobook Three
Elf Mk 1, 2, 3 1961–70	..	..	..	Ball	Mini 1959–70 Autobook
1100 Mk 1 1965–67 ..	..	..	..	Ball	1100 Mk 1 1962–67 Autobook
1100 Mk 2 1968	..	..	..	Ball	1100 Mk 2, 1300 Mk 1, 2 America 1968–71 Autobook
1300 Mk 1, 2 1968–71	..	..	..	Ball	1100 Mk 2, 1300 Mk 1, 2, America 1968–71 Autobook

ROVER

60 1953–59 ..	..	..	..	Ball	Rover 60–110 1953–64 Autobook
75 1954–59 ..	..	..	..	Ball	Rover 60–110 1953–64 Autobook
80 1959–62 ..	..	..	..	Ball	Rover 60–110 1953–64 Autobook
90 1954–59 ..	..	..	..	Ball	Rover 60–110 1953–64 Autobook
95 1962–64 ..	..	..	..	Ball	Rover 60–110 1953–64 Autobook
100 1959–62	..	..	..	Ball	Rover 60–110 1953–64 Autobook
105R 1957–58	..	..	..	Ball	Rover 60–110 1953–64 Autobook
105S 1957–59	..	..	..	Ball	Rover 60–110 1953–64 Autobook
110 1962–64 ..	..	..	..	Ball	Rover 60–110 1953–64 Autobook
2000 SC 1963–70	..	..	..	Ball	Rover 2000 1963–70 Autobook
2000 TC 1963–70	..	..	..	Ball	Rover 2000 1963–70 Autobook
3 litre Saloon Mk 1, 1A 1958–62		..	..	Ball	Rover 3 litre 1958–67 Autobook
3 litre Saloon Mk 2, 3 1962–67		..	..	Ball	Rover 3 litre 1958–67 Autobook
3 litre Coupé 1965–67	..	..	..	Ball	Rover 3 litre 1958–67 Autobook
3500, 3500S 1968–70	..	..	..	Ball	Rover 3500, 3500S 1968–70 Autobook

SAAB

95, 96, 1960–64	..	..	..	Ball	Saab 95, 96 Sport 1960–68 Autobook
95(5), 96(5) 1964–68	..	..	..	Ball	Saab 95, 96 Sport 1960–68 Autobook
Sport 1962–66	..	..	..	Ball	Saab 95, 96 Sport 1960–68 Autobook
Monte Carlo 1965–66 ..	..	..	..	Ball	Saab 95, 96 Sport 1960–68 Autobook
99 1969–70 ..	..	..	..	Ball	Saab 99 1969–70 Autobook

SIMCA

1000 1961–65	..	..	..	Ball	Simca 1000 1961–71 Autobook
1000 Special 1962–63	..	..	..	Ball	Simca 1000 1961–71 Autobook
1000 GL 1964–71	..	..	..	Ball	Simca 1000 1961–71 Autobook
1000 GLS 1964–69	..	..	..	Ball	Simca 1000 1961–71 Autobook
1000 GLA 1965–69 ..	..	..	..	Ball	Simca 1000 1961–71 Autobook
1000 LS 1965–71	..	..	..	Ball	Simca 1000 1961–71 Autobook
1000 L 1966–68 ..	..	..	..	Ball	Simca 1000 1961–71 Autobook
1000 Special 1968–71	..	..	..	Ball	Simca 1000 1961–71 Autobook
1100 LS 1967–70 ..	..	..	..	Ball	Simca 1100 1967–70 Autobook
1100 GL, GLS 1967–70	..	..	..	Ball	Simca 1100 1967–70 Autobook
1204 1970 ..	..	..	..	Ball	Simca 1100 1967–70 Autobook

SINGER

Chamois 1964–68 ..	..	..	..	Smith	Hillman Imp 1963–68 Autobook
Chamois 1969–70 ..	..	..	..	Ball	Hillman Imp 1969–71 Autobook
Chamois Sport 1964–68	..	..	..	Smith	Hillman Imp 1963–68 Autobook
Chamois Sport 1969–70	..	..	..	Ball	Hillman Imp 1969–71 Autobook
Gazelle series 2A 1958	..	..	..	Ball	Hillman Minx 1 to 5 1956–65 Autobook
Gazelle 3, 3A, 3B, 3C 1958–63		..	..	Ball	Hillman Minx 1 to 5 1956–65 Autobook
Gazelle series 5 1963–65	..	..	..	Ball	Hillman Minx 1 to 5 1956–65 Autobook
Gazelle series 6 1965–67	..	..	..	Ball	Hillman Minx 1965–67 Autobook

Make				Author	Title
New Gazelle 1500, 1725 1966–70	..	..		Ball	Hillman Minx 1966–70 Autobook
Vogue Mk 1 to 3 1961–65	..	..	..	Ball	Hillman Super Minx 1961–65 Autobook
Vogue series 4 1965–67	..	..	..	Ball	Hillman Minx 1965–67 Autobook
New Vogue 1966–70	..	..	..	Ball	Hillman Hunter 1966–70 Autobook

SKODA

440, 445, 450 1957–69	..	..	..	Skoda	Skoda Autobook One

SUNBEAM

Alpine series 1, 2, 3, 4 1959–65	..	..	Ball	Sunbeam Rapier Alpine 1955–65 Autobook
Alpine series 5 1965–67	..	..		Ball	Hillman Minx 1965–67 Autobook
Alpine 1969–70	..	..	..	Ball	Hillman Hunter 1966–70 Autobook
Rapier series 1, 2, 3, 3A, 4 1955–65	..	..	Ball	Sunbeam Rapier Alpine 1955–65 Autobook
Rapier series 5 1965–67	..	..	..	Ball	Hillman Minx 1965–67 Autobook
Rapier H.120 1967–70	..	..	..	Ball	Hillman Hunter 1966–70 Autobook
Imp Sport 1963–68	..	..		Smith	Hillman Imp 1963–68 Autobook
Imp Sport 1969–71	..	..		Ball	Hillman Imp 1969–71 Autobook
Stilletto 1967–68	..	..		Smith	Hillman Imp 1963–68 Autobook
Stilletto 1969–71	..	..	..	Ball	Hillman Imp 1969–71 Autobook
1250 1970–71	..	..	..	Ball	Hillman Avenger 1970–71 Autobook
1500 1970–71	..	..	..	Ball	Hillman Avenger 1970–71 Autobook

TOYOTA

Corolla 1100 1967–70	..	..	..	Ball	Toyota Corolla 1100 1967–70 Autobook
Corolla 1100 De luxe 1967–70	..	..	Ball	Toyota Corolla 1100 1967–70 Autobook
Corolla 1100 Automatic 1968–69	..	..	Ball	Toyota Corolla 1100 1967–70 Autobook
Corona 1500 Mk 1 1965–70	..	..	..	Ball	Toyota Corona 1500 Mk 1 1965–70 Autobook
Corona 1900 Mk 2 1969–71	..	..	..	Ball	Toyota Corona 1900 Mk 2 1969–71 Autobook

TRIUMPH

TR2 1952–55	..			Ball	Triumph TR2, TR3, TR3A 1952–62 Autobook
TR3, TR3A 1955–62	..	..	..	Ball	Triumph TR2, TR3, TR3A 1952–62 Autobook
TR4, TR4A 1961–67	..	..	..	Ball	Triumph TR4, TR4A 1961–67 Autobook
TR5 1967–69	..	..	..	Ball	Triumph TR5, TR250, TR6 1967–70 Autobook
TR6 1969–70	..	..	..	Ball	Triumph TR5, TR250, TR6 1967–70 Autobook
TR250 1967–69	..	..	..	Ball	Triumph TR5, TR250, TR6 1967–70 Autobook
1300 1965–70	..	..	..	Ball	Triumph 1300 1965–70 Autobook
1300TC 1967–70	..	..	..	Ball	Triumph 1300 1965–70 Autobook
2000 Mk 1 1963–69	..	..	..	Ball	Triumph 2000 Mk 1, 2.5 Pl Mk 1 1963–69 Autobook
2000 Mk 2 1969–71	..	..	..	Ball	Triumph 2000 Mk 2, 2.5 Pl Mk 2 1969–71 Autobook
2.5 Pl Mk 1 1963–69	..	..	..	Ball	Triumph 2000 Mk 1, 2.5 Pl Mk 1 1963–69 Autobook
2.5 Pl Mk 2 1969–71	..	..	..	Ball	Triumph 2000 Mk 2, 2.5 Pl Mk 2 1969–70 Autobook
Herald 948 1959–64	..	..	..	Smith	Triumph Herald 1959–68 Autobook
Herald 1200 1961–68	..	..		Smith	Triumph Herald 1959–68 Autobook
Herald 1200 1969–70	..	..		Ball	Triumph Herald 1969–71 Autobook
Herald 12/50 1963–67	..	..	..	Smith	Triumph Herald 1959–68 Autobook
Herald 13/60 1967–68	..	..	..	Smith	Triumph Herald 1959–68 Autobook
Herald 13/60 1969–71	..	..	..	Ball	Triumph Herald 1969–71 Autobook
Spitfire 1962–68	..	..	..	Smith	Triumph Spitfire Vitesse 1962–68 Autobook
Spitfire Mk 3 1969–70	..	..	..	Ball	Triumph Spitfire Mk 3 1969–70 Autobook
Vitesse 1600 and 2 litre 1962–68	..	..	Smith	Triumph Spitfire Vitesse 1962–68 Autobook
Vitesse 2 litre 1969–70	..	..	..	Ball	Triumph GT6, Vitesse 2 litre 1969–70 Autobook
GT Six 2 litre 1966–68	..	..	..	Smith	Triumph Spitfire Vitesse 1962–68 Autobook
GT Six 1969–70	..	..	..	Ball	Triumph GT6, Vitesse 2 litre 1969–70 Autobook

VANDEN PLAS

3 litre 1959–64	..	..	..	Ball	BMC Autobook Four
1100 Mk 1 1963–67	..	..	..	Ball	1100 Mk 1 1962–67 Autobook
1100 Mk 2 1968	..	..	..	Ball	1100 Mk 2, 1300 Mk 1, 2, America 1968–71 Autobook
1300 Mk 1, 2, 1968–71	..	..	..	Ball	1100 Mk 2, 1300 Mk 1, 2, America 1968–71 Autobook

Make	Author	Title

VAUXHALL

Model	Author	Title
Victor 1 1957–59	Ball	Vauxhall Victor 1, 2 FB 1957–64 Autobook
Victor 2 1959–61	Ball	Vauxhall Victor 1, 2 FB 1957–64 Autobook
Victor FB 1961–64	Ball	Vauxhall Victor 1, 2 FB 1957–64 Autobook
VX4/90 FBH 1961–64	Ball	Vauxhall Victor 1, 2 FB 1957–64 Autobook
Victor FC 101 1964–67	Ball	Vauxhall Victor 101 1964–67 Autobook
VX 4/90 FCH 1964–67	Ball	Vauxhall Victor 101 1964–67 Autobook
Victor FD 1599cc 1967–71	Ball	Vauxhall Victor FD 1600, 2000 1967–71 Autobook
Victor FD 1975cc 1967–71	Ball	Vauxhall Victor FD 1600, 2000 1967–71 Autobook
VX 4/90 1969–71	Ball	Vauxhall Victor FD 1600, 2000 1967–71 Autobook
Velox, Cresta PA 1957–62	Ball	Vauxhall Velox Cresta 1957–70 Autobook
Velox, Cresta PB 1962–65	Ball	Vauxhall Velox Cresta 1957–70 Autobook
Cresta PC 1965–70	Ball	Vauxhall Velox Cresta 1957–70 Autobook
Viscount 1966–70	Ball	Vauxhall Velox Cresta 1957–70 Autobook
Viva HA (including 90) 1964–66	Ball	Vauxhall Viva HA 1964–66 Autobook
Viva HB (including 90 and SL90) 1966–70	Ball	Vauxhall Viva HB 1966–70 Autobook

VOLKSWAGEN

Model	Author	Title
1200 Beetle 1954–67	Ball	Volkswagen Beetle 1954–67 Autobook
1200 Beetle 1968–71	Ball	Volkswagen Beetle 1968–71 Autobook
1200 Karmann Ghia 1955–65	Ball	Volkswagen Beetle 1954–67 Autobook
1200 Transporter 1954–64	Ball	Volkswagen Transporter 1954–67 Autobook
1300 Beetle 1965–67	Ball	Volkswagen Beetle 1954–67 Autobook
1300 Beetle 1968–71	Ball	Volkswagen Beetle 1968–71 Autobook
1300 Karmann Ghia 1965–66	Ball	Volkswagen Beetle 1954–67 Autobook
1500 Beetle 1966–67	Ball	Volkswagen Beetle 1954–67 Autobook
1500 Beetle 1968–70	Ball	Volkswagen Beetle 1968–71 Autobook
1500 1961–65	Ball	Volkswagen 1500 1961–66 Autobook
1500N 1963–65	Ball	Volkswagen 1500 1961–66 Autobook
1500S 1963–65	Ball	Volkswagen 1500 1961–66 Autobook
1500A 1965–66	Ball	Volkswagen 1500 1961–66 Autobook
1500 Karmann Ghia 1966–67	Ball	Volkswagen Beetle 1954–67 Autobook
1500 Transporter 1963–67	Ball	Volkswagen Transporter 1954–67 Autobook
1500 Karmann Ghia 1968–70	Ball	Volkswagen Beetle 1968–71 Autobook
1600 TL 1965–70	Ball	Volkswagen 1600 Fastback 1965–70 Autobook
1600 Variant 1965–66	Ball	Volkswagen 1600 Fastback 1965–70 Autobook
1600 L 1966–67	Ball	Volkswagen 1600 Fastback 1965–70 Autobook
1600 Variant L 1966–70	Ball	Volkswagen 1600 Fastback 1965–70 Autobook
1600 T 1968–70	Ball	Volkswagen 1600 Fastback 1965–70 Autobook
1600 TA 1969–70	Ball	Volkswagen 1600 Fastback 1965–70 Autobook
1600 Variant A, M	Ball	Volkswagen 1600 Fastback 1965–70 Autobook

VOLVO

Model	Author	Title
121, 131, 221 1962–68	Ball	Volvo P120 1961–68 Autobook
122, 132, 222 1961–68	Ball	Volvo P120 1961–68 Autobook
123 GT 1967–68	Ball	Volvo P120 1961–68 Autobook
142, 142S 1967–69	Ball	Volvo 140 1966–70 Autobook
144, 144S 1966–70	Ball	Volvo 140 1966–70 Autobook
145, 145S 1968–71	Ball	Volvo 140 1966–70 Autobook

WOLSELEY

Model	Author	Title
1500 1959–65	Ball	BMC Autobook Three
15/50 1956–58	Ball	BMC Autobook Three
6/99 1959–61	Ball	BMC Autobook Four
6/110 1961–68	Ball	BMC Autobook Four
Hornet Mk 1, 2, 3 1961–70	Ball	Mini 1959–70 Autobook
1100 Mk 1 1965–67	Ball	1100 Mk 1 1962–67 Autobook
1100 Mk 2 1968	Ball	1100 Mk 2, 1300 Mk 1, 2, America 1968–71 Autobook
1300 Mk 1, 2 1968–71	Ball	1100 Mk 2, 1300 Mk 1, 2, America 1968–71 Autobook
18/85 Mk 1, 2 1967–71	Ball	1800 1964–71 Autobook
18/85 S 1969–71	Ball	1800 1964–71 Autobook